Squirrel Pie
A Memoir

Deborah Brannigan

Squirrel Pie: A Memoir
Copyright © 2025 by Deborah Brannigan

All rights reserved. No part of this publication may be reproduced, distributed, or transmitted in any form or by any means, including photocopying, recording or other electronic or mechanical methods, without the prior written permission of the author, except in the case of brief quotations embodied in reviews and certain other non-commercial uses permitted by copyright law.

Without in any way limiting the author's [and publisher's] exclusive rights under copyright, any use of this publication to "train" generative artificial intelligence (AI) technologies to generate text is expressly prohibited. The author reserves all rights to license uses of this work for generative AI training and development of machine learning language models.

Printed in the United States of America

Hardcover ISBN: 978-1-965253-39-7
Paperback ISBN: 978-1-965253-40-3
Ebook ISBN: 978-1-965253-41-0
Library of Congress Control Number: 2025909875

DartFrog Plus is the hybrid publishing imprint of DartFrog Books, LLC.

301 S. McDowell St.
Suite 125-1625
Charlotte, NC 28204
www.DartFrogBooks.com

*For Tara,
the solid ground beneath my feet.
Thank you for the showing me the way home.*

Prologue

It is well after midnight and still eighty-five degrees. Even for August, this oppressive, humid heat is unreasonable. The open windows provide no relief; only the chirping of crickets wafts through the tattered screens.

I kick away the cheap polyester sheets in frustration, then freeze at the sound of keys scraping in the front door lock. Despite the heat, a shiver cascades down my body, and I lie motionless in bed listening to the heavy footfalls on the carpet.

Two weeks ago, Mac went out to buy a pack of cigarettes. He has just returned.

I should pretend to be asleep but I get up instead, moving down the hallway to the darkness at the edge of the living room. He stands still in the center of the room, as if he is waiting for me.

The room is so dark that I miss the warning signs. I have lived with Mac for nearly two years now, since the age of sixteen, and have learned to recognize when he has been drinking. But this night I don't see the knitted brow or the eyes so black that no light seems to get in or out of them.

"Where were you?" I ask.

Before I can take another breath, he slams me back against the wall of the hallway and presses his right forearm hard against my throat, winding a section of my hair tightly around his left hand.

"None of your fucking business."

He swipes my legs out from under me, and I crash onto the floor. Out of the corner of my eye, I see a sliver of five-year-old Ian as he cracks open his bedroom door, then quickly closes it while warning his older sister, "Dad's home." Like a school fire drill, the kids have learned a set of safety protocols. They will jump back into bed and pretend to be fast asleep.

When the first kick comes toward my midsection, I see Mac's boot in great detail. Mac wears heavy black motorcycle boots made of genuine leather, with straps across the front and back that are lined with steel grommets and joined by a metal ring at the ankle. The boots cost more than three of his paltry paychecks from the local foundry. Knockoffs will become trendy in the future, but on that hot August night in 1982, Mac's boots are the real deal, worn by motorcycle gang members and wannabes like Mac.

The kick seems to come in slow motion, and I manage to get my hand between the boot and my belly to absorb some of the impact. My middle finger stings with agonizing pain. It is most likely fractured, but all I can do is tuck it to my chest, curl into a ball, and roll toward the wall with my backside exposed.

My mind refuses to focus on what's happening and instead conjures up an image of a "roly-poly," which is what I must look like. I drift back in time, to a scene from my childhood. My little brother, Mark, and I have just discovered a cluster of pill bugs in the dirt between the bushes and the brick of old Mrs. McVeattie's house on Avon Street. Our bare knees are embedded in the rocky soil, fingers plucking up the prehistoric-looking creatures while they attempt to escape into the safety of Mother Earth. We declare victory as each bug transforms into a perfect ball of impenetrable grey armor, the armadillos of the insect world. We roll them around in the palm of our hands, counting to see who has the most. It doesn't take long to become bored, and we discard them carelessly, letting them drop to the ground from our hands.

The kicking stops. Mac is also bored. I lie motionless for what seems like hours, waiting to hear the creak of the couch springs, the thump of each boot hitting the floor, and finally the snoring.

When I'm sure he's out cold, I lift myself up, unsteady on my feet, and lean against the wall for a few moments. I hear whimpering from the kid's room and make my way there using the wall as a crutch. Even in the dark, I see them flinch in their beds as the door opens.

"It's okay now. He's asleep."

I shuffle into the bathroom to do some triage. My face is unscathed, no black eyes or bloody nose this time. My back, however, is bright red and already turning blue. The middle finger on my right hand is swollen like a purple grape at the joint. I'll never know if it's fractured because there will be no trip to the doctor.

Instead, there are flowers.

The next morning, Mac buys me a bundle of gladiolas and begs for my forgiveness, as he always does. For the next three weeks, I take quiet pleasure in asking him, "Does it look like it's getting better?" as I raise my middle finger, which I've splinted with sticks and duct tape.

It is my subversive form of defiance, a *fuck you* that goes unnoticed by him but makes me feel fierce and cowardly at the same time.

I have endured countless beatings prior to this one, and there will be countless more to come. This summer night in 1982 is neither the beginning nor the end; it's somewhere near the middle. What makes this night stand out from others is that I am nearly eight months pregnant.

I don't know it now, but I'm carrying a daughter who will one day save my life.

But that's still in the future. Three more years of abuse will go by before I leave for good.

In the end, the last straw will not be a beating, nor the years of poverty and countless lies. In the end, it will simply be spilled milk.

CHAPTER 1

Avon Street

Most homes that line our block of Avon Street in the mid '70s are modest three-bedroom, one bath brick bungalows. They are neat and tidy, not at all ornate, just like their occupants. Moms stay at home while dads drive off every morning to trade jobs as pipe fitters, machinists, plumbers, or welders.

My dad, Hugh, is a manual welder in a Detroit auto plant. That job was his ticket out of the Glasgow slums in Scotland where he grew up, and he is forever grateful to the Motor City. Every year on Family Day he proudly parades us around the Chrysler stamping plant, where free hot dogs and aluminum ashtrays with the company logo are handed out to any kid who wants them.

The *Mad Men* era of the '60s fades into the '70s of my childhood. The kids on Avon Street, including me, practice smoking with candy cigarettes and metal ashtrays, and our dads stop at the bar after work every night, eventually arriving home half-tanked. The word *alcoholic* is not in the mainstream vocabulary yet, and getting blind drunk is equivalent to ripping apart a phone book in the unwritten rule book of manly behavior.

Every kid in the neighborhood insists their dad is the toughest man on the block. Curbside arguments go on for hours as we debate whose dad could beat up which superhero. Years later I realize it is the moms, not the dads, of Avon Street who are made of steel, wrapping any chaos and turmoil under invisible cloaks of cheery normality.

Nobody locks their doors in our community; I can walk into any neighbor's house as if it is my own. During the summer, we barricade both ends of the street for block parties and set out food-laden tables, folding chairs, and coolers filled with Budweiser and PBR. Kids enjoy homemade pigs in a blanket and raisin pie while dads gather in a cluster around the coolers, their voices rising, falling and sliding sideways as the day progresses.

At least once each summer a heavy rain swells Lake St. Clair at the end of the block and turns Avon Street into a raging river. When the sky turns emerald green and the birds stop singing, parents dart outside to cover the sewer drains with newspapers. Once the storm subsides, we hit the murky water with inflatable rafts and inner tubes, making the block our own water park until the paper dams give way.

Summer break ends abruptly after Labor Day. For the next nine months, boots crunch over brittle fallen leaves or ice-covered snow as we walk in groups to Avon Elementary School, picking up friends on their doorsteps. Occasionally, a fistfight breaks out along the way, and we form a cheering and booing ring around the scuffle to block any meddling teachers. These fights often involve one or both of my brothers, and if my little brother Mark is involved, I join with fists flying. If you pick a fight with him, you must contend with both of us.

With our matching platinum blonde bangs, hazel eyes, and translucent Celtic skin, Mark and I are often mistaken for twins. Like twins, we have an invisible tether that joins us at the hip. We ride our pedal bikes everywhere. We share Halloween candy. We tie yellow towels around our necks and call ourselves the Mustard Men, a superhero duo that derives invincible powers from drinking Plochman's yellow mustard.

Steve, my older brother, is a stark contrast to Mark's teddy bear demeanor. Steve has a thick mop of dark curls and is always looking for a fight. He is the neighborhood bully, even beating up friends at his own birthday party.

Mom claims Steve changed when he was five years old and fell from a ten-foot wall when we lived in Canada. All I know is that Mark and I are often handy targets for his uncontrollable anger.

We scribble defense tactics and escape routes onto slips of paper that are rolled up and strategically hidden from Steve. We recruit allies from our neighborhood to form the Steve Hater Club, and most kids on our street carry an official membership card. We sit in my sunny bedroom for meetings, drawing crayon pictures of Steve engulfed in flames, chased by wolves, or stabbed by Satan's pitchfork. We disband only when my Catholic guilt persuades me that it would be me, not Steve, stabbed by Satan's pitchfork if the club were to continue.

My brothers and I fight, but we also play together a lot, along with the other kids in the neighborhood. Like birds drawn together by a magnetic field, we fly out our front doors and assemble in the same spot on the curb every morning. Billy is our unofficial pack leader, with Steve as his trusty side kick and enforcer. When Billy proclaims that we're playing baseball, we scatter to retrieve mitts, bats, and balls, then return to him so he can lead us in a raucous procession down Avon Street to the elementary school ball field. It never occurs to me that I am a girl running with a pack of boys. I'm never treated differently... at least until I turn twelve.

Halfway through a tackle football game, Steve punches twelve-year-old me in the stomach, knocking the wind out of me. This is not unusual; games are often delayed due to somebody triggering his temper.

Steve stands over me grinning as I double over, gasping for air.

"Don't you ever hit her again," Billy says, stepping between us.

I don't know who is more surprised, me or Steve, but something has changed, and apparently that something is me. My sturdy square body is beginning to soften and curve, and it becomes crystal clear to me in that moment that all of the forbidden zones I am developing mean I am no longer part of the pack.

It is during this same time that my baby sister, MaryAnne, arrives.

At the ripe old age of thirty-six, Mom has sent quite a shockwave through the neighborhood with the news that she is pregnant. Several men on Avon Street wink and dig their elbows into my dad's ribs, calling him a sly old dog. My parents have never discussed pregnancy, or anything about having kids, with my brothers and me. We don't know if it takes days, weeks, or months to grow a baby. We just come home from school one day, and there is MaryAnne, swaddled in a pink blanket. When I hold her, it is love at first sight. She fits into the crook of my arm much better than any stupid football.

Besides having a new baby sister, the other big change in my life is that in the fall, I leave Avon Elementary School to begin seventh grade at Kennedy Jr. High. Every day I walk back and forth to school with my best friends, Cheryl and Melody, talking the entire time.

Cheryl has bright orange hair and broad shoulders, with a solid sense of herself that makes her impervious to peer pressure. Everybody — from nerds to tough girls to jocks — likes Cheryl, and in the tumultuous sea of teenage insecurities and hormones, she is my lighthouse.

Melody, however, is always helping me row toward the rocks. She is my co-conspirator in anything that promises adventure. She is built sturdy like me, except with hair so black it shimmers blue in the sunlight. If there is a bad choice to be made, Melody and I are eager recruits.

Kennedy Jr. High is full of new faces and personalities and, best of all, new boys. The familiar boys of Avon Street are dull compared to somebody like Jeff Dunbar, whose high cheekbones and long feathered hair make me swoon. He has the same effect on most of the other girls in my class, too, including Melody.

Melody and I compete to capture his affection, and after weeks of "devotion tests" like carrying Jeff home on our backs so his feet never touch the snowy sidewalk, I win the girlfriend contest.

Jeff lands me my first job, washing dishes at Wong's Garden, a family-owned Chinese restaurant in a blue-collar neighborhood just a few miles from my own. Nobody speaks a word of English, and the staff are kind and respectful, offering smiles and bows when Jeff and I arrive and depart each night.

My fingers blister from pulling blazing hot tin platters and silverware from the industrial dishwasher, load after load. The job pays two dollars an hour, cash, and I love it. It feels great to make more money than my brothers do on their paper routes, and while my fingers may be burnt, I don't have to ride my bike in bad weather at 4:00 a.m. I am on the work schedule every week and never miss a day, except for when Dad asks me to take off and help with housework while Mom is away.

Where Mom has gone and how long she'll be "away" is a mystery. One day we come home from school, and Mom is washing dishes, scrubbing floors and ironing clothes, reminding us to clean up for dinner and do our homework. The next day she isn't.

"Your mother's gone away for a rest," Dad says, staring at his shoes.

I'm not sure when we figure out that Mom is at a mental health facility. Like politics, religion, and sex, mental health is a topic considered too taboo to discuss in polite conversation — and apparently also with your own family — so we acclimate to this new reality without a word.

I keep working at Wong's, saving cash to fund my dream of moving to Australia where I can surf and have a pet koala bear. My plan evaporates the day my parents announce we are moving twenty-five miles up the I-94 corridor to New Baltimore, Michigan.

New Baltimore is considered "up north" in 1979. Suburban creep has not reached that far yet, and the few new housing developments are surrounded by dirt roads and acres of soybeans. People drive there to buy tomatoes and apples from roadside farm stands or attend the annual Bay O' Rama Fish Fly Festival.

Despite the hint of manure in the air, New Baltimore is a tranquil setting for young families and, in Mom's case, an inpatient mental health facility. We never learn if it is the idyllic surroundings she views from her assigned room or the idea of starting a new chapter in her life that convinces Mom we need to pull up our Avon Street roots and move to a cookie cutter subdivision in the middle of nowhere. We just start packing.

Cheryl and Melody promise to visit me but being two years from a driver's license and lacking cell phones or the internet, New Baltimore might as well be a thousand miles away. My friends, my job, my whole identity is gone in a moment, and I am devastated. Even though Avon Street had plenty of quirks and secrets, the tightly knit community had been my cocoon, a familiar place to sprout my wings.

That cocoon is now torn open, and I begin to spill out of it, a gooey, unformed mess.

CHAPTER 2

A New Tribe

Dad often recounted the story of the day in 1969 when he pulled the moving truck up to our house on Avon Street and every man on the block came over to help. Bellaire Street proves to be no Avon Street, and as the day drags by, we unload our moving truck without a single neighbor coming to lend a hand.

We are the first occupants of our brand-new house, which lacks any soul or warmth. Every third house in the subdivision is a clone, with minor variations of color or landscaping. All of the homes are bright, shiny and new — and have the personality of earwax.

It is the start of summer break, and my brothers and I are like seedlings scattered on a concrete sidewalk, hoping to take root in a welcoming crevice. I haven't made a single friend in our new subdivision, which is devoid of teenage girls, so I spend the long days of summer practicing dance moves with three-year-old MaryAnne. I listen to records for endless hours in my giant bedroom and hang Led Zeppelin posters on every square inch of wall space. *Led Zeppelin II* and *IV* are my favorite albums; Jeff stole them from his sister as going away gifts, throwing them out her bedroom window to me along with her green velvet jacket. A true romantic.

Labor Day finally arrives, signaling the start of another school year. Mark is off to middle school while Steve and I head to Anchor Bay High School. I am a freshman without friends, and I cling to Steve as we board a school bus for the first time in our lives. I trail in his wake as he reaches the top step next to the bus driver and scans for a seat. He hesitates and I detect fear in his eyes, something I have never seen before.

"Take a seat," the bus driver says. "I have a schedule to keep."

I nudge Steve toward the front row, and we sit in silence along the route. The bully and enforcer of Avon Street is gone, and it dawns on me that I am actually seeing my brother for the first time.

"Quit staring at me," he says with a shoulder check before turning to look out the window.

Our bus pulls up in front of the high school along with several other buses, all erupting with teenagers. Steve steps off the bus and marches straight ahead.

"See ya," he says, leaving me on the sidewalk.

I'm not prepared for the chaos of my first day. It seems like I'm the only person who doesn't know where to go. I wander through the hallways, comparing my class schedule to room numbers as I pass by. All around me there are reunion celebrations with girls hugging and boys high-fiving. *Loser*, I think to myself, and feel my cheeks get hot.

"Come sit here."

The words snap me out of my head. I am frozen just inside the entrance of my first period classroom. Other students bump into me as they scramble for seats, and I scan the room to locate the source of the command.

"Sit here."

A girl locks eyes with me and drops her shoulder bag onto the empty desk next to her to save the space. Relief washes over me, and I rush to sit beside her.

Her name is Carol, and she has long, mousy brown hair with blonde highlights around her face. Her chin-length bangs are permed and hang over her ears on each side, making her look like a Standard Poodle. She is long-limbed, beautiful and stern-looking at the same time, her expression softened a bit by lip gloss and mascara. Carol seems like a tough girl with a soft side, and I like her immediately.

"Where you from?" she asks.

"I just moved here from St. Clair Shores."

"Where the hell is that?"

I explain that I grew up on Avon Street, which is just one block north of 13-Mile Road at Jefferson Avenue.

"Oh, over there."

"Where you from?" I ask, trying to mimic her cool indifference.

"Detroit. West Side."

Carol doesn't need to say more. I grew up on the safe side of 8-Mile Road, and she grew up in the war zone.

I end my first day with two new friends, Carol and Johanne. Johanne is in my third period class and, like Carol, extends the proverbial hand of friendship first. She is tall and willowy with ash blonde hair in a tight perm that comes to her jawline. Her smile is unnaturally wide and seems permanently affixed to her pretty face. Johanne is part of the popular girl crowd, the cheerleaders and soon-to-be prom queens.

I alternate between them as lunch dates in the cafeteria. Conversations with Johanne's friends are always punctuated with giggles and center on boyfriends, diets and clothing. These are local girls, and I am certain they wouldn't last ten minutes on the west side of Detroit.

Carol's tribe is more eclectic; non-conformists conforming to their role as outcasts. Richard is dressed in coat tails one day and a dog collar the next. Vicky is built like a pro linebacker and already has the raspy smoker's voice of a 1940s steel worker. The cast of characters changes at this table, and conversations range from new music to the bullshit teacher of the day.

I bounce between these groups for a couple of months until the day of reckoning comes. I walk into the bustling lunch hall, gripping my plastic tray with both hands. Johanne and Carol stand at the same time and wave me over to their respective tables. They catch sight of each other and then look back at me. I pivot toward Carol and set my tray down next to Richard, who is dressed in a vinyl Devo jumpsuit. Johanne doesn't talk to me much after that day.

The multiverse theory says an alternate universe is created for every decision made, and sometimes I wonder about that alternate version of me and who I might have become if I'd continued to sit with Johanne and the cheerleaders instead of Carol and the fringe crew. Would alternate me graduate with honors and go to Michigan State University? Would she marry the tennis captain and have three adorable, dimpled children? Would she slide into middle age with grandchildren and handcrafted scrapbooks? I imagine alternate me would be happy. Safe and content, perhaps even bored.

One thing is certain — alternate me would have bypassed the nightmare scenario that is beginning to unfold.

CHAPTER 3

Hazard Pay

I spend every weekend at Carol's house drinking and listening to rock music in her garage with our group of teenage loose ends. We pool our money, and her father buys us a case of beer. His only rule is that it never leaves the property because he believes it is better to have us at home drinking than out driving around.

In an effort to be unique like everybody else in our group, I create an alias for myself. My name is now Crystal, based on a female superhero from Marvel Comics, one of only two at the time. There are nods of approval all around when I announce this. I am too naïve to know what crystal meth is and that I have just implicated myself as a hard-core drug user with the selection of this new moniker.

During the week, we do anything but go to school. We get on the bus at home and get off at school, then walk into the woods across the street to smoke and drink. Strict rules and boring study halls are no match for the intoxicating sense of adventure and belonging. Sometimes I show up for art and creative writing classes, but it's not long before my absences skyrocket and my grades plummet. Nobody at home seems to notice.

"Crystal, you still looking for work?" Vicky asks as she puffs on a cigarette one morning in the woods.

"What is it?"

"Babysitting."

I roll my eyes. Vicky is not surprised; she knows I hate babysitting.

"These are really cool people, Crystal — they ride Harleys and shit. I went to their house with my brother for a party. Besides, they pay really good money."

"How much?"

"Five bucks an hour."

Now I am interested. Vicky grins at me like the Cheshire Cat from *Alice's Adventures in Wonderland.* What I really want is another dishwashing job or maybe landscaping, anything that requires physical effort. I grew up playing hard with my brothers and learned early that I was physically strong, but away from the baseball diamonds and backyard football games, it doesn't do me much good. Babysitting is the only viable job option for teen girls in New Baltimore.

I am the worst babysitter. I move the clock ahead two hours so I can announce bedtime at six p.m. If a bath is on the schedule, the kid is wrinkled, shivering and blue by the time I get off the phone and return with a towel. I hate every minute of it, and the pay is miserable at one dollar an hour. Five dollars an hour, though, might make it tolerable.

Vicky sets everything up for Saturday afternoon, and I arrive right on time and walk up the long, muddy driveway to a small brick bungalow. Weary folding chairs and empty coolers languish on the front porch. Three Harley Davidson motorcycles lean into the muck of the driveway, lined up like horses outside a Wild West saloon.

I have just reached the first step when two men in black leather pants and vests come out the screen door. They look me up and down without saying a word, then stride to the motorcycles. The rickety screen door slams once again as a bearded, long-haired man steps out to greet me.

"I'm Mac," he says, pulling his hair into a ponytail. "We're going for a ride. Should be back in a couple of hours. The kids are inside."

There is no tour of the house, no list of emergency numbers, no introduction to the kids. I know from Vicky that there are two kids, a four-year-old girl and her younger brother. I yank the screen door open and step inside as the three Harleys roar onto 23-Mile Road.

The living room is cluttered, and it takes a moment for my eyes to adjust to the darkness. Every window is closed, and the air feels stale. The smell of cigarette smoke and boiled hot dogs is so heavy that I unconsciously run a hand through my hair to keep it from settling in. A sudden movement in the hallway startles me, followed by a tiny body slamming full force into my legs. It's the girl, grinning at me like the Joker. She pushes at my thighs to move me toward the well-worn couch.

"You want me to sit here?"

The girl continues to push on my legs until I sit down on the couch, then she climbs into my lap and launches into a passionate but unintelligible dialogue. Her vocabulary consists of grunts, gibberish and maniacal shrieks, followed by hysterical laughter, all while punching and slapping the side of my head. Her hair is matted with dark brown strands that reach in every direction. I intercept the next slap, catching her tiny hand before it can land on my face. Her fingers are both sticky and gritty and I instinctively let go and wipe my hand down the thigh of my jeans. I begin to panic, wondering why nobody mentioned that one of the kids has special needs. Her attention is diverted when her brother shuffles into the room. Unlike his wildling sister, the boy reminds me of a sweet cherub. He climbs onto the couch and smiles at me before resting his head on my arm.

"Hi there, little man."

I begin to put my arm around him, and the girl slaps it away. I don't know if she is being jealous or protective. She directs her gibberish toward her brother, who seems to understand every word, and they dismount from the couch and vanish into the darkness of the hallway.

The girl is back in a flash with a naked and tattered plastic baby doll. She bounces into my lap and forces the doll's head toward my mouth in a violent display of "kiss the baby." I push the doll away and it falls to the floor. She leaps from my lap and runs down the hall again, then returns faster than a shot with a wrinkled T-shirt that she tries to pull over my head.

She runs off once more when I grab the T-shirt, and this time I follow her down the hallway into the first room on the left. I stand in the doorway, confused. There are two small, unkempt beds amid a chaos of clutter. This must be the kids' bedroom, but why is there a swing latch mounted to the outside of the door, with a padlock hanging from its loop?

A small hand slips into mine while I'm trying to make sense of the door. The little boy grins and pulls me toward one of the beds, then scoots himself under it. He reappears with a sleeve of Saltine crackers and offers them to me.

My heart breaks and I'm repulsed at the same time. I retreat to the kitchen and set my gift of Saltines on the cluttered counter. My hands are shaking. Maybe I should call somebody, tell them about the lock that's obviously meant to trap the kids in their room, but who?

I spot a pack of Kool menthol cigarettes to my right and pull one out. I'm not a smoker, but I inhale my way through it, using that first cigarette to light another one. I pace and smoke and curse, at a loss for what I'm feeling, much less how to handle it.

I take both kids out into the sunshine to clear my head. The girl immediately rockets down the driveway toward the busy traffic of 23-Mile Road. I hold her brother on my hip and lunge for her. Somehow, I manage to hook my free arm around her waist mere yards from the blur of passing cars and trucks. The boy yanks my red tube top down to my belly button, and a dozen car horns applaud the show before I can set him down and pull my top up.

Confined again to the interior of the house, I feel like I'm trapped in a macabre carnival fun house where reality is distorted. I raise the shades up in the living room to watch the driveway, waiting for the warden of the prison to come back and set me free.

The thunder of returning Harleys three hours later sets off a chain reaction in the house. I grab my hobo purse from the kitchen counter and have it over my shoulder before they're even in the driveway. Ian and Tyan — I have discovered the kids' names in the last hour — drop everything and run from window to window, slapping the glass panes and jumping up and down. I collect my fifteen dollars from Mac without a word and evaporate from the house, vowing never to set foot in there again.

The orange glow of dusk is descending over the subdivision when I get home. I walk through the door of our plain vanilla, cookie-cutter house on Bellaire Street, never so glad to be there.

MaryAnne is tapping out a tune on the piano with our Maine Coon cat, Marco, at her side. Mom is at the kitchen table engrossed in a crossword puzzle, and the drone of the TV lets me know Dad is watching hockey in the family room. I open the fridge and retrieve a Tab cola to wash the stale taste of nicotine out of my mouth.

"How'd it go?" Mom asks.

"Horrible! If that guy ever calls again, I'm not home."

"That bad, eh?"

She returns her attention to the crossword puzzle, not asking for any details, and I don't offer any.

MaryAnne enters the kitchen with a book in her hand. She looks like Cindy Brady with her blonde curls pulled up in two tidy bunches and held in place with butterfly rubber bands and red plastic barrettes.

"I got a new book," she says, holding up a Dr. Seuss hardcover for me to admire.

"Let's go," I say, and we climb the stairs hand in hand to her princess-themed bedroom.

It is Saturday night, and I know a crowd is assembling at Carol's house, where albums are playing at high volume and the cooler is filled. I opt to stay home, sitting on my sister's canopy bed while she reads *Green Eggs and Ham.*

MaryAnne's perfect diction is a stark contrast to Tyan's gibberish. Sitting cross-legged on the bed, I have a new appreciation for the faint smell of fabric softener rising from the pressed pillowcases and linens. I am exhausted and stop trying to make sense of the padlocked bedroom door. I push the image out of my mind, curl up under the Strawberry Shortcake comforter, and ask MaryAnne to read another story.

Boring never felt so good.

CHAPTER 4

Oh Brother, Where Art Thou?

Cooler weather dwindles the population of truants in the woods, but I know I will find Vicky there when I hop off the bus Monday morning. Sure enough she is there, alone in the clearing with one arm wrapped around her midsection for warmth and the other holding a half-smoked cigarette. Her trademark grin spreads from ear to ear as I approach.

"How were the little monsters?" she asks.

"Very funny!" I reply. "What the hell were you thinking, setting me up for that?"

Vicky drops her head back and lets out a nicotine-soaked belly laugh, like she had been waiting a lifetime to deliver a punch line to some joke.

"What's up with the girl anyway?" I ask. "She's like a wild animal."

"Sad, ain't it?" Vicky says, her smile evaporating with a shake of her head. "I heard the parents had a stash of mescaline in the house and she ate a bunch of it."

I have trouble believing that a four-year-old could ingest mind-altering acid without being hospitalized and the parents being thrown in jail, but I nod my head in agreement anyway.

"Did you see the padlock on their bedroom door?" Vicky asks.

"Yeah, and their window is nailed shut too. Why?"

Vicky's reply is casual, as if she's commenting on the carpet color. "You said it yourself. Wild animals."

Vicky clearly has nothing more to say about the matter, and it puzzles me. Am I overreacting? Have I led such a sheltered life that I don't know "normal" when I see it?

A small delegation of fellow miscreants begins to congregate around us, so Vicky and I stop talking. We stand in a circle rubbing our hands and stomping our feet for warmth, until somebody suggests starting a small bonfire. When several people move to gather twigs and branches for kindling, I decide it's time to leave.

•••

I approach school like it's a buffet these days, picking and choosing the classes I want to attend. Ms. Sorenson's third period art class is always at the top of my list.

I creep in the side door of the school just as the bell rings to end second period. Classroom doors fly open and bodies of all shapes and sizes spill out. I ditch my jacket and gloves before sliding into Ms. Sorenson's class mere moments before the second bell rings.

Gay Sorenson is the living stereotype of an eccentric artist. Middle-aged and wearing oversized glasses with round black frames, her shocking white hair is cut in a messy bob. Her wardrobe is filled with homemade works of art like fur skirts, leather pants, and jockey hats. Ms. Sorensen doesn't just teach art, she embodies it, and her enthusiasm is infectious.

Today, however, is different. Today she is at the front of the class, crying, with my brother Steve standing next to her.

"It's okay," Steve keeps saying, patting her shoulder.

Empathy is foreign to my brother, to my entire family for that matter, and it's awful to watch him fumble through it. I look away, ashamed for me and for him, until Steve takes his seat next to me.

Through choked back tears, Ms. Sorenson explains that vandals broke into the school over the weekend. They shattered the display case in the hall and ripped up the latest art exhibit, which held Steve's artwork.

The class rumbles at the news. It's no secret that Ms. Sorenson treats Steve more like a protégé than a student. He's talented, and she excavates his gift, teaching him ways to master it. He's definitely the teacher's pet, yet nobody seems to resent him for it.

I look sideways at Steve, trying to gauge his reaction, but there's nothing. He stares down at his desk, crimping the corner of his notebook. The rage-filled brother I grew up with on Avon Street has evaporated since moving to New Baltimore. This current version of Steve is calm and artistic — someone who enjoys a good laugh, is liked by his peers, and doesn't beat up his siblings.

My parents attribute this inner peace to Steve finding a group of nerdy friends — or maybe just outgrowing the violent outbursts. It's years before any of us realize that his peace actually comes from a bottle. Alcohol tranquilizes his rage and stifles the terrible bully, bringing relief for him and us, too. Nobody asks Steve where all his anger went. All we know is the gentle, sweet boy who existed before the ten-foot fall is back.

"Art is not just lines on paper," Ms. Sorensen says to the class, her voice rising. "It is not just marble or clay or oil paint. Art is your soul communicating with the world."

My brother looks up at Ms. Sorensen at the exact moment she turns to face him.

"This is a violation of your soul, Steven, and I'm sorry this happened to you."

Her words hang in the air until the sound of sirens cut them in half. Fire trucks are heading down the dirt road across the street to extinguish a bonfire that's now raging in the woods.

CHAPTER 5

A Long Walk Home

I join my flock of outcasts at Dodge Park, over twenty miles from New Baltimore, to enjoy the outdoors one last time before winter lays down her blanket of snow. We arrive in groups of twos and threes at different times, depending on how much luck each of us had catching a ride. Hitchhiking is a common mode of transportation in 1979 for those with no wheels but lots of time.

Hours tick by at the park as we get lost in Frisbee, beer, and the rock music of 101 WRIF blaring from a portable radio. The sun is dim before we scatter and start the arduous trek back to New Baltimore. I begin my journey with Tim, a regular hitching buddy from school. It takes numerous rides before landmarks begin to look familiar.

Tim and I are dropped off on Gratiot Avenue and part ways. He heads back toward Cotton Road, and I stick my thumb out on 23-Mile Road, deciding to hitchhike the last three miles home rather than walk it in the growing cold.

Within minutes a beige, four-door sedan rolls to a stop a few feet in front of me. I open the passenger side door and climb in next to a middle-aged man wearing a baseball cap.

"Thanks," I say as I tuck my long blonde hair behind my ears and situate my hobo purse on the seat next to me. "Just drop me in front of Vitale's fruit market."

The crunching of gravel gives way to the smooth hum of tarmac. I look out the window and push the seat belt out of my way. Seat belts are still optional in cars and even though this car has them, I never strap in when hitchhiking.

"How old are you?" the man asks.

"Fifteen."

"Have you ever been fucked?"

My antennae go up and my palms begin to sweat. Somehow my heart rate and my voice remain steady.

"That's none of your business," I reply as my right hand begins to wander over the landscape of the door, searching for the handle.

"You're not going home," he says with a crooked smile, jerking the sedan onto the I-94 entrance ramp and gripping the wheel tighter.

He seems excited by what he just said and what he is about to do.

I, on the other hand, show zero emotion. I don't plead for mercy. I don't sob. In fact, I don't react at all; I just stare straight ahead. Thanks to Steve, I have more than ten years of hand-to-hand combat training under my belt, and plenty of proof that showing any reaction would only add fuel to fire.

Steve's assaults on Mark and me were so relentless that our babysitters came once, then refused to return to our house on Avon Street. Steve would lie in wait for us inside cabinets or behind doors. He was lightning fast and would have me on the floor in a stranglehold before my mind could piece together what was happening. I'd learned to wear my bulky mood ring on the middle finger of my right hand as a makeshift brass knuckle, and I kept a giant comb in the back pocket of my jeans in case I needed to jam it into an eye socket. I even had a long, wooden-handled filet knife in my purse.

So as soon as the words "you're not going home" leave the man's mouth, I become incredibly calm. My vision and breathing slow until time seems to stand still. The entrance ramp grows shorter in front of me, and I mentally calculate five seconds until the point of no return. Then I cross my arms over my midsection, my left hand finding and gripping the wooden handle of the knife in my purse. With one swift movement, I pivot on my left knee and thrust the edge of the blade to his throat. Both my hands are now on the handle, and they are rock steady, along with my voice.

"Stop the car or I cut your fucking head off."

The car fishtails as he slams on the brakes and skids to a complete stop. Somehow, I keep my balance and my eyes on him. We are sideways on the ramp, mere feet from the highway.

I inch backward on the seat until my backside brushes the passenger door, then reach my right hand behind me in search of the door handle. I falter for a moment when I find it, not knowing if I need to lift it up or swing it back. I turn my head to look at the door handle and he seizes the opportunity, thrusting his meaty fingers into my long blonde hair just as I pull the handle and kick open the door.

My right leg dangles from the car while my right hand grips the door frame. He tries to drag me back in as I try to pull myself out. My left hand still has a white-knuckled grip on the knife, and I begin to swing it blindly behind me. The blade glances the dashboard, the steering wheel and then something soft and fleshy.

He grunts and releases my hair, then kicks hard at my low back. I spiral out the door and land face-first, then roll onto my feet braced for battle. There is no need. His taillights are already fading down the highway, heading north. My purse was kicked out with me, and I grope in the grass for its scattered contents — house keys, Aqua Net, Cover Girl blush trio.

It's only when I reach the streetlight at the top of the entrance ramp that I release my grip on the knife and shake my fingers out. I'm thankful there are no oncoming cars, and I feel safer among the streetlights, gas stations and fast-food restaurants that line 23-Mile Road.

Under the streetlight's yellow haze, I take a minute to inspect myself and the knife. There is a faint, one-inch streak of blood on the blade. I crane my neck around to inspect the backside of my bell-bottom jeans, but there is nothing. I stretch my arms and rotate them from topside to underside, but again, nothing. I frown, realizing I inflicted only a minor flesh wound on the driver.

I do not contemplate going to the police, not even for a second. Not only would I be grounded for life, but I imagine the police shaking their heads at my cutoff shorts and flimsy tank top, certain that I'd been asking for it. My fifteen-year-old brain sees what happened as an inconvenience, an irritation. I never consider that I am probably not this predator's first attempt, and decades later, the thought that I probably was not his last will still haunt me.

I wipe the blade on my sock and return the knife to its rightful place in my purse, handle up. I resign myself to the fact that I will be walking home on wobbly legs, my heart racing from the adrenaline aftermath.

Just shake it off, Debbie.

It is a long walk to our house on Bellaire Street. I unlock the front door and step inside, noticing how empty it feels even though my siblings are asleep in their bedrooms.

I open the fridge and grab a Tab, then shut the door a bit too hard. I freeze in place, listening for the sound of my parents coming downstairs to investigate. There's nothing but silence, so I pop the metal cap on the bottle and take a long drink. Adrenaline has left my mouth parched and the burn of cool soda is just what I need.

I sit in the quiet dark at the kitchen table, realizing just how much I miss my life on Avon Street.

CHAPTER 6

Never Say Never

Michigan winters last an eternity, with signs of spring creeping in painfully slow. The crocus are the first to peek through the snow, followed by bright daffodils. Then smart convertibles with heaters on and tops down appear in the strengthening sun and winter is forgotten.

My memories of a would-be rapist and wilding kids with padlocked bedroom doors fade with time, and eventually I begin to question if either event ever really happened.

"Deborah, is that you?" Mom calls from the kitchen as I walk through the front door.

"Yeah, it's me."

I enter the kitchen and nearly collide with her outstretched arm, which is holding the phone.

"It's a babysitting job."

"Who is it?"

"That man with the two kids you watched a few months ago."

"I told you I didn't want to babysit for them again!"

"Tell him yourself."

She deposits the receiver into my hand and walks into the living room, out of sight. I take

a few breaths before barking "Hello" into the phone.

"Hi, umm, Debbie… Hey, are you, uh…" Mac stammers.

This doesn't sound like the same tough motorcycle guy I met, the one with waist-length hair, a bushy beard, and a leather jacket.

"Would you be able to watch the kids for a couple hours on Wednesday? I'm in a real bind."

"Sorry, I'm busy."

There is such a long pause that I check to see if the cord has disconnected from the phone's receiver.

"I can pay whatever you want. Ten dollars an hour?"

"No, I'm really busy."

"My wife left," Mac says. "She abandoned us. I know they're not the easiest kids to watch, but they've had it rough lately."

The memory of Ian offering up his stash of Saltine crackers washes over me. I'm silent as my head and heart negotiate, and my hesitation signals Mac that he's on the right track.

"I need to see the lawyer, and the kids really like you. Ian still asks me when you're coming back. I just don't want my kids to end up in foster care."

I take a deep breath. "You said ten dollars an hour, right?"

My head wins this negotiation, overruling both my heart and my intuition.

• • •

Wednesday arrives and my dread deepens with every step down the muddy driveway toward Mac's house. He opens the door just as I'm about to knock and ushers me inside with a broad smile.

"Thanks for doing this. You have no idea how grateful I am."

The garage sale decor of the living room has been tidied up. Clutter has been cleared away, furniture dusted, and the window shades lifted. The cloying scent of cheap lavender spray, however, is losing its battle against the smell of a recently flushed toilet. The kids fidget nearby on the couch. Tyan is like a tightly coiled spring while Ian sits quietly, both kids held in place by their father's stern gaze.

"Remember what we talked about," Mac says, looking at the kids until they nod their heads in acknowledgment. Turning to me, he adds, "I won't be more than two hours."

He leaves and the living room is too quiet. Tyan and Ian look from me to the front door, then back at me. When the Harley roars to life, a pressure valve pops inside the kids. They bound from the couch to the windows, slapping wildly on the glass while jumping up and down. My heart sinks.

"That's enough," I say.

The kids continue their manic revelry, unfazed by the sound of my voice.

"That's enough!" I yell, stomping my foot on the floor.

The kids stop and stare at me. How about that? It works!

"Now sit down!" I yell, pointing at the couch.

They sit, smiling up at me as if we are playing a new game. I dig through my oversized purse and pull out a small stack of folded plain paper, smoothing it flat on the coffee table. I then produce a sandwich bag full of assorted crayons and dump them onto the table.

The kids don't move from the couch, only sit there looking puzzled.

"Don't you want to color?"

I draw a big flower then hand the crayon to Tyan. A light seems to go on inside her and she drops to her knees at the table, scribbling wildly over the flower. I give her another sheet of paper and she picks up a fistful of crayons, creating an explosion of color in jagged lines across the paper and onto the table. Ian joins in, drawing small squiggles on his sheet.

"How about a snack?"

I dig into my purse once more and pull out a three-pack of Cracker Jack. I open one, spilling a small mound of caramel popcorn onto the table in front of each of them.

It takes two blinks of an eye for all of it to disappear. The sight of their sticky cheeks flecked with popcorn bits and papery peanut skins makes me laugh.

At some point I dig out the other two boxes, handing one to each child. Tyan snatches Ian's box and they run down the hallway, disappearing into their bedroom. They return seconds later, and I know that two boxes of Cracker Jack have just been added to the makeshift food pantry under their beds.

They open their hands, wanting more. I try to explain that's all I have, but Tyan is upset and talking so fast I can't understand her. She lunges for my purse and I grab her wrist, afraid of her finding and wielding the knife that's tucked inside.

She bares her teeth to bite me, and I let go of her arm. Dropping to all fours, Tyan barks like a dog, snapping at my feet. Ian stands off to the side, watching. I start to sweat, but suddenly Tyan stops mid-snarl and pops up off the floor.

The faint rumble of a motorcycle comes closer. The kids are at the windows in a flash, pounding the glass and jumping up and down again. One hour and twenty minutes since Mac left, according to the clock next to the couch.

The motorcycle chokes off, and the kids scramble back to the couch before the kickstand clunks open. They sit still, hands in laps, as Mac steps through the door.

"That was quick," I say while he shakes his long hair free from the helmet.

"Yeah, I just had to sign some papers and write a big check. You know how lawyers are—they bleed you dry when you're down."

I don't bother to tell Mac that at age fifteen, I do not know about lawyers.

"How were they?" he asks.

"Really good," I reply, and mostly mean it.

"I guess I owe you these," he says to the kids as he reaches inside his leather jacket and tosses them two bags of M&Ms. "Now go play in your room."

They shoot from the couch like torpedoes and are headed for the bedroom when Mac yells, "Wait! Come back and say goodbye to the pretty lady."

Did he just call me pretty?

Ian and Tyan wrap their arms around my legs and hug me tightly, then run off to their room once more.

"They really like you, Debbie. They don't like many people, but they sure like you."

I shrug, not entirely convinced. Mac reaches back and pulls a black wallet from his rear pocket. It is attached to a belt loop with a long silver chain.

"I owe you fifteen dollars, right?"

"Ten dollars is more than enough," I say, now ashamed of my over-inflated rate.

"You sure?" he asks, fishing around in the folds of his wallet. "Well, this is embarrassing. I didn't go to the bank yet, and all I have is six dollars. I can run back out…."

"No, it's okay. Six dollars is just fine, really."

I stuff the six dollars into my bell-bottoms and pick up my purse.

"You want a beer?"

I pause, not accustomed to having a grown-up offer me a beer.

"Never mind," Mac says with a wave of his hand. "I'm sure a girl like you has a few boyfriends to spend her time with. It's just been one of those weeks, and I'd like to have a conversation with somebody who's normal."

I shift my purse to my other side, buying more time. The truth is that boys rarely talk to me and grown-ups never do. But this grown-up is offering me beer and conversation like I'm somebody. I consider staying, but common sense tells me to go home.

"I should probably get going," I say, and pivot toward the door.

"Wait," Mac says. "You don't want to forget this."

He lifts my ratty leather jacket from the arm of the couch. I rescued this eyesore two months ago from a garage sale box marked *Free*. Despite my efforts to sew the torn lining and soften the brittle leather with shoe wax, it still looks like roadkill. Mom constantly threatens to throw the jacket in the trash the minute I take it off, so I wear it all the time, even inside.

Mac passes the jacket to me, and I drape it over my arm, embarrassed by its shabby appearance.

"You've got great taste, by the way," he says.

"I do?"

"Yeah, that's a Lesco jacket. It'll last a lifetime if you treat it right."

I take my jacket, beaming with pride. It's a Lesco jacket! I'm not sure what that means, but it sounds special.

"You know what?" I say, setting down my purse. "I'll take that beer."

CHAPTER 7

Boiled Frog

The transition from babysitter to girlfriend happens without notice or courtship. Over the following weeks, I return a few more times for paid babysitting jobs. Each time, Mac fishes through his wallet and complains how lawyer fees are taking money from his children's mouths. Each time I assure him it's no big deal and agree to take whatever he can afford, which is never much.

He makes up for a lack of cash with an abundance of compliments. "The kids can't wait to see you," he says, or "I don't know what I'd do without you." And then there's my favorite, "You're so grown up." Mac has left a trail of these sugar-coated phrases over the last few months, and I have eaten up every one of them. Compliments from adults aren't entirely new to me. Teachers compliment my writing and artwork, but I don't give what they say much weight, assuming that giving compliments is one of the requirements of being a good teacher. But Mac's compliments are different. They're about *me*, not my work. And it feels like he means them.

Mac intrigues me. With his long hair and Harley Davidson motorcycle, I feel sure he has already seen more adventure in his life than my boring parents or teachers ever will. He feels wild and dangerous, a man who lives by his own rules, a sharp contrast to my diminutive, submissive father. What would it be like, I wonder, to be with someone like Mac?

Beer and conversation quickly become routine. Babysitting turns into "hanging out," and if Mac needs to go run some errands, well, I'm cool with that because that's what friends are for. His occasional compliments become more flirtatious with each visit. In the frog in the pot of boiling water analogy, I am just about poached.

One day in early summer, I arrive at the house to watch the kids. The muddy drive is now sunbaked clay that slaps hard against the soles of my moccasin boots. I have spent weeks embroidering *Led Zeppelin* across the back of my denim cutoffs and am proudly wearing my handiwork.

The door opens before I reach the first step of the porch, and Mac leans against the door jamb, his grin widening with each step I take. The July sun is eclipsed by the cool shade of the living room, and my eyes take a moment to adjust. Something is different about the house today.

The dishes are washed, the floors are mopped, and the smell of cigarette smoke is infused with chemical pine scent. And the house is quiet. Too quiet.

"Where are the kids?" I ask, following Mac into the kitchen.

"They're staying at my friend Mary's for a few days," he says, fishing two cans of Pabst Blue Ribbon out of the fridge. He closes the fridge door with an elbow while extending a cold can of PBR in his other hand. "Looks like I get you all to myself, beautiful."

My face burns as I take the beer, and my hands begin to sweat.

"No need to be embarrassed," Mac says when he sees my red face. "You'll have to get used to me calling you beautiful." He steps in close, puts his hands on my waist and begins to kiss my lips. "Don't be shy now," he whispers into my ear, his hands crawling up the back of my shirt.

I'm not shy, I'm frozen. For months, I'd thought we were building a friendship. This sudden detour into a physical relationship has left me paralyzed with a mix of terror, guilt and shame. How could I be such an idiot? What did I think was actually going to happen with this man? I am seven years old again in a musty cinderblock basement.

• • •

Mom's brother moved to the US from Scotland a few years before our family did. He helped Dad get his job at the auto plant and is a regular visitor to our house. I think he's rich because he owns several acres "up north" with lots of horses, chickens, and pigs. Right now, Uncle Mark is trying to convince me that one of his new ponies is waiting for me in the dank basement of our home on Avon Street.

"I don't believe you," I say.

"It's true, Debbie. Come on, I'll show you." His hand swallows mine as he leads me down the steep stairway to the basement.

"Where is it?" I ask, making a loop around the enormous metal furnace squatting in the center of the basement.

"He's a miniature pony. He's in my pocket."

I creep closer, my curiosity overruling my child's intuition, which knows this feels wrong. Uncle Mark has his back to me and speaks softly. "It's okay, he won't hurt you," he says, then turns to face me with his erect penis in his hand.

"That doesn't look like a pony!"

"He was just born," my uncle says. "You need to put your hand around him to keep him warm."

"I don't want to." I have no idea what this fleshy thing is, but I know that it is *not* a pony.

Uncle Mark reaches for my hand, wrapping it around his penis and stroking himself with it.

I turn my head and watch the sun streaming in through the small window near the top of the cinderblock wall. My eyes trace the path of dancing particles, trying to count them as they glint and fall to my red leather shoes and dust the lace cuff of my white ankle socks.

Later that night, I sit in the bathtub as Mom lathers up my hair.

"Lean back so we can rinse out the bubbles," she says.

I am starting to lean backward when she props me back up.

"What's in your hand, Deborah?"

I unfurl my fingers to reveal a shiny quarter that I've been clutching for hours.

"Where did you get that?"

"Uncle Mark gave it to me for petting his pony."

Lightning could not strike me any harder than the shriek that comes out of my mother. Something is wrong, and it's obvious I did it, but I don't know what it is and she doesn't tell me.

When Dad comes home, Mom whisks him off to their bedroom, their muffled words growing louder and louder. I wait, anxious, not knowing what my punishment will be.

My anxiety ends up stretching out for weeks. I keep waiting, and yet my punishment never arrives. The pony incident is never mentioned again.

Uncle Mark returns to our house for parties and holidays, and the following summer I am sent to stay at his farm for two weeks with my cousin, Anne. He never touches me again, but when he sits in our living room, laughing and drinking with my parents, I become a little more invisible.

• • •

Mac clasps one of my hands and pulls me along the hallway into his bedroom. A mattress lies on the floor with no sheets. It's thin and I can feel each spring impressing half-circles into my back. I scan my memory, searching for what I'd done to make Mac think I wanted to have sex with him. I shouldn't have worn the lip gloss, I decide.

Stop whining, I tell myself. *You wanted to be treated like an adult. This is what adults do.*

I turn my head and count the threads of my embroidered denim shorts, now crumpled on the floor beside me. One, two, three, four…

CHAPTER 8

An Apple Falls from the Tree

I don't know what to feel the next day, so I feel nothing. Burying shame into the pit of my stomach is a default setting, which makes it easier to convince myself that Mac loves me. Not just loves me, but *needs* me, which is the ultimate enticement to this budding co-dependent.

Unsure of how I fit into this new world, I allow Mac to define me. My immature long ponytail is replaced by a more sophisticated, collar-length perm. Groovy floral-patterned blouses are pushed to the back of my closet as black Harley Davidson T-shirts become my clothing of choice. Within a few months, my appearance, my thoughts, and my beliefs align with Mac's vision of who I should be.

I tell myself we're in love. In my teenage mind, love equates to a set of sequential steps: flirting, going steady, sex and getting married. I have completed most of them now, so it doesn't matter that I've just turned sixteen and Mac is twenty-eight with two children.

For months, I come and go as I please at school and at home. I have my own key and let myself in at all hours. Even Carol, whose cool dad buys us beer, envies my unfettered freedom.

My parents rarely question where I've been, and when they do, all I have to say is "babysitting." They don't check the phone numbers I leave or ask why I never have any money from all the work I seem to be doing.

Looking back, my parents were far too entrenched in their own sagas to notice that I had started one of my own. Their struggles created emotional patterns that took root early on and, despite their best efforts, they never were able to let them go and see what was happening to their children.

• • •

Wee Bridget "Bridie" Donegan was a beauty, with long golden hair and legs that would be the envy of any New York dance girl. She was twenty-four when I was born, already a mother with eighteen-month-old Steve at home.

Mom was number seven out of nine siblings. A black and white photo of her younger sister, Barbara, sits atop the piano in our living room. In it, Barbara is two years old, with dimpled cheeks and ringlets of dark hair, a cherub on earth. She holds a large ball of yarn in her chubby hands, laughing at the photographer.

It was 1945 when Mom stole a slice of cake from the grown-up table at a neighborhood party and hid outside to eat it. Barbara, who had just turned three, came teetering after her, but not wanting to share her cake or be found out, Mom told her to go away.

The bus driver never saw Barbara as she stepped into the busy street. The impact was so forceful that one of her tiny shoes was found at the opposite end of the block, standing upright and completely separated from the accident.

Mom never forgot that shoe. When she withdrew to her bed for days, no longer willing or able to participate in daily life, she would hold Barbara's photo in her hand and call me into her dark room. Without tears, she would recount the accident, describing the shoe in vivid detail, as if I were a priest who could go back in time and absolve the sins of her five-year-old self. I believe her tender soul took refuge inside that scene, replacing the pain and chaos of the accident with something comprehensible: a tiny shoe lying far away from the lifeless body of her little sister.

She also hid from the deaths of her two brothers. Her older brother Sammy was serving in the Royal Army when his Jeep flipped, killing him on her tenth birthday. Her younger brother Alex died of a heart defect before she turned sixteen.

These tragic events did nothing to strengthen the relationship between Mom's parents. Despite having nine children together, the Donegans did not like each other very much. Shouting matches, dishes breaking, and extramarital affairs were part of everyday life. Sammy was the third child to die, and according to Mom, her father never recovered, dying just a couple of years later. Her mother coped with the loss of her children by staying out late and drinking, alternating those activities with weeks of deep depression.

• • •

Dad also learned early the futility of expressing his emotions. He grew up just a few miles away from Mom, but unlike her raucous family of nine siblings, Hugh Brannigan came from a quiet home. He was the youngest of three siblings, with a mop of thick, dark hair and bright blue eyes—a momma's boy by his own admission. His body grew lanky and lean, well-suited for wrestling, and he excelled at it. After winning the Gold Cup for Glasgow, he rode the bus home alone, unheralded, the same way he had traveled to the event. My grandfather dismissed his wins on the mat. The wins weren't for soccer, so they weren't worth talking about.

The tenement building in Govan, the district of Glasgow where Dad grew up, resembled a Charles Dickens orphanage in photos, with lots of young boys in short pants with dirt-smeared cheeks staring at the camera. There is not a blade of grass anywhere, and the entire building seems to be coated in soot.

Dad shared a tiny bedroom with his older brother and sister, and his parents pulled a makeshift curtain across the front room to sleep in the kitchen. Three families lived on each floor, all sharing one communal toilet in the hallway. Once a month Dad paid two pence at the public bathhouse for a cold bath. He has worn a full set of dentures since his early twenties because he never had the benefit of a toothbrush.

Like most boys without means, Dad left school at age sixteen to learn a trade so he could scrape together an honest but sparse living at the Harland & Wolff shipyard like his father. My grandfather worked full-time there through the week, then tended bar twelve hours a day on weekends. He smoked a lot and drank even more, until a stroke left him paralyzed and wheelchair bound at fifty-six.

The real tragedy was that, even though he lived another twenty years, he died without telling Dad he loved him. He didn't withhold the words out of contempt or disdain; he just wasn't capable of saying them.

• • •

Neither of my parents grew up with any models on how to express or receive love. But as fate would have it, their bruised and untethered souls crossed paths at a dance hall in Glasgow. Mom was about to leave for the night when she felt a tap on her shoulder; it was Dad, nervously asking for a dance.

Their courtship was a tumultuous rollercoaster of ups and downs. Mom followed her sister to Canada but then returned. She dated other suitors and left again. Unfazed, Dad continued his pursuit, and shortly after my mom turned twenty-two, the rollercoaster came to a screeching halt. She was pregnant with Steve, and they married within weeks.

To support our growing family, Dad picked up more hours at the shipyard, but it was a constant struggle to pay bills. He accepted this daily grind and borderline poverty because it was all he'd ever known — and a bit better than what he'd grown up with.

Mom, however, knew there was more out in the world. She had seen it in Canada. Weary of the pub culture and the apathy that grew like bacteria at the shipyard, she was determined to keep our family from sliding into Glasgow's industrial abyss. In pursuit of more, we moved from Scotland to Denmark to Canada to America, all before my fifth birthday.

While living in Canada, Dad landed a good paying job as a manual welder in one of the booming Detroit auto plants. For over a year, he commuted to the US, driving the Detroit-Windsor Tunnel on Monday mornings and returning Friday night. If there was overtime, he didn't come home for weeks.

Mom was twenty-six, raising three children in a ramshackle house. With no friends, no car, and no alternatives, she rolled up her sleeves and somehow made it work.

Growing up, I didn't see the struggles brewing in our family, especially with my parents. All I knew was that Dad was fun-loving when he was home, and Mom kept our lives in order with her rules and strength of will.

As fate would have it, this little apple was about to fall hard from the family tree.

CHAPTER 9

Intercession

Mac's rusty sedan sputters and coughs down the two-lane road along Lake St. Clair, and I begin to doubt it will survive the twenty-minute trek into Algonac to pick up Ian and Tyan. They have been staying with Mac's friends, Mary and Donna, for over two weeks now so Mac could *get some shit done*. I didn't even realize Mac had any female friends and I'm a bit nervous to meet them.

"How do you know them?" I ask.

"I guess you could say through work. Donna's work, that is."

Mac's grin is mischievous and unsettling. I don't know what the joke is, and I don't ask.

"You're gonna love these two," he tells me. "They're a real trip. They eat a lot of carpet, if ya know what I mean."

I do not know what he means, but before I can ask, he slows the car and points out the passenger window.

"That's where Donna works!" he says.

It is a gray cinder block building with no windows. The faded sign out front says *Anchors Away – Full Nudes* with a neon anchor that blinks from left to right. It's not even noon and the gravel parking lot is nearly full. I am still trying to make the connection between Donna, the strip club, and Mac when he makes a sharp left turn into a mobile home park.

We pull in beside a small white mobile home and are ushered inside with bear hugs and cheek kisses from Mary. The space is tiny, like a camping trailer, but the smell of tangy tomato sauce makes it feel cozy and inviting. Mary is nearing middle age and is dressed in baggy jeans and a frumpy sweatshirt with an odd lace collar. She adjusts her thick glasses while boasting loudly about her daughter's recent academic award at school. This unwanted attention prompts the embarrassed girl on the couch to relocate to the rear of the trailer with her stacks of books.

"I'm on the PTA, the playground patrol, and I coordinate all the school bake sales. There's no hiding from me!" Mary yells lightheartedly toward the disappearing teen.

Two young boys are a tangle of arms and legs as they wrestle in the hallway. The bathroom door opens and Donna exits, stepping around them.

"Thake it outhide, boyth," she says. Her lisp is pronounced, and I wonder if she's doing a cute Daffy Duck impression for them.

Donna is dressed in a tight-fitting red mini dress that flatters her toned body and heavily tattooed arms. Her strawberry blonde hair is thick and lustrous, and I assume she must be at least ten years younger than Mary. The boys are ushered outside through the small room that acts as both a living room and a dining room before Donna turns toward Mary and smiles broadly.

I'm startled to see that several front teeth are missing, causing her face to collapse and aging her at least twenty years. Mary leans in and kisses Donna on the lips.

Oh! They're lesbians! I think, immediately transfixed. This colorful couple is so far from my beige, cookie-cutter life that they feel magical and mythical, like Big Foot or a unicorn. I can't wait to tell Carol. I bet she's never met any lesbians.

"I need milk," Tyan says.

For the first time, I notice Ian and Tyan sitting quietly at the small kitchenette table. They are eating Beefaroni with spoons and have napkins tucked under their chins.

"That's not how we ask for things. Try again," Mary answers.

"May I have some milk, please?" Tyan asks.

Who are these kids? They bear no resemblance to the dirty-faced wildlings that ate with their bare hands. Even Mac shakes his head in disbelief.

"How did you do that? They're using silverware!" he says.

"Patience and praise are all these two angels need," Mary replies.

"Well, thanks for keeping 'em," Mac says. "I know they can be a real pain in the ass."

"Nonsense," Mary says. "They just need a little guidance, that's all."

It takes thirty minutes to pull Ian and Tyan away from the trailer and into the sedan. They slather kisses and hugs all over Mary and Donna, who grow misty-eyed. Tyan clutches her Beefaroni spoon to her chest, refusing to leave it behind, and Mary just kisses her forehead and tells her to bring it back next time. Then she waves and wipes tears from her cheek as we pull away.

• • •

The late summer sun burns a red line along the part of my hair while Mac and I watch the kids from the small cement porch on rickety folding chairs with fraying nylon seats. Mine sags as if it had been used to store a bowling ball. Mac calls it the low rider chair, but I just call it uncomfortable.

The kids obviously love Mary and Donna, but I can tell they are happy to be home. Tyan digs rocks from the dirt driveway with her prized spoon, and Ian sorts them into random piles. It must be fun because they've been at it for hours. A small cooler sits between Mac and me, stocked with ice and cans of PBR. The ice doesn't cool us down, but the PBR makes us not care.

"Are your parents still married to each other?" Mac asks.

"Yeah, they've been together for like thirty years."

"That's great because the children of married parents stay married forever, too, so it means we are going to grow old and gray together."

Mac winks when he says this last bit, like he's gifted me the universe. My first reaction is to point out the obvious — he's in the middle of a divorce and his parents are still married, which makes his theory total crap. Instead, I say nothing and smile weakly, my face starting to burn from a mix of embarrassment from his flattery and my own rising fear. I just turned sixteen a few months ago and he's talking about growing old together? Mac senses my inward retreat and drops the subject. He has been talking this way more frequently, as if a life together is already a matter of fact.

I waffle about it. I have my own bedroom at home with Led Zeppelin posters on every wall and my own telephone, so why would I want to give that up and raise two wildling kids with him? But then Mac talks about the long road trips we will take on his motorcycle, and I start to long for that imagined freedom. There would be no more early morning bus rides to school, no more bullshit homework, no more depressed mother and browbeaten father to deal with. We'd host weekend parties at "my house" where booze would always be free and plentiful. We would be the most popular couple in New Baltimore, and I'd be the envy of all my friends.

Mac and I never talk about anything as heavy as "feelings," but we do talk. He asks for my opinions and tells me I'm smarter than any teacher at Anchor Bay High. The kids bring me their crayon art to admire and want to know when I'm going to be their mommy. Their questions feel rehearsed, and yet I wonder how they will get by without a mother because, according to Mac, his soon-to-be ex-wife Darlene doesn't even want to visit them. He tells me she was the one who put the padlock on the kids' door so she could go out partying for hours. She's never been a good mother, Mac says, then adds, "You're the kind of mom they deserve."

Most days I split my time between Carol's house and Mac's. One Friday night Mac insists on dropping me off at Carol's to meet my friends, reasoning that if they're my friends, eventually they'll be his friends, too. We are treated like celebrities when we pull into the driveway on his restored 1945 Harley Davidson Panhead. A circle of teens surrounds us before the kickstand hits the pavement.

Mac shakes out his ponytail and turns down a beer from Carol's brother, saying he can't stay long. He answers a few questions about his motorcycle before donning his helmet again and roaring back out the way he came. Mac now knows where to find me.

I gain a lot of street cred arriving on the back of that motorcycle. Word spreads fast, and before long the popular kids at school begin to ask me about my "cool boyfriend" and his vintage motorcycle. Heads turn when I pass in the hallway, leaving a wake of chatter behind me. Whether it's good attention or bad doesn't matter. All I know is I'm no longer invisible.

I pull a swath of hair under my nose and give it a sniff as I walk to Ms. Sorenson's art class a few weeks later. My hair reeks of cigarette smoke, and I curse under my breath because there's no time for me to cloak it in Aquanet. I don't smoke, but just about everybody who skips class and heads to the woods does.

I forget my hair anxiety when I see Ms. Sorenson leaning against the wall talking to Mr. Kucharski, the jewelry teacher next door. These are the two coolest cats teaching at Anchor Bay High. The '70s may have ended last year, but neither one of them seems to have noticed.

Ms. Sorenson is in her typical faux-fur skirt, lace-up boots and bright red beret, items that are benign compared to her necklace: a six-inch, robotic-looking metal sculpture dangling from a chain that was probably protecting a bicycle last week. Mr. Kucharski, known to the students as Mr. K., completes the Mod Squad look with his corduroy bell-bottoms, black mutton chop sideburns, and bushy moustache.

"Hey Debbie, have you filled out your class selections for next semester?" he asks.

"Nah, Mr. K., I'm in the B's so it's last pick for me."

Class selection is first-come, first-serve and prioritized alphabetically. If your last name is Allen, you get first pick at the best electives in the first semester, but then second semester it is Zawinski's turn.

The only electives shaping up for me are sewing and accounting, so I'm not keen to fill out my selection card. Somewhere in the back of my mind I am still contemplating the option of touring the country on the back of a Harley Davidson.

"If you don't turn something in, you'll be assigned classes nobody else wants," Mr. K. says, furrowing his brow.

"Yeah, but I dunno, I might not come back next semester."

Ms. Sorenson exchanges a glance with Mr. K. as she steps into the classroom. Her look says, "I told you so," and I know immediately that she's heard the hallway chatter about my cool boyfriend. The bell rings, and I ease toward the door as well.

"Come see me before next period," Mr. K. says. "I'll write you a pass if you need it."

I haven't been to fourth period in weeks and Mr. K. knows it. I nod my agreement anyway and slip into Ms. Sorenson's class.

Class ends and I wait for the stream of students to trickle out of Mr. K.'s room before putting on my best "I don't care" face and striding in. His jewelry class is coveted by many, attended by few. Only juniors and seniors can apply, and each student must be approved by the vice principal. The high cost of materials is also a deterrent.

The room reflects the prestige of the class. There are long, polished wood worktables with magnifying glasses mounted on reticulating arms, along with a few metal anvils secured to the tops. Tall display cases stand as glass monoliths along the windows, each containing intricate silver rings or pendants with gemstones. The space feels sacred.

Mr. K. is wrapping small tools into a leather pouch at one of the worktables. I wait until he finishes tying the cord around it before I step into view. He looks up with a smile.

"Debbie, thanks for coming by. Have a seat."

He motions to the stool opposite him. There is a large teacher's desk against the wall, but legend has it that Mr. K. has never sat behind it. He likes to work alongside his students, showing them the craft as well as teaching it. The heavy wooden stool screeches in protest as I hike myself up onto it.

"So, Debbie... Talk to me about your future. What are you hoping to create in life?"

Mr. K. asks this question without a hint of condescension or authority, only curiosity. Nobody has ever asked me this question, including me. I try to answer, but my mouth freezes and no words form.

Mr. K. drops his interlaced fingers from his chin to the tabletop in front of me. I stare at the bulky silver rings on his fingers, the long strands of dark knuckle hair trapped beneath each one. Several moments pass.

"That's a tough question, isn't it?" he says, rescuing me from the quicksand of panic I am drowning in. "How about you just tell me why you're considering leaving school? Are you in trouble?"

Years will go by before I realize what "trouble" Mr. K. is actually referring to. In the moment I assume he's asking if I'm about to be arrested.

"I'm not in any kind of trouble, Mr. K., I swear it! I'm just bored." I add this at the last minute, before realizing that I mean it. School is only important in homes where parents look at report cards. Besides, college is not an option for me, so why fill my head with useless things like science or social studies?

"I get it," Mr. K. laughs. "You've got a creative mind, and it's hard to sit through those boring classes. But it's the boring classes that will keep your life running smoothly."

I roll my eyes.

"I understand that nobody wants to come to school and be bored every day," he continues, "but if I get you into my jewelry class next semester, would you promise to come back?"

"What? But I'm not a senior… How?" I'm stunned and my words won't knit together as they should.

"Don't worry about how. You leave that to me."

There is a lump rising in my throat and tears welling behind my eyes. All I can do without coming apart is nod my agreement. Mr. K. goes on to explain there is a waitlist for the class and he is moving me to the front of the line. He also tells me that he'll do his part, but I've got to do mine as well.

"You need to start taking your education seriously, Debbie, and that starts with showing up to *all* of your classes. Vice Principal Fowler won't approve this deal unless you're serious."

He gives me a stern look over the top of his wire-rimmed glasses, waiting for me to acknowledge the arrangement. Words still can't leak beyond the lump in my throat, so I nod again.

"Shake on it," Mr. K. says, extending his hand with a huge grin. His hand swallows mine, giving two firm shakes, and all my tension disappears. I laugh, able to breathe again.

"Can you write me that pass, Mr. K.? I think I'm late for typing class."

CHAPTER 10

Mirage

It is no surprise that Mr. K. keeps his word and works out a deal with the vice principal. It is also no surprise that the vice principal has stipulations. Each day I must get signatures from every teacher on my schedule, verifying my attendance. What *is* a surprise, however, is how comforting this new structure feels.

When I step off the bus Monday morning, I'm greeted by the usual gang heading toward the woods.

"Are you coming with us?" Dan asks.

"Wish I could, but I've got this stupid thing," I reply, waving my sign-in sheet.

The gang groans in unison, muttering about the tyranny of it all, and then continues across the street, vanishing into pine-scented darkness. By the end of the week, they stop asking.

I struggle to stay awake in history class but make an honest effort in the others. It takes a few days for classmates to stop gawking at the prodigal sophomore when I take a seat. It takes a few more days for me to stop caring about them. By week three, I find my stride and discover that I'm capable of good grades. I forget why I stopped going to Mrs. Harris's creative writing class, which is now my favorite.

• • •

"Do you want to read something I wrote?" I ask Mac, dangling two sheets of notebook paper near his face. We haven't even been on the couch for ten minutes, but I'm proud of my latest writing assignment.

"Not really," he replies, reaching for a pack of Kool menthols on the coffee table without even looking at me.

He flicks open a Zippo lighter, lights the cigarette, and blows a cloud of smoke into the room — all while looking straight ahead.

"I think it's pretty good. It took me a long time. Mrs. Harris even read it to the class."

"You know I think all that school bullshit is a waste of time."

I can tell Mac's getting annoyed, and I drop my hand to my lap, crushing the papers along with my enthusiasm. I fight the tears welling up behind my eyes and try to swallow the feeling of insignificance caught in my throat.

"Jesus, are you gonna cry?"

I want to say, "This means something to me" or "Please look at me when I talk to you." I want to say so many things, but instead, I say nothing and stare at the water stain on the coffee table.

"For crying out loud, don't be such a baby!" Mac says with a sigh. "Look, I didn't want to say anything just yet, but you might as well hear it now. We're leaving in a few days."

"What do you mean?"

"The kids need family around them. I can't get their mother to pick up the phone, and I can't raise them by myself. I have family in Ohio, and they want all of us to move there."

"Oh?" It's the only reply I can muster because I am disoriented and confused. I've never heard Mac talk about family in Ohio or even hint about moving there.

"It's *all* of us," Mac adds. "That means you, too."

"My parents would never let me go to Ohio," I stammer. "And what about school? I can't just quit."

"Yes, you can."

"What? How? I mean, I can't." I am stumbling over every word now.

"You just stop going. It's that easy."

Before I can ask my next question, Mac answers it. "You don't tell your parents. You just pack up some clothes and you leave like a big girl."

Mac explains that he is taking Ian and Tyan down to Ohio on Thursday and will return Sunday. Then he will spend two weeks packing things up before leaving for good. My choice is either to go with him or say goodbye forever.

• • •

Two days later Mac heads to Ohio with the kids. I have his mother's phone number on a scrap of paper, and I agree to call him Saturday at noon. For a few months now I have called Mac from a payphone outside Vitale's Fruit Market, a one-mile dirt and gravel walk down Callens Road. We use these calls to plan the week ahead, deciding what days I will come over.

Nobody finds it unusual that I make regular trips to the payphone because our home phone is disconnected. Dad lost his job again, and this time it has dragged on longer than his unemployment benefits cover. Not long after the phone service is shut off, my mom begins to pay for groceries with food stamps.

I plug three quarters into the phone, which gets me ten minutes of long-distance talk time. The phone rings twice and a woman answers, her quirky drawl coming through loud and clear on the line.

"Hallo there, Ace High Tavern!"

I don't say anything, wondering if I misdialed.

"Hallo? Anybody there?"

"Umm, I was looking for Mac McCall?"

She says no more to me but shouts, "Mac! Git on over here. Phone call for you."

"Hello?" This time it is Mac's familiar voice.

"Hi…I thought I had a wrong number when I heard Ace High Tavern."

"Yeah, my parents own a bar here in Trimble. That was my mom you talked to."

"That's so cool," I say, picturing a quaint, small-town pub with brass beer taps and a polished wood bar backed by mirrors reflecting a rainbow of liquor bottles.

"Hang on a minute," Mac says. "I've got somebody here that wants to talk to you."

"Hewow?" Ian's three-year-old voice comes on the line.

"Hey! How are you, my little big-man?"

Ian hesitates, and I hear mumbling in the background. "I miss you," he says, obviously repeating what he was told. "Grammaw has chickens!"

Mac gets back on the line and wastes no time with small talk.

"Have you thought any more about what I said?"

"Yes, but I just don't know. My parents, school, my sister, I don't think I can leave them yet."

"Your parents?" Mac laughs. "They'd probably appreciate having one less mouth to feed. Didn't you tell me they were struggling to keep the lights on?"

"Well…"

"And school? A classroom is nowhere to learn anything. It's just a sanctioned prison for brain-dead kids. I thought you were more grown up than that."

"Well, I…"

"Your sister will be in first grade next year. She'll make friends, and pretty soon she won't even remember she has a sister. Nobody there needs you. *We* need you."

I'm speechless. Death by a thousand papercuts must feel better than this. *Nobody needs me?*

"Are you still there, Debbie?"

I start to answer when an automated voice comes on the line, repeating that I need to insert twenty cents to continue the call.

"Come to the house on Tuesday and —"

Mac is cut off by the operator, and I am grateful to hear only the humming buzz of the disconnected line.

Later that night, Dad whips up his specialty for dinner, battered and deep-fried SPAM slices. But I no longer see it as my favorite greasy indulgence. Instead, I see a low-priced alternative to the chicken and beef we used to eat.

The next day I watch MaryAnne run through a sprinkler in the backyard with Claire, her playmate from down the street. She is no longer that chubby-cheeked baby I once carried on my hip. Her long limbs are tanned, and she reaches for Claire's hand as they jump over the sprinkler's head. I imagine them boarding a school bus, going on double dates, graduating high school and heading off to college. Already I see a fierce independence blooming in MaryAnne and can easily imagine her surrounded by people whose lives will be marked by creative genius rather than outsider status.

When I step off the bus Monday morning, I am tempted to join the usual procession heading into the woods. I feel adrift, cut off and just plain lonely. The world looks different to me after the phone call with Mac.

I am taking a half step toward the woods when Mr. K. steps out of his sedan in the parking lot and waves to me. I blush, as if he could see what I was contemplating, then quickly turn on my heel and walk to the double doors.

There is a crowd gathered outside my creative writing classroom. Somebody has jammed a pencil into the keyhole and broken it off. Mrs. Harris is upset, and she keeps trying, unsuccessfully, to open the door.

The school natives are getting restless. Mrs. Harris has no control over us, and she never has. Paper airplanes and erasers often fly in her direction when she's explaining something, so when she tells us to go to study hall while maintenance fixes the lock, half of us head in that direction while the other half disperse.

• • •

The day continues to go downhill for me. Shortly after I arrive at typing class, Mr. K. appears in the doorway. He pantomimes to Mrs. Ford that he needs to see me. She nods and motions for me to step into the hallway.

"What's up, Mr. K.?"

"Hey, Debbie. Your materials fee needs to be paid before the next semester starts. I sent a letter to your parents but haven't heard back."

"That's weird."

This is a total lie. I know full well that my parents never read the letter because I threw it away. I check the mailbox every day when I get off the bus, censoring anything that comes from school.

"Give this to your parents, please," Mr. K. says, handing me an envelope. "It's my schedule. I stay late most days, and I'd like them to pick a day to meet with me."

"About what?" I ask, nearly choking on the panic rising from my gut.

"I'd like to figure out a way to make sure you succeed in jewelry class. Your phone is disconnected, so I'm assuming things are tight at home."

I nod, embarrassed. Mr. K. is probably thinking about a payment plan or some form of charity. I'm also afraid, because my parents have no idea that I have an attendance problem or that Mr. K. has gone out of his way to help me, thanks to our disconnected phone and my mailbox censorship. What will they do when they find out they owe money they don't have?

I can't focus in typing class; all I manage to produce by the time class ends are three pages of typos smeared with Wite-Out. I walk all the way to my next class before realizing I left my books under the desk chair. The second bell rings as I run back to the other side of the building. The typing classroom is now filled with the next batch of future administrative assistants. I walk to "my" desk and ask the girl seated there to hand me my books.

As I head back toward the door, Mrs. Ford steps in front of me and puts her hands on my shoulders.

"Sorry, Mrs. Ford, I'm late for…"

My words are cut off by the tears streaming down her face as she looks at me. Mrs. Ford is like Aunt Bea from Mayberry, your favorite relative who is always kind and looks out for you. But I have never exchanged more than two sentences with her, and this sudden display of public emotional intimacy is bewildering and more than a little terrifying.

I turn into a granite statue. Everybody in that classroom is now looking at me as if I punched their grandma. I stay silent while she struggles to speak.

"You have so much potential, but you're making bad choices." Her chest heaves and she bites her lower lip before continuing. "If…I…were…your… mother…" Her words tumble out slowly, one at a time. She takes a deep breath and pushes out what's left. "I would be so worried about you!"

Mrs. Ford steps away, leaving me dumbstruck. Several heads in the class tilt together, whispering back and forth, and a roomful of eyes are on me. I don't know what just happened, but I do know that I never want to step into this classroom again.

I stumble into math class, ten minutes late. My heart is pounding and my arms are shaking, and it's not from carrying a load of books and running down the hallway.

"Miss Brannigan, do you have a late pass?" the teacher asks.

"No sir."

"Well, then you'll be marked as late. One more and it's detention, got it?"

"Yeah. Got it." I make no attempt to explain; I only bury my burning red face in my consumer math textbook.

• • •

The day drags by, and I am eager to end it. My last stop is the school office to hand in my attendance sheet.

"Where's Mrs. Harris's signature?" the assistant asks, frowning.

"We didn't have class today because the lock was jammed. She told us to go to study hall."

She looks at me like I have committed murder in front of her.

"Ask her! It's the truth!"

"You can be sure I will," she says, turning away with my sheet in hand, heading toward Vice Principal Fowler's office.

I hesitate a moment, unsure if I'm supposed to wait. Out the window, I see buses pulling away, and I dart out of the office, throwing open the double doors just in time to see my bus turning out of the lot. I heft the stack of books onto my hip and start the four-mile walk home.

SQUIRREL PIE

The sky is turning purple by the time I reach our street. When I open the door, something feels off. The house is too quiet, and I stand in the foyer a few minutes, listening and wondering if anybody is home.

Dad is sitting on the arm of the couch in the living room to my right. He doesn't seem to see me. His head bobs slightly while his body sways side to side, like he's under some kind of spell.

"Dad?"

He tries to look my way but instead falls forward, slamming his face on the floor. He is motionless and, to my untrained eye, 100 percent unconscious.

"Mom!" I yell, hoping she is in the house somewhere.

"What is it?" The answer comes from upstairs, behind her bedroom door.

"Dad fell on the floor. I think he's sick."

"Let the bastard stay there."

I stand limp in the foyer for what seems like forever, not knowing what to do. I look up the stairwell, willing Mom to appear and take charge, but the only thing that comes down is silence. I kneel next to Dad and put a hand on his back. He mumbles, rolls on his side, and starts to snore. I drape a crocheted blanket over him, hoping I won't catch whatever flu he must have.

It never occurs to me that he is black-out drunk — I won't find that out until I'm eighteen. I don't know that the automotive industry is slowly replacing manual welders with robots, so Dad gets laid off regularly now and copes by drinking more. I also don't know that Mom is becoming more tightly wound and controlling with every passing day as she loses her battle to keep our household running and cover for Dad's chronic alcoholism.

I leave my stack of books on the floor and close the front door behind me. I walk to the payphone and dial Carol's number.

"Hey, it's me. Is it okay if I spend the night?"

"Sure," she replies, no questions asked. "My brother will be there in about ten minutes to pick you up."

In the morning, I pull on one of Carol's T-shirts and we catch the bus to school. I don't think twice about it this time; we walk straight into the woods and stay there all day, talking with friends as they rotate in and out of our conversations.

I spend the day contrasting my options in the back of my mind. I can report to the office each day with my sign-in sheet, swallow my humiliation and return to typing class, then figure out how to pay Mr. K for materials without my parents getting involved. Or I can just walk away, which is beginning to seem like the best option. Maybe Mac is right, and school is nothing but a self-imposed prison. Why not just set myself free?

Late that afternoon, Mac steps onto his front porch when he sees me walking down the driveway. I get to the bottom step and look up at him.

"When do we leave?"

CHAPTER 11

Escape Plan

Mac does not sweep me off my feet in a passionate embrace when I agree to go. Instead, he is all business and logistics. I'm not involved in the planning so much as I am told where to be at what time: Callens Road behind my parents' house, next Wednesday, 6:00 a.m.

"Do *not* tell anybody," Mac says, as I am about to leave his house for the last time. "That means your friends, your teachers, your brothers and most of all, your parents. *Nobody.* You got that?"

I nod mutely.

"Just go home and act normal. Pack a few things and I'll see you Wednesday morning."

All week I hide from teachers and check the mailbox for incriminating letters from school. I may present a cool outward demeanor to friends, but I am a jumbled-up mess inside my head. I don't want to leave my siblings, or my large bedroom with my very own phone and my collection of Led Zeppelin posters, but I also don't want to stay. I consider putting my thumb out and hitchhiking to anywhere.

Tuesday arrives too soon. I hop off the bus from a long day of not being at school and check the mailbox on my way to the front door. Among the overdue bills and junk mail is a letter from Anchor Bay High with the words *Third Attempt* written across it. I quickly fold it in half and slip it into my back pocket.

I peer inside Steve's Delta 88 as I pass on my way to the front door. A 12" flat-head screwdriver sits in the passenger seat, the only key required to start it. It's a disaster of a car with rusted holes in the floorboards and torn vinyl seats, but Steve treats it like a Mercedes. I may not know how to drive yet, but right now I'm ready to learn if it will get me out of here.

Mom is in her usual place at the dinette table, working on a crossword puzzle, when I walk into the kitchen.

"Mail call," I announce and plop the stack onto the table. "Mostly bills."

"Take those to your father. Let him deal with them."

I haven't seen my parents in the same room all week. They fight silently, exchanging harsh looks but never words. To me, it's worse this way because we are all expected to play our part and pretend nothing is wrong.

At some point they'll exchange pleasantries and the tension will break, but that doesn't appear to be happening anytime soon. This time the silence feels exceptionally heavy, and it adds to the weight I'm carrying in my chest.

I take the stack of bills into the living room where Dad is sleeping on the couch with the TV on. I set the mail on the coffee table and drift back into the kitchen.

"Where's Mark?"

Mom answers without lifting her eyes from her puzzle. "Playing guitar at Pete's house."

"Where's MaryAnne?"

She sighs to let me know she's tired of me interrupting her crossword. "She's with Claire."

I don't bother to ask where Steve is. A few months ago, he volunteered to move his bed from the upstairs room he shared with Mark to the basement, just beyond the sump pump. He rarely leaves the basement these days, preferring to be left alone.

Of my two brothers, Mark has always been more open-hearted and welcoming. He seems to draw people to him without even trying, the latest proof being his large group of guitar-playing middle school friends. But our Mustard Men superhero capes from Avon Street have long been retired, so it is Steve I spend more time with lately — especially given his rediscovered sense of calm.

My hand grips the basement doorknob but stops short of opening the door. He's probably working on an art project. I stand for a moment, watching Mom scribble answers onto newsprint, and release my grip. Turning, I slip upstairs to pack a few things.

I set my alarm that night but there is no need. I barely sleep, waking every half hour. At 5:30 a.m. I brush my teeth, then hold my breath as my closet door squeaks along its tracks one inch at a time. I retrieve a tall kitchen garbage bag filled with clothes and hug it to my chest as I creep past my parents' bedroom door and down the stairs.

I stop at the front door and wonder how long it will take my parents to realize I've left. A day? Maybe two? Can I leave and not say anything?

I set the bag of clothes down and inch back up the stairs to my room to scribble a note that says I'm starting a new life and for them not to worry about me. I don't know what else to say, so I fold the note in half and lay it on my dresser. This time, when I make it down the stairs, I head to the basement.

Steve knows about Mac. He's met him a few times, and Mac has bought six packs of beer for him. Steve has never shared an opinion about Mac and doesn't seem to have any.

"Hey, wake up," I say, shaking his shoulder.

"What the hell do you want?" His eyes flutter but he doesn't sit up.

"I'm leaving. I won't be on the bus and I'm not coming home. Don't say anything about Mac to anybody, okay?"

"Yeah, okay." His eyes are open now, looking at me. "See ya later?"

"Eventually."

He rolls over and that's it. I grab my bag of clothes at the front door and make my way to Callens Road where I wait in the dark. Ten minutes go by, then twenty. The sun is starting to rise, and soon the neighborhood will be awake and see me and my bag of clothes standing by the dirt road.

The faint sound of crunching gravel in the distance grows louder. Headlights round the corner toward me. This is it. The van rolls to a stop, and the side door wheezes open to reveal Mac, waving me inside. "Come on!" he says while extending an arm to pull me inside. For the briefest moment, I hesitate. I don't think of my family or friends. I think of Mr. K. and how I'm betraying his trust.

"Let's go!" Mac hisses, louder this time.

I clasp his hand and fall into the van, my garbage bag rolling toward the rear. The metal cargo door grinds closed with a definitive thud. The only seats in the van are the two upfront, along with the only windows. Mac gestures directions from the passenger seat to the driver, a stern-looking man I've never seen before.

I struggle to find my balance on the metal floor as the van rumbles down Callens Road. A warm hand reaches out to steady my swaying body, followed by a deep voice.

"It takes a minute to get used to it. Sit cross-legged and it'll help."

The hand and voice belong to Graham, Mac's riding buddy. He is dressed in full biker regalia, and while premature balding and love handles keep the word "handsome" just out of his reach, no amount of gear can alter his boyish face and movie star dimples. I have always liked Graham and suspect he uses the biker persona to hide a kind heart.

"Thanks, Graham."

"I didn't think you'd do it," he says. "It looks like some nice houses back there. Why would you leave all that?"

We glance toward the front of the van, knowing this talk would not meet Mac's approval. He has a map spread across the dashboard, his finger roaming along one line then back again. With the road noise, the rock music from the radio and the confusion around directions, he can't hear us.

"I don't really know why. I mean, school sucks. It's nothing more than a prison, and the kids really need me. Their mom doesn't even care about them."

"It's not like that," Graham replies, shaking his head. "Darlene is good people."

"Good people? But she doesn't even visit."

"You wouldn't come around either if somebody beat you with a motorcycle chain."

I am speechless, unable to connect the dots. What kind of psycho would beat another person with a motorcycle chain?

Graham shifts to a crouching position before looking toward Mac again, then reaches inside his leather vest and withdraws a folded scrap of paper. He tucks it into my hand and says, "Just in case" before switching position to the opposite side of the van, facing me.

I start to unfold the paper, but he gives me a look that says not to and so I don't. Three hours later, we finally pull into a service station for a pitstop. The restroom is filthy, smelling of sour lemons. I close the stall door with a paper towel, then pull the folded paper from my jeans pocket. It is step-by-step driving directions back to Bellaire Street.

CHAPTER 12

Prodigal Daughter

We crossed the Ohio state line long before the service station, and the longer we drive, the more rural and hillier the landscape becomes. It occurs to me that I have no idea where the town of Trimble is.

Mac and Graham take turns sitting in the back of the van with me. The sour-faced man is Tom, who never leaves the driver's seat. He glances at me in the rearview mirror but does not acknowledge me in any other way. I suspect Mac left out a few details when he agreed to pick me up, and Tom's probably not happy about transporting a teen runaway across state lines.

Mac has shown no excitement or affection since I tumbled into the van. His short visits to the back seem like an interrogation, not a new start on life.

"Did anybody see you leave?"

"No."

"Did you tell anybody you were leaving?"

"No," I lie, remembering the way Steve looked at me.

"What time do you usually get home from school?"

"Around 3:00."

"Okay, we've got a few hours before they start looking."

Self-doubt washes over me. I just want Mac to put an arm around me and say I did the right thing. Instead, he sits opposite me, smoking cigarettes and distributing beer to Graham and Tom. Nobody offers me a drink and I don't ask.

Before long the van is filled with cigarette smoke and I'm sick to my stomach. I hug my knees to my chest and rest my forehead on them. My long hair, grown out from the shoulder-length perm Mac had suggested, cascades around my face, arms, and knees. Alone in my blonde teepee, I quietly weep.

"We're here," Mac says, nudging me awake from an unexpected sleep.

The van veers from the pavement and wobbles unsteadily over uneven, rocky terrain before rolling to a stop. I shimmy out the side door, dragging my garbage bag and wincing at the brightness of a sun I haven't felt or seen all day.

Tom peels away without a word or a wave. We stand in a large gravel parking lot in front of a building so generic it could be mistaken for a home, a church, or an old-timey schoolhouse. Faded red letters above the door saying *Ace High Tavern* are the only clue of what to expect inside. It takes a moment for me to reconcile my prior image of a trendy sports bar with this wood-slatted, paint-peeled, crooked-framed structure.

I walk into the dimly lit bar and all talk ceases. A few customers around the room trace my steps toward what must be Mac's parents, Jan and James, behind the bar.

"Well, hello darlin'," Jan says to me with twinkling eyes. "You look sweet as sugar. What kin I git ya?"

She is as round as she is high, five-feet-nothing of pure hospitality with close-cropped hair. On most women the look would be severe, but on Jan it accentuates the high cheekbones of a pinup girl drowning in middle age.

Before I can answer, James sets a sweaty bottle of Coke in front of me. He is tall and lean with a stern look etched into his face, the opposite of Jan. He turns without a word to retrieve a bottle of beer, then limps back as if one leg is paralyzed or perhaps a few inches shorter than the other. Swinging a bar towel onto his left shoulder, he plants the beer in front of Mac.

"Just where do you intend for her to stay?" James asks.

"At the house," Mac replies.

"Think again." James says this a little louder, and Mac's jaw stiffens.

"Now, let's not ruin our visit," Jan says. She ushers James to the other end of the bar, rubbing the small of his back and speaking softly to him. Twenty minutes later she returns with a verdict.

"Take the car and go on up to the house. Put your things in Vickie's room."

We head for the door while James stands at the bar sink rinsing glasses, ignoring our goodbyes.

We stop in front of what looks like a child's crayon drawing of a house: a crooked square with a triangle roof and two rectangle windows. A half dozen chickens round the corner into the dusty front yard. *This can't be that bad*, I think to myself.

The inside of the house looks incomplete, as if the builders called it quits after four walls. There are blankets nailed to the ceiling to define bedrooms, like a giant blanket fort.

"Where's the bathroom?"

"Be careful," Mac replies, pointing to one of only two interior doors.

The bathroom floor is rotted through in several spots. Baby chicks peck in the dirt below. The toilet creaks and shifts as if struggling to maintain my weight. One glance at the shower stall and I decide I will wait to bathe — I don't care how long. I emerge from the bathroom swatting at my bare legs, now covered in bites.

"Damned fleas," Mac says. "Put on some jeans and socks."

I pull on a pair of jeans and tuck them into tube socks, not caring how I look. I keep them on all night, even though they're a useless suit of armor against the flea-infested mattress we sleep on.

The following day is a series of endless errands. "I need to see a guy" is the only information Mac gives me. I ask no questions.

Mac and Graham make stops at several houses. Each time I am left in the backseat of the old Dodge Dart Graham showed up in that morning, with the window cracked, scratching my flea bites. By late afternoon, I am wondering if this is any better than sitting in a classroom all day.

"I'm hungry," I say when Mac and Graham return to the car, smelling of beer.

"One more stop," Mac replies.

We pull into the gravel lot of the Ace High Tavern. I take a seat at the bar next to Graham, and Mac heads straight to the bathroom. Without a word, James sets down another bottle of Coke in front of me, along with a beer for Graham. I say thank you, but he is already limping to the other end of the bar.

"He's warming up to you," Graham jokes.

"I don't think he wants me here."

"It's not you he's mad at. Try not to take it personally."

We clink bottles and take a long draw.

"Where are the kids?" I ask.

"They're with Mac's sister Ruthie."

"Ruthie? I just found out about Vickie. He's got another sister?"

"Get ready for a newsflash. He's got three sisters: Vickie, Ruthie, and Deb."

"I don't really know anything about Mac, do I?"

"We've been friends for years, and I still don't know much about him. I bet you'll be happy to leave here tomorrow."

"We're leaving tomorrow?"

"He doesn't tell you much, does he?" Graham says, shaking his head. "The plan is to hit the road by noon. But you should get details from Mac, not me."

With that, Graham heads to the restroom. He returns with Mac a few minutes later, and they stand together near the door. I don't know if they're making plans, talking bikes, or cracking jokes. I drink my Coke, read the bottle labels along the bar, and wait.

• • •

The next morning Jan cooks fresh eggs from the coop and fries green tomatoes from the garden. I eat like I haven't seen food in days, which isn't far from the truth. This is the first hot meal I've had since leaving home. I even miss my Mom's burned crescent rolls and microwaved frozen peas.

There was a time when Mom tried to be the equivalent of Julia Child. She would spend days preparing a traditional Scottish dish from scratch: beef barley soup, stew with suet dumplings, steak and kidney pie, and raspberry-custard trifles for dessert.

This pride extended to us kids and our clothing, as well. I wore traditional wool kilts to school, and all of us sported hand-knitted sweaters, personalized with kittens for me or hockey players for Mark and Steve. Even our Halloween costumes were hand-sewn creations that took her weeks to construct.

Things started to change after MaryAnne arrived, and by the time I reached junior high, dinners were in foil-covered partitioned trays or plastic microwavable bags, and our clothes came from clearance racks. This was also about the time that Dad began making routine trips across the border to Canada, where codeine-laced Tylenol could be obtained without a prescription. "Mother's little helpers," Dad called them, watching Mom retreat to her bedroom to sleep for days.

"Did you get enough, darlin?'" Jan asks as I deposit my plate in the large farm sink.

I assure her that I could not fit another bite as the unmistakable roar of a Harley Davidson chokes off in the front yard. Mac dismounts from his red and white 1945 Panhead while Graham rolls the Dodge Dart to a stop close behind.

They left hours ago to pick up Mac's bike. From where, I don't know — I am just excited to be returning to Michigan on the back of a vintage Harley. Finally, the road trip I'd been promised!

My garbage bag suitcase is hoisted into the trunk of Graham's car. Mac piles duffle bags and toys over the top of it and slams the trunk shut. Two days after arriving, we are heading back without the kids.

"Don't worry about it," he says when I ask for more details. "They'll join us later."

Mac fires up the Harley and motions for me to climb on behind him. Everything on this motorcycle is original, including the saddle seat, which I quickly learn is not made for two. Mac scoots forward, but I hang off the backside, the rim of the seat digging into my buttocks. There is no sissy bar to lean my back on, and if we hit a bump, I will surely fly off backward. I wrap my arms around Mac's waist and weave my fingers into a death grip.

Twenty minutes on the highway, and I know without any doubt that this is a mistake. I imagine sliding off the back, my body ping-ponging off car hoods before splatting against the cement divider. When I try to look at the road ahead over Mac's shoulder, my half-shell helmet catches the wind and nearly chokes me on its way to the backside of my head. The incessant sting of bugs and gravel on my cheeks convinces me to bury my face into the back of Mac's leather jacket for the rest of the trip.

It is dusk by the time we roll into the parking lot of a motel. There is no name for this tucked-away burrow, only a hand-drawn sign in the office window that reads, *Weekly $35, Monthly $120*. My guess is the inhabitants prefer it that way — it seems like a place for the hopeless and the hiding.

We dismount from the Harley and curtains in several windows pull back as residents peer out. Mac goes into the office while I try to regain my land legs. I am trembling head to toe from a mixture of hunger, cold and fear. All I want is to wrap myself in a blanket and go to sleep.

Mac unlocks the door of an efficiency unit and flips the light switch. Cockroaches skitter across the floor, taking refuge under the bed and mini fridge. An eye-watering stench of ammonia does nothing to mask the acrid smell of old vomit. The dark-paneled studio has a double bed and a built-in dresser, with only a half-wall separating it from the living area. The small kitchenette along one wall reminds me of the set Santa brought me as a child.

Everything in the place is cheap, miniature, and oppressive, and I find myself wondering how many suicides took place here.

I sit on the faded floral sofa, and it crunches like cellophane. Mac turns the thermostat dial, and dozens of cockroaches cascade out of the wall vents. The tears I'm holding back start to roll down my cheeks. Mac tosses his leather jacket on the couch and sighs with irritation.

"You just need a good night's sleep," he says, turning away from me.

Things do not look better in the morning light. I stand before the rust-stained shower stall dripping with sulfur-scented water. *You can do this*, I coach myself as I crank the water spigots and step in, socks still on my feet, to wash away three days of dirt and sweat.

I emerge from the bathroom smelling like rotten eggs and gas station soap. Mac has a selection of biscuit sandwiches and hashbrown patties spread across the scorch-marked dinette table. He hands me a paper cup with the McDonald's logo.

"Do you take cream with your coffee?" he asks, grinning. He is pleased with himself, with his ability to provide.

"I don't know. I've never had coffee."

"Oh…Guess not, then."

"How long are we staying here?"

"It's a good hiding spot while the cops are looking for you," Mac replies, back to business. "I paid for two weeks."

"Two weeks?"

"We'll see how it goes."

Two weeks become four, and finally Ian and Tyan join us. For weeks Mac has been telling me how desperately they miss and need me, so I expect them to be excited when they see me. Neither kid acts as if they even remember who I am. I feel foolish for my over-inflated sense of importance as I watch them fall asleep on the sofa. They sleep end-to-end and wake up smelling of stale cigarettes.

Mac heads off to work each morning, leaving me with the kids. I rarely leave the confines of the room, terrified I'll be hauled off to juvenile detention. Instead, I focus on cleaning and making friends with the manager, Linda, a thin blonde who reminds me of a high-strung Chihuahua. She lets me use all the bleach and soap I want.

I learn to make sloppy joes, tuna casseroles, and fried bologna sandwiches for dinner. My days are filled with laundry, cooking, and dishwashing. I'm only sixteen years old but already worn out. I miss my friends and my family — I even miss school — as the days turn into weeks.

I borrow some lined paper from Linda and draft letters to my parents, writing several iterations of *I'm sorry* and *Forgive me*, always ending with *Please don't send me to juvenile detention*. I keep these drafts under the mattress until I can get them just right, and plan to ask Linda to mail the final versions.

As luck would have it, no stamps or envelopes are required. I am halfway through mopping floors on a sunny Saturday when somebody knocks on the door. While I'm wringing out the mop, the knocking repeats, only louder. I open the door and Linda is standing behind two male police officers.

"Hey, Nicole, I told them you were my niece, but they wanted to make sure," Linda says, winking.

"Are you Debbie Brannigan?" the older of the two officers asks, and it's obvious he's not buying that Linda's my aunt or my name is Nicole.

"Yes, sir."

"You need to come with us."

Without another word, I'm escorted to the police cruiser. The back door closes behind me, and as we pull away, I watch Linda get smaller out the window, standing dumbstruck with Ian and Tyan tugging at her pant legs.

"Are you taking me to jail?" I ask, peering through the wire grate that separates me from the officers. The younger one drives while the older one fills out paperwork on a clipboard.

"Jail? Of course not," says the young one.

The other officer sets the clipboard on his lap and turns to face me. "Is there trouble at home, Miss Brannigan?"

"Well, I'm going to be in trouble now for sure," I reply.

"No, that's not what I mean. Do your parents harm you?"

"No. It's nothing like that."

"Then why did you run away?"

I shrug, suddenly unable to speak. My reasons no longer make sense to me, so I can't even think of how I might answer.

In less than ten minutes, the cruiser pulls into my parents' driveway. It dawns on me that I have been a mere five miles away for the last four months. I could have walked home easily. I trudge up the driveway with both officers following and stand at the front door with my head bowed. The older officer reaches past me and rings the doorbell.

I look up when I hear Mom gasp. Her hands are covering her heart. "Thank God!" Mom sounds relieved but her face looks angry. There is no hug. Instead, she places her hand on my shoulder and says, "Let's all go into the kitchen."

The officers decline coffee and get right to business.

"Mrs. Brannigan, would you like to file criminal charges against Mr. McCall?" the older officer asks.

"Charges? What kind of charges? She wasn't kidnapped."

"Statutory rape, for starters."

"Rape? Certainly not! She went willingly, and this man has children. I'm not putting him in jail."

"Ma'am, your daughter is only sixteen years old. This man is twenty-eight...."

Her hand flies up in front of his face like a crossing guard halting children at the curb. "I will not put a man with children in jail for something he didn't do. This is a family matter, and we will deal with it as a family. Thank you for bringing her home."

I resist the urge to object or at least roll my eyes at mom's words. I know full well that nothing will be dealt with. Just like Dad's drinking, Mom's mental health, and Uncle Mark's petting zoo in the basement, this too will be buried and never spoken of.

After a few seconds of absorbing the futility of the conversation, the officers stand to leave. The older officer hands a business card to Mom, telling her to call if she changes her mind or has any further questions. She walks them to the door while I stay at the kitchen table. I hear the door close, and then Mom is back in the kitchen, hands on her hips.

"I ought to knock the stuffing out of you, Deborah."

Mom has never raised a hand to any of us, although she barks orders, makes demands and issues threats. She may be tiny, but I've never seen anybody so small walk so tall.

"I'm sorry," I squeak out.

"Do you know how worried your father and I have been?"

"I'm sorry."

"Your father will be home shortly, and then we'll sit down and establish some rules. If this man wants to date you, he'll have to do it properly."

I say nothing because I'm not sure I heard her correctly.

"Did you hear me, Deborah?"

"You want to meet Mac?"

"Yes. If he wants to date you, we'll expect him to meet with your father tomorrow."

I can't believe what I'm hearing. No jail time. No juvenile detention. I'm not even being grounded. They want to meet Mac?

MaryAnne comes through the front door with Claire. She skips into the kitchen and freezes when she catches sight of me. She starts to cry, then runs and collapses in my lap.

"Why did you leave?"

I've only been gone four months, but she seems to have grown several inches in my absence. I hug her tight while she sobs.

"You'll be staying with MaryAnne until we sort things out," Mom says. "There have been a few changes since you left."

I pass my bedroom door on the way to MaryAnne's room and peek inside. All my furniture and posters are gone. The giant mural of Led Zeppelin's "Swan Song" I'd painted is covered by a wallpapered scene of a tropical beach, and my parents' furniture and clothing now fill the space. I wonder how long they'd waited before erasing all traces of me.

MaryAnne reads me bedtime stories, and we drift off into a deep sleep. The sun has

barely risen when the bedroom door flies open and the overhead light switches on.

"Time to get up!" Dad announces in the doorway.

"What time is it?" I yawn.

"It's 7:30. Time to get ready for church."

"Church? I'm not going to church!"

"As long as you're under this roof, you are going to church!"

"Then I won't live under this roof!" I yell back in a rare show of defiance. I've been raising two kids and running a household for four months now. I don't need my dad to tell me where to go and when.

My parents joined a small congregation when Dad began attending AA several months before I left. It is the type of church that meets in ever-changing rented spaces. Congregants speak in tongues, and the pastor anoints his flock with oil. This flock is small, so members know each other intimately. I am certain an entire service was devoted to praying for my sins, and the thought reddens my face with shame.

Mom appears in the doorway, wanting to know what all the fuss is about. Dad's finger jabs toward me, then up to the ceiling, in some attempt to show a direct line between me and a higher power.

"As long as she's under this roof, she's going to church!" he yells.

"Go get a shower," Mom says. "I'll handle this."

We face each other, mirror images of crossed arms and tight jaws.

"You heard your father."

"I can't face those people."

"Those people? Those people prayed for you!" she says, confirming my suspicions.

"I am *not* going! You can't make me."

"Well, maybe you should just go back to Mac."

She delivers this line like a poker chip tossed on the table, calling my bluff. I fumble, not expecting it.

"Fine!"

"You should leave today."

So I do.

CHAPTER 13

The Big Bang

In just twenty-four hours, one universe expands while another collapses. There's no need for me to hide from public scrutiny or fear juvenile detention anymore, but all hope of hanging out in Carol's garage is now gone, along with my youth.

Mac arrives at the house to pick me up, apprehensive of a trap. Like me, he doesn't believe the turn of events. I lead him into the kitchen where my parents sit waiting.

Mac is full of "Yes, sirs" and "Yes, ma'ams." He towers over Dad, and yet it is odd to see this bushy-bearded man in motorcycle boots almost cowering in front of my stick-thin father with his Coke-bottle glasses and white tennis shoes with black socks.

"Let's go have a wee chat, man to man," Dad says, leading Mac into the living room.

Mom and I stay seated at the kitchen table, our eyes meeting for only a few seconds over the newspaper we are pretending to read. Mac and my father emerge an hour later, shaking hands.

"She's all yours," Dad announces, sweeping his arm in my direction.

Mac and I leave the house and head back to the efficiency unit. My emotions are ricocheting between relief and utter dread.

"What did you talk about?" I ask.

"He told me I had to marry you."

"What did you say?"

"I said I would, of course. If it keeps me out of jail, I'll marry the dog, too."

"When?"

"Hell, I just said I would. We can drag this so-called engagement out for two years, until you're eighteen. Then it won't matter."

Mac's rejection is lost on me. Instead, I am comforted that he wants me for another two years.

• • •

Two weeks later, Mom stops in for a surprise visit to meet the kids. Fortunately, the space is clean and the kids are dressed neatly. Clean doesn't cover up desperate poverty, though, and Mom's face registers her disappointment.

"I hope this is temporary," she says, raising an eyebrow. I just shrug.

Mom isn't the only visitor that week. Darlene is coming, and Mac is in a heightened state of anxiety. He helps me clean for the first time and is uncharacteristically particular about how things look. There is a new tea pot on the Formica dinette table, along with two matching teacups and an assortment of biscuits and cookies.

"Why are you doing all this for her?"

"We're in a custody battle, Debbie. I'm not going to give her anything negative to say about me in court."

"What am I supposed to do while she's here?"

"You can't be here. As far as the court knows, you're just the babysitter."

"Where am I supposed to go?"

"I don't know. Go for a walk. Don't come back until the curtains are open."

Mac gestures toward the dirty sheers hanging over the window by the couch. I pack a bologna sandwich in my purse and wander the parking lot for a few minutes before knocking on Linda's door.

It is dusk when the curtains part, my stay at Linda's long over-extended. Mac is in a foul mood when I return. He wipes cookie crumbs from the table, avoiding eye contact as I step through the door. Ian and Tyan surround me, showing off the new toys that Darlene brought them.

"My mommy gave this to me," Tyan says, thrusting a brand-new baby doll into my groin.

"Tyan!" Mac yells. "You call her Darlene, not Mommy. Understand?"

Tyan simply nods and thrusts the doll at me once again. "Darlene gave this to me."

"What a pretty baby —"

"Darlene is my mommy, not you!" Tyan yells while slapping me on the hip. "You're a dumb-dumb."

"Yeah, a dumb-dumb," Ian giggles, and slaps me on the thigh.

"That's not very nice," I say, looking to Mac for backup.

"I don't have time for this shit. I'm grabbing a beer with Graham. I'll be back in a couple of hours."

He pulls on his black leather jacket and slams the door behind him. What just happened? Both kids hug my legs and plant kisses all over them. I don't know if they're apologizing for calling me names or if they feel bad about the anger their father directed toward me.

I get them fed and changed into pajamas before pulling out the nighttime blankets. They lie down on the couch, feet to feet. Since we have no TV or children's books, I recite a tale of "Hot Diggity," an improvised character that has many quirky adventures. It is a tale Mom would tell us at bedtime, before Dad took over our bedtime rituals.

By 10:00 they are both out cold. I retreat to the bed, which is behind the couch separated by a half-wall. The only things to read are Mac's *Easyriders* magazines, and I flip through the glossy photos of restored motorcycles, my eyelids growing heavy. A glance at the digital clock tells me it is nearly midnight, so I get under the covers and go to sleep.

I am startled awake by the door closing in the next room. I sit up and check the clock. 2:00 a.m. Through sleepy eyes, I see the outline of Mac staggering to the foot of the bed.

"Hey, are you —" I start to say.

I don't see his fist in the dark. My head snaps backward, and something warm runs from my nose, but before I can get my hand to it, a blow to the side of my head sends me off the bed onto the floor. Only then do I realize Mac is beating me with his bare hands.

I sit up and Mac grabs two fistfuls of my hair, pulling me up to my feet, and then slams my head into the wall. I don't cry out because one thing that growing up with Steve taught me is that crying only encourages more punches. Instead, I aim my foot toward his groin and push him backward.

"Mac! Please stop! You're drunk —"

He comes toward me again, fists clenched. I throw myself onto the bed and curl into a fetal position, hands laced behind my head. I lose count of how many times I am punched before Ian wanders in.

"Daddy?"

The rapid-fire punches halt. Mac slumps onto the bed, beside me.

"Go back to bed," he slurs.

Ian pauses, then obeys. I hear his feet shuffle on the floor, the blankets rustle on the couch, then quiet. Mac falls backward onto the bed and starts to snore right away. I don't move a muscle for minutes. When I'm convinced he is in a deep sleep, I unfurl my body and roll off the bed.

I close the bathroom door before flicking on the harsh overhead light. My face is a growing mottled palette of blues and reds. I run a cold, damp washcloth across my mouth, my nose, my cheeks. The coolness of the cloth helps lessen the heat building behind my skin.

I turn off the bathroom light before opening the door. On tiptoes, I creep to the bed and slowly pull my pillow away. Without a sound I find my way to the couch and place the pillow on the floor in front of it. I lie down on the linoleum and cover myself with a scratchy towel from the bathroom.

My mind replays the last twenty minutes, searching for an explanation. I'm trying to pull logic out of chaos but am coming up with nothing. I'm brought out of my racing head by a movement in the dark. Ian's small hand reaches down from the couch and strokes my hair.

Only then do I bury my face in the pillow and cry.

THE BIG BANG

• • •

In the morning the kids and I play a game of "Who's the quietest?" and I promise a big surprise to the winner. They eat cereal and change out of their PJs like they are professional mimes, not making a sound. I usher them out the door to play in the parking lot with their new toys.

Mac snores long into the early afternoon. At 2:30 he rises to empty his bladder, then wobbles into the kitchen area. I keep my back to him, pretending to dry dishes. He slides an arm around my waist before asking, "Do you know where my…"

I turn to look at him and he stops mid-sentence.

"What the hell happened to your face?"

"You don't remember?"

Mac's face drains of color and he turns away, the guilt plain to see. "I was drunk! Darlene pissed me off so much yesterday… I didn't mean to… I'm going to make it up to you, okay?"

He pulls on his leather jacket and goes to the door.

"Just don't go anywhere. I'm going to make it up to you right now. I promise." The door closes and the Harley fires up a few minutes later.

Don't go anywhere? Where the hell could I go?

I sit on the crunchy couch and wait. Thirty minutes later Mac returns and hands each of the kids a paper bag he extracts from his saddle bags. Then he enters the kitchen with a dozen blood-red roses wrapped in clear cellophane from the grocery store.

Mac makes sloppy joes for dinner and even washes the dishes. He hands me a music magazine with Led Zeppelin on the cover. "You still like Led Zeppelin, right?" he asks, then tells me to go lie down and relax. He puts the kids in their pajamas and tucks them in on the couch.

I'm flipping through the magazine when Mac comes in and sits on the edge of the bed.

"You deserve better than this."

I put down the magazine but say nothing.

"I'm getting us out of here. You're going to have a house with a yard and a garden and anything you want."

I continue to stare at him, remembering the many times Steve punched me over the years. I tell myself this sort of thing just happens sometimes. Boys probably hit girls all the time.

"This will never happen again," Mac says. "I swear it."

And I believe him.

CHAPTER 14

Home Alone

We move in the next few weeks to a brick home about thirty minutes away from town. It feels luxurious, with three large bedrooms, a full basement, and even a tub in the Harvest Gold bathroom. Nothing but rows of corn and fields of potatoes surround us along Schoenherr Road. Ten-acre lots separate the scant number of neighbors dotting the landscape.

We need everything from dishes to furniture, so Mac and I spend an entire day at the Goodwill store. It may as well have been a Saks Fifth Avenue; it feels decadent to pick out whatever I want.

I furnish the house in the style you'd expect from a sixteen-year-old with no sense of function or fashion — fake velvet couch, bulky mismatched end tables, a dining set made from old whisky barrels, and an antique wash basin just because. It is not so much shabby-chic as hobo-shopping-cart, but I love it all.

Domestic life falls into a routine. Mac sells his beloved Panhead Harley to Graham, and now there is a copper-colored Cutlass Supreme in the driveway. I get up early each morning with Mac to pack his lunch and see him off to work.

I'm not sure what kind of work Mac does. I know he works at the New Haven foundry, shoveling something into or out of a large machine. He comes home covered from head to toe in a fine black powder every afternoon.

Once he is gone, I have an hour to myself before I wake the kids. I use this time to do sit ups and push-ups and run circles in the living room. Mac has given me the nickname of "Tubby" and says he doesn't mind a little extra cushion if I keep it under control. I wear a size two, but he says, "a two becomes a twenty when there's zero effort." He even buys me one of those belted fat-shaker machines at a garage sale and puts it in the living room.

Tyan is in special education kindergarten and catches the bus for a half day of school. I'm thankful to have Ian home with me in the mornings to curb the boredom. He loves to snuggle on the couch and help me fold laundry. I will be lonely when he starts kindergarten next year.

When Tyan is deposited back home, I pack a blanket and take the kids out to the woods behind the house. I set a daily challenge to find the biggest pinecone or the prettiest rock. They forage the woods while I sit on the blanket and contemplate how long I could live out here, alone, if I had to.

I am always within view of the house, sure to see Mac's car returning from work. While Mac showers black silt away, I attempt some form of dinner. Hamburger, tuna, and chicken livers are all staples that I have learned to either casserole or fry into something edible. After dinner, I handwash dishes while Mac has a few beers in front of the TV. Teeth are brushed, pajamas put on, and the day repeats itself in the morning.

Weeks pass this way, then months. Darlene has not come for another visit, and I know better than to ask any questions. There is a hard frost on the ground before her name is mentioned again, when Graham and getaway driver Tom come to visit on a Saturday night. They hoist a large cooler of beer from the van and bring it into the kitchen.

Tom remains cool and indifferent to me, acknowledging me with nothing more than a head nod. Graham trails in behind him, all smiles and bear hugs for me and the kids.

"How's it going, kiddo?" he asks.

"Okay, I guess. There's not much to do out here."

"Everything's been okay, though? No trouble?"

Graham looks at me, more intently now, but I'm not sure what he's asking, so I just shrug.

"You may want to go to bed early tonight," he says, leaning close to me. "We've got a couple cases of beer here."

At that moment, Mac appears and slaps Graham on the back.

"I hope you're not hitting on my old lady!"

"Nah, Mac, I was just asking how it's going. This is a real nice place."

"I'm just giving you shit, man. Tubby, get this man a cold beer!"

I pull the tabs on three cans of PBR and hand them out, then I leave the kitchen as they take over the keg barrel chairs and drink beer after beer.

I sit on the floor of the living room, handing out crayons and coloring books to the kids to keep them quiet. The sun is a heavy plum dipping below the horizon when I hear Tom ask, "So what's going on with Darlene?"

I drop a yellow crayon before it can reach Ian's outstretched hand and glance toward the kitchen table. Graham locks eyes with me for a moment, then raises his eyebrows and looks over my shoulder in the direction of the bedrooms. I sweep crayons off the coffee table and stack the coloring books.

"Time for pajamas!" I announce. Ian and Tyan protest but quiet down as soon as I promise to read a bedtime story.

The voices grow louder in the kitchen, and my story of Goldilocks is interrupted with "Teach that bitch a lesson" and "Kill the bastard before it's born." From what I can piece together, Darlene is pregnant and one of Mac's former friends is the father.

"Bad Daddy!" Tyan yells. She has lost all interest in Goldilocks and slaps at the air to make her point. I tell her to hush, putting a finger to my lips. "Bad Darlene?" she asks, looking sideways at me. Before I can assure her that nobody is bad, I hear the keg barrel chairs scrape linoleum and Mac's slurred voice.

"There's a payphone at 23-Mile road. The cops won't be able to trace it."

The plan hatched by these drunken fools is to drive to a payphone and call the Detroit police department to report a murder. More specifically, to report Darlene's murder. Mac wants to swarm Darlene's house with cops "just to fuck with her." I don't understand why, but I do know I want to be in bed, asleep, before they return.

Three pairs of heavy boots thump across the carpeted living room, out the front door, and down the gravel driveway. The van motor starts up, followed by the Cutlass Supreme. The silence that follows is unnerving.

"Bad Daddy?" Tyan frowns, still trying to puzzle out who's responsible for all the commotion. I sure hope not, I think to myself.

SQUIRREL PIE

I lie awake, too tense for sleep. Two hours go by, then four, and I fall asleep sometime around 1:00 a.m. Sun pouring through the open windows wakes me, and I hear Tyan giving orders to Ian in the kitchen.

Two mountains of cereal rise from small plastic bowls. Tyan sits with her spoon poised, waiting for Ian to pull a gallon of milk from the top shelf of the fridge. I return all but a modest portion of cereal to the box and pour milk into both bowls. As they eat, I go to the front door and look out. The driveway is empty.

We are home alone. I feel equal portions of relief and panic, each competing for control.

An idea for an art project comes to me. I tell the kids to pick out their favorite picture from a bedtime book. They choose a full-page illustration of the three little pigs trotting home in overalls with lunch pails swinging. I start to pencil in a large-scale mural on their bedroom wall. They clap and bounce with excitement.

The mural takes all day. We even color it with cheap watercolors, which works much better than I expected. The sun sets with no sign of Mac returning. I plug in the electric skillet and fry the few remaining potatoes with large slices of onion and throw in an egg at the end. It is surprisingly good.

He'll be home tomorrow, I think. We always grocery shop on Saturdays and barely have enough to last us a week. I take inventory of the fridge: mayonnaise, ketchup, margarine, milk, and two eggs. The cupboards hold nothing more than half a box of generic cereal, four slices of white bread, and a single pear.

I stay up late with the TV on and fall asleep on the couch. The off-air signal wakes me around 2:00 a.m. I trudge into the bedroom and sleep fitfully until sunrise. When the kids come into the kitchen, I pour the cereal a little less liberally than usual and splash each bowl with milk. I put the jug to my lips and drink my breakfast in two gulps.

I am distracted. All morning long, I open and close the refrigerator door compulsively, hoping for a miracle. I open and close the front door just as frequently, peering down the road for any sign of the Cutlass. Panic is clearly the winner today.

"I'm hungry," Tyan says.

It's now mid-afternoon and bellies are rumbling. The panic prevents me from thinking straight, so I lock myself in the bathroom to clear my head. It takes several deep breaths to come up with an idea.

"Get your coats," I announce to the kids. "We're going to the woods."

They scatter to put on boots and coats. I retrieve a giant metal spoon from the kitchen drawer and pull a pillowcase from the bed. We march out the back door, snapping brittle twigs beneath our boots. We look like a human steam train, puffing white condensation with our breath. We reach our usual spot in the woods and the kids stop, but I continue forward.

They say nothing and fall in line behind me. We walk and walk and walk until I am about to give up. Then the trees thin out and I see the plowed field just beyond. I begin to trot, then fall to my knees at the edge of the field. I hand the pillowcase to Ian and Tyan, instructing them to hold it open. I dig at the soil with my giant spoon, not knowing what kind of harvest I am going to get.

Jackpot! Gorgeous brown potatoes dangle from tangled roots, and I dump them into the pillowcase. I hug the lumpy, makeshift bag to my chest, and we trot back home with mere minutes of sunlight left. I stash the potatoes in the basement, afraid the police might come knocking on the door looking for stolen produce. Then I wash several large potatoes, and we eat like kings.

I wake with the Monday morning alarm to find the bed empty again. A new level of panic sets in as I realize Tyan's bus will pull up in little more than an hour. I scour the kitchen, attempting to pack a school lunch. I send her off with a mayonnaise sandwich and half a pear.

When Mac doesn't come home Monday night, I send her off with an identical lunch for Tuesday. She gets off the bus with a note pinned to her chest that reads *Tyan needs a more nutritious lunch*, and my eyes well up with tears.

On Wednesday morning I write *FLU* in large letters on a sheet of paper. When the bus driver pulls into the driveway, I step onto the front porch and hold up the paper. She nods and backs out the way she came.

SQUIRREL PIE

There is no cereal or milk. I boil, mash, and fry potato cakes smeared with the final dollops of margarine and mayonnaise. The kids groan when I set breakfast on the table. Then I go back to bed and curl into a ball because panic requires more energy than I have left.

Under the covers, I go over my limited options. I have no car. I have no phone. I have no money. I am down to one option. When it warms up, I will trek five miles to the closest payphone and make a collect call home. If I'm lucky, Steve will answer. If I'm not so lucky, Mom will.

I know she will come straight away with bags of groceries. She visits every few weeks and never comes empty-handed. The coloring books and crayons all came from her last visit three weeks ago. When I thanked her, she sniffed and replied, "Well, somebody has to do something for these wee'uns."

But generosity or any sign of softness makes Mom uncomfortable, so her gifts are wrapped in sacrifice. I don't know if I can swallow the amount of shame that telling her I need help will require.

It is just past noon when I bundle up the kids for our ten-mile round trip hike. We are halfway down the driveway when the sound of an approaching car stops us in our tracks. The gravel road kicks up a large cloud of dust and out of it emerges the copper-colored Cutlass Supreme. Mac pulls into the driveway, and the kids rush to greet him.

He looks rough with bags under his eyes and hair unkempt, but he is not covered in black powder, which tells me he hasn't been to work. I catch up to the kids as Mac closes the car door behind him.

"Where the hell do you think you're going, Tubby?"

"I was going to walk to a payphone and call my parents. We have no food in the house."

"So you run to your mommy and daddy? You're pathetic."

"Mac, we have nothing. The school sent a note home with Tyan about packing better lunches."

"Are you saying I can't take care of my kids?" he fires back, the rage rising in his eyes and voice.

"I'm saying you left here four days ago and —"

"Shut your fucking mouth!"

Mac punches me in the stomach so hard I double over and crumple to the ground. Ian and Tyan pile on top of me, forming a protective shield. He peels them off in one swift movement, like small Band-aids, and pulls my head up by a fistful of hair. Tyan is cowering behind Mac, but Ian is wrapped around his leg like a spider monkey.

"No, Daddy!"

Mac retains his grip on my hair and with his free hand yanks Ian's hair so hard it sends him spiraling backwards. He lands in a heap next to Tyan, and Mac returns his focus to me, dragging me onto my feet by my hair.

"You want food? Get in the car!"

He opens the car door and shoves me face down into the back seat. Ian lands in a heap beside me.

"You two can suck your thumbs together."

Tyan climbs into the front seat next to Mac. She cranes her neck to look at us and whispers, "Bad Ian. Bad Debbie."

Mac drives with his jaw clenched, not saying a word. The car glides to a stop in the Kroger parking lot. He digs a bill out of his leather wallet, balls it up and throws it at me, bouncing it off my forehead.

I clasp the wadded-up bill in my hand and exit the car, keeping my eyes lowered. Ian scoots out behind me and grips the back of my jacket as we walk into the store together. I situate Ian in the cart before smoothing out the bill. To my dismay, it is only a ten-dollar bill. We typically budget $60 a week for groceries and are always hungry.

I head straight to the no-brand aisle. Every item is packaged in a white label with two diagonal red stripes. *No brand, my ass*, I think. They may as well print *Low Income* on them.

I buy pasta, rice, beans, lard, a brick of some cheese product and pigs' feet. I add a loaf of white bread from the day-old shelf and hold my breath at the register. We cash out a few pennies over ten dollars, and while I'm trying to decide what to put back, the cashier scoops a few pennies from a small bowl to make up the difference and says, "Have a nice day."

Back at the house, I unpack the meager grocery bag in the kitchen. Nobody speaks a word, and I hear the bedroom door close. Mac's boots hit the floor one at a time, and within minutes his snoring breaks the silence.

I cut thick slabs from the brick of fake cheese, pull out a few slices of stale bread and grab our usual "picnic blanket."

"Let's go to the woods," I whisper. We exit the house on tiptoes, closing the back door behind us, and then run like mad to the woods.

Cold and waning sunlight force us back home two hours later. We enter as quietly as we had exited. Mac is in the kitchen and smiles broadly at us.

"Come on in and warm up! I'm about to boil some spaghetti for dinner."

We proceed with caution, and when Mac leans over to kiss me, I flinch. His face reddens, and he opts to kiss the top of my head instead.

We eat spaghetti with ketchup and fried bread. Mac offers to do the dishes, and I just nod in agreement. Teeth are brushed, pajamas put on, and I pray this day will not repeat itself in the morning.

CHAPTER 15

A New Normal

Entire weeks go by without incident. There are days when Mac brings home random gifts and seems genuinely happy to be at home with me and the kids. The next day he arrives with a furrowed brow and dark eyes. On those days, I send the kids outside and agree with everything he says. I do my best to make everything perfect and then make myself as small as possible.

If I'm lucky, a violent outburst is avoided. Other times it may be a kick to my backside that sends me sprawling to the carpet. Uncertainty over which version of Mac will appear is more unnerving than the violence itself. Every muscle in my body is tensed, and every word from my mouth is weighed upon the scale of pros and cons before I utter them. I am on high alert, non-stop, but somedays no amount of effort can divert his rage.

• • •

"Where's the shampoo?"

Mac is standing in the middle of the living room soaking wet, a towel loosely wrapped around his waist. Inky black trails trace his path from the shower. We use a generic pink liquid soap to clean dishes, body, and hair. I run to the kitchen and retrieve the plastic bottle from the windowsill.

"Here you go. I washed the dishes and forgot to put it back."

"I asked you for shampoo, not this shit."

"This is what we always use."

"Are you calling me a liar?"

"No, you're right. We must have used all the shampoo."

"You mean *you* used it all!"

Mac backhands me like a pro tennis player. The liquid soap bottle lands hard on my right temple and eye. Ian and Tyan scatter into their bedroom and slam the door. I am holding my eye with one hand and shielding myself with the other when his towel falls to the floor, leaving him stark naked.

He looks down at himself in confusion, like he's just awakened from a deep sleep. Blushing, he picks up the towel and returns to the shower. I am in the kitchen when I hear the bathroom door open, then the bedroom door close. He does not come out again until the morning alarm.

My face is still various shades of blue and green three days later when Mom pulls into the driveway. I rush the kids to their room, yelling at them to take a nap before slamming the door closed. I creep into my bedroom and hide behind the door.

Mom continues knocking at the front door, and just when I think she may give up and go home, I hear the knob turn and she is inside the house — I failed to lock the door when Mac left for work. "Deborah!" she yells from the living room. I remain quiet but I hear the bedroom door squeak open down the hall. Tyan begins to giggle, and I curse at her under my breath.

"Come out here, both of you."

I hear the door swing open and two sets of feet pad down the hallway.

"Hi, Grandma!" the kids say in unison, and I imagine mom's reflexive wince. It's been nearly a year, and she still can't hide her discomfort with this new title.

"These go in the kitchen, not under your beds. Understand?"

"Yes, Grandma. Thank you, Grandma!"

"Deborah! I know you're here."

I scramble my hair to make it look like I've just awakened and pull a section of hair down over my right eye, hoping to obscure the damage. Taking a deep breath, I walk down the hall into the living room, rubbing my eyes and yawning. Ian and Tyan are at the kitchen table with Happy Meals from McDonald's.

"Hey, Mom. We were just taking a nap."

"Bullshit! You were hiding that black eye from me."

"Oh, this? Ian had a rock in his pocket, and when he put it in the laundry chute—"

"Just stop it! Do you think I'm bloody daft?"

Mom's Scottish accent and slang always become more pronounced when she is angry. Tyan laughs through a mouthful of cheeseburger. "Grandma said bloody."

"There'll be no apple pie if you keep up that smart mouth."

Tyan resumes eating, and Mom returns her attention to me.

"So, this is the life you want for yourself?"

I say nothing, staring at my bare feet.

"Grown-up life isn't what you expected, eh? You've made your choices, Deborah, and now you see what the consequences are."

We stand together in a long silence. Then she sighs with exasperation and hands me a Filet-O-Fish sandwich.

"Sit down and eat. You probably haven't had a decent meal in days."

We sit on the couch, eating from greasy wrappers and not saying much. It takes great effort to swallow my sandwich, forcing it beyond the hard knot lodged in my throat. Nothing more is said about the black eye or grown-up consequences.

Mom updates me on things at home — MaryAnne's piano lessons, Steve's latest art award, and a new rock band Mark has joined. These updates are my only window to a world that I no longer live in. A family I no longer belong to.

I feel forsaken when she leaves.

• • •

Four days before Easter Sunday, Mom pulls into the driveway. She hauls large bags from the trunk of her car as Ian and Tyan watch her from the living room window, bouncing with excitement. She hands new clothes and stuffed animals to each of them. Tyan parades around the living room in her new Easter hat, grinning from ear to ear, and Ian holds a velveteen rabbit to his cheek, hugging it while he sways side to side.

Laughter fills the room, and even my mom is smiling. Tyan plops her Easter hat onto one side of my head, and I reach up to straighten it. Mom grabs my wrist, pulling my arm out straight in front of me.

Bruises wrap around my upper arm, and it is clear that somebody has gripped me hard enough to leave purple imprints of their anger. Mom lifts the sleeve on my other arm to reveal a matching set, and the room becomes silent.

"That's a bad daddy," Tyan says.

"Another rock in the laundry chute, Deborah?"

"He didn't mean to, Mom. He apologized."

"Of course he did." She tilts her head to the gladiolas standing tall in the antique pitcher of the wash basin. "I suppose he bought those as well. Is that all it takes?"

"I don't know," I say with a shrug.

"I see. So, you're not ready to accept any responsibility yet?"

I don't understand what she means, but I don't ask her to explain. I just stand there, not knowing what to say or do next. Mom puts on her coat and lifts her handbag over her wrist. Without looking at me directly, she says, "I hope you have a happy Easter" and then closes the front door behind her.

• • •

Easter Sunday comes and goes like any Sunday. Tyan wears her hat for weeks until one day she gets off the bus without it. She traded it for a Ho Hos snack cake at lunch. Ian dropped his stuffed rabbit somewhere along the trek from the woods to the house. We search for days but never find it. When he cries about the loss, Mac tells him stuffed animals are for girls and sissies. Ian dries his eyes with his shirt sleeve and never mentions the rabbit again.

The entire month of May passes with no sign of Mom. By mid-June it has been a solid two months since her last visit. She'll come on my birthday, I think, but June 25th passes and the red station wagon never pulls into the driveway.

I make my own cake with Ian's help. It is top heavy and leans to one side, but we are proud to set it on the kitchen table after dinner. Mac wears a mischievous grin as he hands me a small, gift-wrapped box. Inside is a ceramic figurine of a grinning piglet in a bathtub, cleaning its back with a scrub brush. The word "Tubby" is painted on the base.

"Isn't it perfect? I had to get it."

I laugh along with him and say thanks, then scrape my half-eaten slice of cake into the trash.

The following afternoon, we are heading to the woods for a cheese sandwich picnic when the sound of a car pulling into the gravel driveway sends us running back to the house. I'm expecting the red station wagon, but it is Steve's Delta 88 junker.

Ian and Tyan run ahead, chanting "Uncle Steve." My brother is out of the car and playfully rubbing "noogies" on the tops of their heads when I catch up.

"Happy Birthday, Sis! I brought you something."

We walk to the trunk of his car, where he hands me a bucket of sliced pickles. He hoists a case of frozen burger patties onto his shoulder before slamming the lid. "Let's go make some Whoppers."

Steve works part-time at Burger King and has managed to steal this bounty for my birthday. I should be disappointed in his criminal behavior but I'm not. I have lived with Mac for nearly a year, and this is Steve's first visit. He seems impressed by the house and large yard, and I'm grateful for the food and his company.

I start frying burger patties at the stove while Steve retrieves a six pack of beer from the back seat of his car. He offers me one, but I decline — I've never actually liked the taste of beer.

"I'll leave a few for Mac," he says, then tosses an envelope onto the kitchen table. "Mom wanted me to give this to you."

"Is she okay? I haven't seen her since before Easter."

103

"She's not coming over anymore."

"What do you mean? Like, never?"

"She says you need to move back home and take responsibility, blah, blah, blah. You know how she is. You're supposed to be like Dad and read her mind, then do everything her way."

Move back home? I didn't know this was an option. I've been told to take responsibility. I've been told to face the consequences of my poor decisions. But nobody has said, "You can come home."

Steve is still sitting on the couch when Mac arrives from work. My heart is racing, and I pray silently that "Good Mac" has come home today. The door swings open, and Mac grins at the sight of Steve. There is no furrowed brow or dark eyes, and I sigh inwardly.

"Hey man, I brought some beers," Steve says. "Get showered and help me drink them."

After Mac cleans up, they sit together on the couch making small talk, watching TV and drinking. I put the kids to bed, then slip into the bedroom with the envelope from Mom. I'm hoping for a letter, maybe an invitation to come home and work things out.

There is no letter, just a birthday card with a twenty-dollar bill inside. The inscription reads, *Happy Birthday, Deborah. Use this money wisely. Love, Mum.* I crumple the card in a napkin and tuck it under the top layer of garbage in the kitchen can. I don't want Mac to read it and learn that I have money.

I stuff the bill into one of Ian's socks and toss it down the bathroom laundry chute. It lands in the basement near the washing machine. In the morning, I will add it to the stash of coins and small bills I've collected on nights when Mac is too drunk to recall having money in his pant pockets.

I am certain that I will use this money wisely.

CHAPTER 16

How'd That Happen?

My seventeenth trip around the sun continues in a steady trajectory toward rock bottom. One day blurs into the next and I feel aimless, alienated from my friends and family. Relationships fade when there is no way to connect, and the last phone call I had with Carol was months ago when Mac spent his entire paycheck on a three-day drinking binge.

That day, he drove to a payphone and told me to start calling my friends and ask them to buy a set of speakers.

"Get one of them to buy these or we don't eat today!" he says, handing me a list of features for the speakers and a handful of change. I sit in the passenger seat with the receiver while Mac coaches me from the driver seat.

"Hey, Carol. How ya doing?"

"Hey, girl! Where have you been? I haven't heard from you in forever."

"Well, I'm just living out in farm country now."

Mac jabs my leg, telling me to quit bullshitting and get to the speakers.

"So, Carol, I was wondering if you or your brother might want to buy some speakers? They're really good and you can have 'em real cheap."

I choke on "cheap" and feel myself shrinking into the seat.

"Speakers? What the hell do I need more speakers for? Are you okay, Crystal?"

I turn to Mac and shake my head to let him know she's not interested. His face turns red, and he motions for me to read the features from the paper. This all feels so hollow, and I don't want to do it, but the look on his face means trouble if I don't.

"They're really good ones, Pioneer…."

"Crystal, forget the speakers. Is everything good with you or what?"

"Um, yeah, it's good." I look at Mac and shake my head once again to signal that Carol is still not interested.

"Just hang up the fucking phone," he says, and I cut the call short with Carol, relieved to end the humiliation.

"Now call Vicky."

It takes less than ten minutes to repeat the same call with the same outcome. I don't care about the money or food. All I can think about is that I will probably never hear Vicky or Carol's voice again. I feel utterly alone.

Nearly six months of solitude go by before Steve pulls his Delta 88 into the driveway again, one week before Christmas. He brings another card from my parents with the same sentiment and twenty dollars inside. I'm thankful for the money but also gutted. The card means my parents do not intend to visit on Christmas.

We sit in the living room while Ian shows Steve how his new dump truck works. Mac gave it to him a couple of months ago, an unspoken apology for kicking him so hard on his backside that he split his lip on the coffee table three feet away.

Mac is an enigma with Ian. He seems to love him fiercely, pulling him into his lap and calling him "my boy." But on nights when Mac comes home with a furrowed brow, he takes it upon himself to "toughen him up."

Ian has a tenderness about him that angers Mac when he drinks, and while I have formed some type of emotional barrier over the last year and a half, Ian cannot. He is always open-hearted, no matter the consequences.

Steve and I sit together and watch whatever happens to be on TV while the kids play on the living room floor. He doesn't say much, just stays with me until Mac comes home, and then they drink beers until the kids go to bed, one man quelling his anger with alcohol and the other feeding it.

By now it is clear to me that alcohol quiets the rage in my brother, allowing us to soften toward each other. The gifted artist inside him also surfaces, and his artwork earns him a scholarship to the Center for Creative Studies in Detroit.

Steve's addiction to alcohol will eventually strip him of the ability to draw a straight line or write his name legibly. By the time he reaches the age of fifty, he will be toothless, friendless and on a liver transplant list, and will continue to choose alcohol's soothing relief for the rest of his abbreviated life.

• • •

The year ends better than it started, thanks in part to a new friend Mac has made at work, Bob Rogan. Bob is thickly muscled with an ample belly and a perpetual smile on his face. He does not ride a motorcycle or disappear on drinking binges, and it's obvious he loves his wife, DeeDee, a tall woman with a lean build and a rich voice. They live in New Haven near the foundry with their five children, ages six to fifteen.

Bob is constantly arranging barbecues and fishing trips for his family and neighborhood friends. They invite us to a weekend fish fry and I am excited to be taken away from the solitary confinement of the Schoenherr Road house, but also apprehensive about meeting new people. I so rarely leave the house that I barely remember how to hold a normal conversation anymore.

When Mac turns the corner onto Bob and DeeDee's street, it is clear which house belongs to them. Cars are parked up and down each side of the block, and people funnel in and out of a small brick bungalow carrying plastic drink cups and paper plates and wearing broad smiles as they hug and greet each other.

Ian and Tyan are swallowed up by a group of children who rush to greet them. Several men from the foundry greet Mac with a smile and nod as we head up the walkway, and yet Mac doesn't acknowledge me, which makes my social anxiety climb higher. We are the only white people here — what if nobody wants us around?

Mac locates DeeDee in the kitchen and introduces me. She puts her wooden spoon down on the stovetop and rests an arm around my shoulders.

"My goodness, you're a little thing." Turning to one of the many children in the kitchen, she says, "Nay-Nay, fetch her some of that banana pudding."

A little girl about eight years old hands me a paper plate with a mountain of homemade banana pudding, along with a plastic spoon and napkin. DeeDee keeps her arm across my shoulders as she guides me through the packed house, introducing me to every aunt, uncle, and cousin there. Within minutes I forget that I am the only white girl at the party. All I feel is the joy that passes from one person to another under that roof.

I feel like family.

• • •

Mac returns home from work one day not long after the fish fry with a small white envelope. His black fingerprints are superimposed across the gold lettering that says, *You're Invited.* DeeDee is having a Tupperware party and I'm invited! I have learned that Bob is Mac's boss, so there's no doubt I will be attending.

I awaken on the day of the party with mild nausea, but I don't mention it to Mac because nothing is going to keep me at home today. A familiar twinge in my right groin stops me, mid-stride, on my trek to the kitchen.

"Forget something?" Mac asks, frowning.

"I'm going to put socks on. The kitchen floor hurts my feet when it's this cold."

I retreat to the bedroom to curl into a ball and breathe through the discomfort. This sharp pain has halted me several times over the last year. When I tell Mac about it, he claims it is a common "female plumbing problem" and to stop complaining and get used to it. I straighten up, put on socks and go make breakfast.

We arrive at Bob and DeeDee's house at 2:00 p.m. and I'm ushered into a living room full of women while Mac and the kids head out to the backyard. It is early April, and the afternoon sun has burned away the morning frost to reveal a perfect spring day. Mac joins a small cluster of men standing around a smoldering firepit while the kids play tag.

I am sandwiched on the long couch in the living room by a row of black women in flower print dresses. I am handed a paper plate that somehow gets filled with small cakes and cookies. The women insist I am going to blow away in the next breeze if I don't put some meat on my bones.

There are games to play for Tupperware, and these women compete like it is the Olympics. This is serious business, and they are hell-bent on winning free items. It's great fun, and when I win a three-piece set, they cheer and clap for me. I stand to collect my prize and double over at the sharp pain in my groin.

There is a collective gasp, and my face goes red immediately. A dozen motherly hands reach out to help me, but I wave them away. "I'm okay," I say, but this group of women are not buying it at all. DeeDee has already summoned Mac from the backyard.

"Debbie's sweating and can't stand up straight," she says. "You need to take her to the doctor right now."

"She's okay," Mac replies, shrugging his shoulders. "She gets like that, you know, when it's that time of month."

"That time? What do you know about 'that time'? I ain't no doctor, but you sure in hell ain't no woman. Don't be telling me or her how it's supposed to be."

Mac opens his mouth but closes it fast. DeeDee turns her attention to me.

"Baby, is this normal for your monthlies?"

Her voice is gentle, and I shake my head before telling her that I'm not having my period right now. Maybe I should be embarrassed to utter this in front of a room full of strangers, but somehow, I'm not.

"That settles it," DeeDee says to Mac. "Take her to Mt. Clemens General. The kids will stay here until you get back."

Mac doesn't argue for once. He helps me with my coat, and we are in the car heading to Mt. Clemens General hospital within minutes.

I brace myself for his anger, but it doesn't appear. He asks only if I'm going to be okay. Mac seems fearful, and I'm not sure if it's my well-being or DeeDee's wrath he's more concerned about.

The emergency waiting room is almost empty. I am whisked back to an exam room while Mac contends with paperwork. A handsome but haggard-looking doctor orders bloodwork and an ultrasound. Long hours seem to pass before the doctor returns, flipping papers on a clipboard. His haggard look is replaced with something that appears more akin to disapproval.

"Are your parents here?" he asks.

"No, sir."

"Well, you have a large cyst on your right ovary."

"Is that bad?"

"It's nothing serious, but there's something else. You're also pregnant."

I'm stunned, bewildered, and the question *How?* forms on my tongue.

"We can take care of this today, if you want."

The doctor looks hard at me, waiting for a response. At that moment, I have no idea what he's talking about. Is he offering me counseling or parenting books?

"If you have insurance, I can write it up so they pay for it."

The light goes on in my brain. He's asking if I want to terminate the pregnancy, the pregnancy I've known about for less than two minutes. The only thing I know about abortions is that having one guarantees an eternity in the flames of hell.

"No, thank you," I reply, my voice shaking.

"Suit yourself. Take these papers to the checkout desk. Good luck."

He holds the door open and ushers me out. I head in the direction of the checkout desk while he disappears into another exam room. I'm almost to the desk when Mom appears in the hallway, blocking my path.

"Well?" she asks.

"Well, what?"

"Well, what did the doctor say is wrong with you?"

"He doesn't know."

I lie outright. This is the first time I've seen Mom in almost a year, and I can't bring myself to tell her that I'm pregnant. I'm certain she will disapprove, and then I'll never see her again.

"Doesn't know? That's bloody bullshit! I'm getting to the bottom of this."

She marches down the hallway in search of answers, right as Mac heads toward me from the waiting room. He sees the confusion on my face and answers me before I ask.

"You're a still a minor," he says. "The nurse called for consent and insurance information. Fifteen minutes later, your mom was here."

He looks over my shoulder, and I turn to see Mom coming back down the hall. Her face is ashen.

"The doctor says you're pregnant." She places a hand on my shoulder, leaning on me for support.

Her comment is posed as both a question and a statement, so I just nod in agreement. I'm waiting for her reprimand when I hear an astonished "What?" from behind me.

I'd forgotten to tell Mac.

None of us move or talk, and time seems suspended in our disbelief. My mom's lower lip quivers and she begins to cry. Then Mac does the same. Before I know it, we are embraced in a three-way hug.

Finally, for just a moment, maybe nobody is mad at me.

CHAPTER 17

A Birthday Wish

Mac is beaming on the ride back to Bob and DeeDee's. There is a tenderness about him that I have not seen before. He stops at a grocery store and insists on buying lunch meat, bread and eggs. "You need to start eating for two," he says. "Just watch it. Having a baby is no excuse to get fat."

Bob shakes Mac's hand and slaps him on the back. "Congratulations, brother. This is a real blessing."

The air is light and the mood joyous. The kids come in from playing outside, and DeeDee tells them we have a big surprise for them. Mac crouches down to their level and they lean in close, one at each shoulder.

"You're going to have a new baby brother or sister soon!"

"Like baby Carl?" Ian asks.

The air goes out of the room, and I can't breathe. Mac takes a moment to compose his words.

"No, not like baby Carl. Now get your coats, it's late."

I am thankful to have Bob and DeeDee there. If not for them, Ian would have been smacked for saying such a thing.

• • •

Darlene gave birth to a healthy baby boy soon after Halloween and named him Carl. Mac's insurance covered the birth expenses because their divorce was not finalized, and this put Mac in a foul mood for weeks.

To celebrate, Mac, Graham, and Tom did an encore performance of the "Darlene is pregnant" drama in the kitchen, only this time they called the Detroit Police department to report a dead newborn at Darlene's address. Mac disappeared for just two days then, but I wished he had stayed away much longer.

I am better prepared for his long absences now. Several of the stolen potatoes in the basement sprouted long roots, which morphed into new potatoes. A fresh crop dangles its roots in a pan of water, like vegetable jellyfish. With every trip to the grocery store, I buy one or two canned items to join the potatoes under the stairs and add to my secret, makeshift pantry.

Weeks of Mac's unpredictable anger follow the birth of baby Carl. Ian and Tyan stare at their plates and eat dinner in silence every night before rushing off to their bedroom to build a fort that always requires one bed be pushed against the door. I had prepared myself for a long, miserable winter ahead when the miraculous invitation arrived for Bob and DeeDee's fish fry.

Things start to get better after that day. Mac spends more time with Bob and less with his leather-clad motorcycle buddies. They have not been around in months, and life is much more stable, although there are still surprises, like the gun Mac brings home one day.

"Look what I've got," he says, holding the revolver up for me to see like a prize he won at the county fair.

"What do you need a gun for?"

"Protection. You never know when somebody might try to break in."

"We don't have anything worth stealing."

"Maybe," Mac says, moving closer to me and bringing the gun close enough to my face I can smell the solvent used to clean it. "But people listen when this baby talks."

I nod my head, falling silent, while Mac walks off to the bedroom, trying to twirl the gun around his index finger like some dime store cowboy.

A BIRTHDAY WISH

• • •

My pregnancy seems to have a positive effect on Mom as well as Mac. She begins to visit again, never speaking of my year-long absence from the family. In my mind, I've been excommunicated, and now we are blessed again, even invited to my parents' home for Easter dinner.

MaryAnne runs to greet me when I walk through the door. She has grown so much in the last year. I bend to pick her up and Mac stops me.

"You shouldn't be picking anything up in your condition," he says. He has turned into such a mother hen, and I dare to feel content, almost happy.

After dinner Mom and I carry dirty dishes into the kitchen, leaving Mac and Dad at the table. I listen in on their conversation while scraping plates over the trash can.

"So, we've got our first grandchild on the way," Dad says.

"Yes, sir. The doctor says the baby will be here September 6th."

"That wedding is more important than ever now. It's not right to raise a child out of wedlock."

"Yes, sir, I agree. But Debbie doesn't want to buy a maternity wedding gown, so we've decided to put off our plans until after the baby."

Their hearty laughter at my expense filters into the kitchen, and I'm tempted to let Dad know that Mac and I have never talked about wedding plans.

I will be eighteen in two months, and on that day Mac will be released from any threat of statutory rape or marriage. I will be more relieved than Mac because marriage just sounds like a prison sentence.

I don't know how Darlene stayed with Mac for so many years or how she is able to be in the same room with him now. When she presses forward on their divorce or visitation rights, Mac launches a fear campaign. He calls the police to her home. He recruits motorcycle cronies to follow her. He does whatever it takes until she backs off.

He never tells me how their battle is going in court, and yet I don't need to ask. Each time Darlene retreats, I pray that she will stay away because it makes my life easier.

But her fight also gives me hope — if she can break free, then so can I. I silently cheer for her every win because, after nearly two years with Mac, I'm now 100 percent certain about who beat her with a motorcycle chain.

Darlene manages to score a point just before my birthday. Without preamble or explanation, Mac announces that we are making a trip to Kmart after breakfast. We never go to Kmart, only the grocery store, and we never shop for "frivolous" items. The thought of new toys sends Ian and Tyan off in a hurry to get dressed.

We stroll the aisles at Kmart, selecting new outfits for both kids. We peruse the sparse selection of maternity clothing, and I'm tempted to continue wearing my unzipped jeans for another three months. I reluctantly add two pairs of polyester pants with large squares of elastic across the front and a plaid smock top to the cart. Mac holds up an oversized shirt that reads, "I'm not fat, I'm pregnant" and drops it on top of the other items without asking me about it.

I turn in the direction of the check-out lanes, but Mac is headed toward sporting goods.

"Where are you going?"

"The kids need suitcases. They're going to Darlene's for a week."

"What? When?"

"I have to drop them off Friday morning."

"That's my birthday."

"Yeah, I know. Now we can go out somewhere nice for your birthday, just the two of us."

Mac walks down the aisle, his legs stretched out like he's taking a Sunday stroll. Darlene has never had the kids for a week, but if he wants to pretend that he doesn't care, I'm more than happy to play along. We add two generic, kid-sized suitcases to the cart and head home with our bounty.

Mac's façade of indifference crumbles as Friday approaches. On Wednesday, when Tyan asks if she can take her stuffed bunny with her, he answers, "Take whatever the hell you want" through a clenched jaw.

By Friday morning the air is thick with hostility as Ian and Tyan drag their mini suitcases to the front door before sitting down for breakfast.

We eat in silence, all eyes on our cereal bowls, until Mac throws his spoon down in disgust.

"What is this shit anyway?"

"Frosted Flakes," I reply.

"Like hell it is! I'm sick of eating this fake, no-brand bullshit. Next time, you get the real stuff!"

"Okay." We all return our eyes to our bowls while Mac paces the living room, all of us waiting for what comes next.

"Ian!" Mac yells. Ian flinches in his seat before looking up from his bowl. "Are you happy that you get to meet baby Carl?"

I send all my mental energy toward Ian, willing him to please, for God's sake, say no. Ian looks from me to Mac, then shakes his head side to side.

"I want you to do something for me while you're at Darlene's, okay?"

Ian says nothing. He simply nods his head and waits.

"I want you to push baby Carl down some steps. Can you do that for me?"

Ian nods again.

"I can't hear you!"

"Yes, Daddy. I'll push dumb baby Carl down the stairs." Ian puts his hands in front of himself and mimes an invisible shove. "Like that!"

"That's my boy! Just like that."

This disturbing exchange nauseates me, but it does the trick for Mac. His mood becomes lighter, and when the kids go to brush their teeth, I ask about dinner plans for tonight.

"I don't care. Make whatever you want."

"You said we were going out for my birthday tonight."

"Oh, yeah, that's right! You're eighteen today, aren't you?" This news brightens his mood even more. He puts his arm around my shoulders and pats my swollen belly. "We've got a lot to celebrate! How about Chinese?"

I ignore the fact that Mac forgot my birthday and instead become excited about dinner out. I remind him Mom is picking me up for lunch at noon, and he closes the front door behind him, swearing to beat me home from lunch.

I marinate in the blissful silence of an empty house, opening all the windows to let in a light breeze. I ease onto the couch and close my eyes, listening to the birds chirping outside.

Tires crunch in the gravel driveway and I get up to look — it's the red station wagon — but why is Mom here so early? A quick glance at the kitchen clock tells me I've slept for over two hours.

Mom enters, balancing a large cake box and a wrapped gift with a bow. Bold pink icing spells out *Happy Birthday*, surrounded by creamy pink roses.

"It's carrot cake, your favorite," she says as she looks around the empty house. "Where are the wee 'uns?"

"They're visiting their mom for a week. Mac is dropping them off now."

Disappointment flashes in her eyes, then she mutters something about how she should have gotten a smaller cake. She pushes the gift to me across the table.

"Here you go, love. Open it now and then we'll head out."

It is a brand-new set of hot rollers. I used to steal hers at every opportunity when I lived at home.

"Now you have your own," she says, and we both laugh.

The driveway is empty when we return from a Mediterranean restaurant. I am beyond full, having eaten two chicken gyros and a plate of French fries, but Mom insists we have birthday cake before she leaves. It is every bit as delicious as it looks, and I am ready for another nap by the time I take my last bite.

"How long does it take to drop off two children?" Mom asks, looking at her watch.

"Darlene lives near Detroit, so it takes a while to get there."

"He could have dropped them off in Chicago by now."

"He's probably buying my birthday present because he didn't have time to pick one up during the week."

I can tell Mom doesn't buy it. I also know she needs to get home before MaryAnne's school bus drops her off. She is barely out of the driveway when I throw my bloated body on the bed and fall asleep.

It is 5:00 p.m. when I rise from my food coma. The house and driveway are still empty, so I take my hot rollers to the bathroom and plug them in. By 6:00 I have golden curls, pink lips, and perfumed skin. Any minute now, I think.

I stop checking the driveway around 9 p.m. and shift into hoping that Mac will not come home. I wash my face, pull on my pajamas and go to bed.

My birthday wish is granted when Mac does not come home that night. Or the next. Or the one after. I don't panic — I sleep when I want and eat an entire carrot cake. Not a bad birthday, I think as I finish the last piece of cake.

It could have been worse.

CHAPTER 18

Broken

Near the end of July, the court awards Darlene a weekend visitation, and Mac must comply within thirty days. One week after the decision, our driveway is filled with a half dozen motorcycles and several cars. They are supposedly here to celebrate Mac's twenty-ninth birthday, but I know it is a rallying of the troops. He has started hanging out with them again since Darlene started winning in court.

I play barmaid for two hours, until words begin to slur and voices rise. I gather my own troops, and we huddle in my bedroom with storybooks and crayons. I already know Mac won't be coming to bed tonight. At least I hope he won't.

"Are you going to take that shit from her?" The voices from the kitchen grow louder. "I can't believe she wants full custody."

"Over my dead body," Mac shouts.

"You mean over *her* dead body," snorts another voice, and the whole room erupts in war cries and fist thumps on the kitchen table. Within minutes, there is a stampede out the front door. Car engines and motorcycles fire up in unison, then fade down the gravel road into the darkness.

Good riddance, I think, as Ian, Tyan and I stand on the bed, watching the dimming taillights out the window. The bedroom door swings open, and we jump at the sudden sight of Mac in the doorway. He sways side to side, held in place by his hand wrapped around the doorknob.

"I'm going out for a pack of smokes. You need anything?"

I shake my head no, afraid to utter anything that might land me in a trap. Ian has dropped to the side of the bed, ready to run for cover, while Tyan remains frozen next to me. Every muscle in my body tightens as Mac stares at my swollen abdomen. I drape a protective arm across it.

"Okay, then."

He closes the bedroom door without a sound, and a few minutes later, we hear the front door close. It's not until the taillights of the Cutlass disappear that we take a collective breath.

In the morning, we venture out of the bedroom. The entire house looks crumpled up and thrown away, just like the discarded beer cans that litter the countertops, furniture and floors. Some are empty and some are half-full, soaking the couch and the carpet. My extra-large belly keeps me from picking any up off the floor.

"We can help," Ian and Tyan say in unison.

They work hard, and within an hour the beer obstacle course is gone and replaced with our tidy living room and kitchen.

"Who wants sausages and eggs?" I ask.

"I do! I do!" the kids reply, bouncing around the kitchen in excitement.

I waddle down the basement steps to retrieve a can of Vienna sausages from my hidden pantry. I slice up the entire can and fry them in with some scrambled eggs. This is a rare treat, but I know we have at least two days on our own, maybe three, so why not enjoy it?

• • •

On day five Mac still has not returned, and I take inventory of the secret pantry items. On day eight, I begin rationing food. I throw the last squirrel from our freezer into a crockpot on day ten. This isn't the first squirrel I've cooked, and I'm sure it won't be the last.

A squirrel bounced off Mac's windshield as he drove home one afternoon. He brought the carcass home, rationalizing that it wasn't roadkill because it was still warm. He boasted that "it's a fresh kill and a free meal," as if he had stalked and brought down a wild boar for dinner. I made a pot pie with it, burying the wild taste in bland frozen vegetables and a hearty Bisquick crust.

Soon after, Mac started shooting squirrels from the tree in front of the house with an old BB gun he'd had as a kid. They've become a staple in the freezer, but I resist making squirrel pies unless times are dire. They represent a new low in my life, a demarcation near the bottom of a barrel I don't want to acknowledge.

By day fourteen, I find myself wishing for another squirrel in the freezer. Tyan goes to school that morning with the last slice of cheese and the butt ends of a bread loaf. No mayonnaise, just a dry, stale, quasi-sandwich, and a Tupperware container half-filled with imitation Frosted Flakes.

We are officially out of everything.

There is no way around it; I have to walk to the store and get food. I've got forty-eight dollars and some change disguised as dirty laundry in the basement. Hesitant to deplete my funds, I take two twenty-dollar bills and leave the remainder in balled-up socks.

I keep Ian home from school. With summer temperatures hovering in the 90s all week and me almost eight months pregnant, I tell myself he could go for help if something goes wrong during the long trek. He can also help me carry bags.

At 9:00 a.m. Ian and I clasp hands and start walking. Between his five-year-old stride and my pregnant waddle, our progress is slow, to say the least. The sun is high in the sky by the time we arrive at paved sidewalks, nearly three miles later. I peel off my cheap plastic sandals to walk barefoot on the hot cement for the remainder of the journey.

We arrive at the small shopping plaza well past noon, dehydrated and covered in dust. The convenience store is like a desert oasis. We share a bottle of Faygo Rock & Rye to cool our throats, and the sugar rush lifts our mood. I splurge on a second bottle for the walk home and load up on jerky, nuts, peanut butter, bread, and snack cakes. I pick only a few canned items, knowing every ounce must be carried back home.

Ian picks out a treat, a brick of Twizzlers, something he says he will share with Tyan. He peels off one licorice twist and puts the rest in his tiny back pocket. "Now I have a wallet like Daddy," he says, referring to the large Harley Davidson wallet Mac keeps in his back pocket.

The walk home is torturous. Within an hour, I'm sure my hips are pulling apart from their hinges. The pain permits me to take no more than ten steps before I need to squat or sit on the hot cement. I don't think we have gone a single mile in over an hour, and I begin to panic. At this rate we won't make it home by nightfall.

Another hour passes, and I swear we are moving backward. I sit on the burning hot sidewalk, trying to build enough resolve to plow forward, when I notice a school bus coming down the road. I joke to Ian that he's going to be in trouble for missing school if they see him. When the bus pulls over to the sidewalk, Ian is ready to run into the woods, terrified he's going to jail.

It is a special education bus, and Tyan is waving at us from the window. The bus door swings open, and a young woman in her twenties with short dark hair and brown eyes descends to the bottom step.

"You look like you need a ride," she says.

"Thanks for stopping."

"It was Tyan that spotted you. Are you okay?"

"I didn't think I was going to make it home."

"You're still a long way from home. Why are you out here anyway?"

"I had to pick up some food. We ran out of everything."

The driver nods her head, pausing before treading into more personal waters.

"Tyan says her daddy ran away from home."

"I'm starting to think that's true."

I adjust the convenience store bags in my hands, unable to look at her. She respects my verbal white flag of surrender and steps off the bus, motioning us to get in. She fires up the engine, and we bump along the dirt roads toward home in silence.

The driver pulls so far into our driveway that we are mere feet from the front porch. She swings open the door and insists on taking my elbow as I lumber down the steps and onto firm ground. She looks at me, then back at the bus.

"I wish I could help you with your bags, but…"

"We can manage. Thanks again for picking us up."

It seems like she wants to say more but decides against it. Instead, she climbs back on the bus and waves as she backs out of the driveway.

Inside the house, I put all the bags onto the kitchen table and leave them there. I need to lie down before my hips give way. I'm not on the couch five minutes before Tyan is at my side, tugging at my shirt sleeve. "What is it?" I ask, irritated. She points to another note pinned to the front of her shirt. Without sitting up, I unpin the note and crumple it into a ball.

"You're gonna be in trouble," Tyan says. "Teacher said you're supposed to read the note."

I imagine Tyan telling her teacher tomorrow, "Bad Debbie smashed your note," so I smooth it out across my belly and unfold it. It tells me, again, that Tyan's lunches are lacking proper nutritional value. And there is a new request this time: to call the office to discuss possible aid programs she might benefit from.

"Big surprise," I say out loud. "Tell me something I don't know!"

I swing my legs over the side of the couch and get up, frustrated. Without looking at either of the kids, I go into my bedroom and slam the door behind me. I'm angry at the whole world.

I open a bedroom window, and when the fresh air and bird song floods in, I begin to cry. I can't stop the tidal wave of grief. I drape an arm along the windowsill and lay my head down on it, my shoulders heaving with sobs of despair.

I cry until I have no more energy and then lift my head at the sudden realization that I cry every single day. Typically, it is when I'm alone, doing laundry in the basement or taking a shower, but not a day goes by without a good cry.

Do most people cry every day?

I ponder the question for several minutes and then decide, yes, most people must cry every single day because life is one long burden.

This revelation strips away the heavy responsibility of happiness from me. If it isn't attainable or real, all my hope can disappear, and emotional numbness can replace despair. At least now I'll be able to roll up my sleeves and keep moving.

I wipe my eyes and head to the kitchen, where I put things away and start on a dinner of macaroni and cheese with bologna sandwiches. I wash dishes. I pack Tyan's lunch box so full of snacks and sandwiches it is comical. I put the kids to bed and read *The Three Little Pigs* for the hundredth time, only now I have no inflection in my voice. I read it like a robot would. I try to summon that part of me which animated story time each night, but she won't surface.

The kids don't beg for a second story like they usually do. Instead, they pull up the covers and say goodnight, almost eager to have me leave the room.

I sit on the couch in darkness for hours before deciding to go to bed, well after midnight. I open all the windows in the bedroom, trying to alleviate the oppressive August heat. I cannot sleep, despite every bone and muscle in my body telling me how much I need it.

I kick away the cheap polyester sheets in frustration, then freeze at the sound of keys scraping in the front door lock. Despite the heat a shiver cascades down my body, and I am frozen in bed, listening to the heavy footfalls on carpet.

Mac is home.

I should pretend to be asleep but instead I get up and move down the hallway to the edge of the darkness that marks the living room. He stands still in the center of the room as if waiting for me.

"Where were you?" I ask.

And with that, Mac swipes my legs out from under me and launches the first kick.

CHAPTER 19

Labor Pains. Maybe.

The Harley Davidson wall calendar flips from August to September. Ian and Tyan go off to Darlene's for a weekend visitation, and the baby's due date comes and goes. Mac has not disappeared or raised his voice since returning from his two-week absence. He also hasn't had a drink since then.

The "morning after" apology I got for that beating was the most extravagant yet. There were flowers, a night out for Chinese food, even foot massages. Best of all was the crumpled man on his knees, tears of regret and remorse, begging for my forgiveness.

This is usually what makes me feel whole again, his declaration of love and how important and valuable I am. This time, however, I just shrug inwardly. I believe he means it for now, but that will change.

It will always change.

Mac returns home from work a few nights later, flustered. He has come to the realization that I am eighteen and no longer under my parents' medical coverage. He paces the living room as he explains there's no way he can pay the hospital expenses of having a baby.

"I asked DeeDee to drive you to social services tomorrow. You need to file for assistance right away."

"I don't want to, Mac."

"You don't get a choice. You don't have any medical insurance, and the baby is going to be here any day."

My eyes well up with tears.

"Look, you just tell them you don't know who the father is or make up a name. They have to give you medical coverage. You can file for food stamps and relief payments, too."

"But I don't want to go on welfare."

"I know that, but we all have to do things we don't want to. I don't want to work in a dirty foundry every day, but I do it so we can eat. You've gotta start doing your part."

"But —"

"You want this baby to have a better life, right? So you're going tomorrow, like it or not!"

Mac storms off to the bedroom, so there is nothing more to be said. Tomorrow I will be applying for welfare, and even though I know somewhere in my mind that welfare's not bad, it feels awful to accept it. Like another low in my life, something my parents, especially Mom, will give me a hard time about. A daughter on the dole.

I console myself with the thought that maybe we can at least stop eating squirrels.

• • •

DeeDee is in the driveway at 9:30 sharp on Monday morning. I waddle over to the car and climb into the passenger seat.

"Good morning," I say with my eyes downcast. When DeeDee doesn't return the greeting or put the car in reverse, I look up.

"Now you go on and give me a smile when you say good morning," she says, giving me one of her biggest grins. I smile for real this time and repeat my greeting.

"That's better. You keep that head up today and don't be ashamed. Everybody needs a little help sometimes."

I spend the entire day filling out papers, waiting in line and answering questions. I'm caught off guard when a case worker asks me for the name of the father. "Robert McGee," I reply, hoping she is not a Janis Joplin fan. I tell her we had a one-night stand in West Virginia, and I have no contact information for him.

Papers are stapled and stamped in triplicate. I am handed a packet and told that a case worker will be assigned to me. It is nearly 5:00 p.m. when DeeDee drops me off at home.

LABOR PAINS. MAYBE.

My backache that began while sitting in a waiting room plastic chair for two hours is getting worse. Soap suds cling to my forearms in the kitchen sink as I knuckle down with a scouring pad. My back twinges again, and I inhale sharply, unable to move. The pain is like white-hot barbed wire that tightens with each breath.

I rationalize that it must be the stress from today's trip to the welfare department, but that's not what it is. My baby is three weeks overdue and has decided to make its way down the birth canal, sunny side up. Since I know nothing about being pregnant, I don't realize this incredible pain is not a good thing.

All I know is I can't sleep with these "muscle spasms." I run a scalding hot bath and watch my china-white legs turn bright red up to the calf as I step in. It takes a few attempts, but eventually I submerge up to my chin. The heat weaves into my muscle fibers and they loosen. I tilt my head back and close my eyes, falling fast asleep.

I feel cold, so I try to pull a blanket over me. Instead, I pull a wave of water over my face that wakes me up. The house is dark and quiet. Everybody has gone to bed, including Mac. I hoist my shriveled body out of the tub and slip on my long nightgown. The bedroom door is open a few inches, and Mac is snoring like a freight train.

As quietly as possible, I slide myself into bed and under the covers. Within minutes, my back convulses with pain again, and I inch my way back to the edge of the bed, sliding out the way I came in. I drop to my knees and put my forehead onto the carpet. I manage to fall asleep in this yoga pose for about an hour, until an urgent need to pee wakes me.

I do my best to dash for the bathroom, but it's too late. Hot liquid is running down my thighs. Flipping on the bathroom light reveals a horror show. Trails of bright red blood stain the front of my nightgown, and there is a swath of blood-soaked carpet behind me, snaking from my feet into the dark abyss of the bedroom.

My first thought is that I've been stabbed somehow — there's just so much blood. Pulling the nightgown up and over my head, blood spatters from the hem onto the bathroom wall. No knife wound, only blood coming from between my legs.

Maybe this is normal. Maybe I'm in labor?

I return to the bedroom and stand over Mac, whispering for him to wake up. No response. I repeat myself just a little louder and this time, I put my hand on his shoulder. His eyes fly open, and he is upright in one swift movement, ready for action.

"What's wrong?"

"I think the baby is coming. We need to go to the hospital."

"Turn the light on. I can't see a damned thing." He whips the bed covers back and swings his feet onto the floor. I flip the switch, and Mac almost falls over as he backs away from the crime scene on the carpet.

"What the fuck happened?" he says, more in disbelief than anger.

"I don't know. I'm bleeding."

"Yeah, no shit! Get in the car."

I swap the nightgown for stretch pants and the top that reads, "I'm not fat, I'm pregnant." It's 2:00 a.m. when we pull out of the driveway, leaving Ian and Tyan asleep in their beds. Mac eases the car to a stop in front of the emergency entrance of Mt. Clemens General Hospital twenty minutes later.

"Go on," he says, motioning toward the large glass hospital doors.

"What do I do?"

"You go in there and you tell them you're having a baby. What else would you do?"

"You're not going to come in?"

"We left the kids at home, so I need to go back," he replies, avoiding my eyes. "Labor takes hours. I'll be back in the morning, and I'll call your parents too, okay?"

Without a word, I open the car door and get out. Mac speeds off before I even turn toward the hospital doors. I watch his taillights turn right, then left out of the parking lot. He really left me here, I think. My throat is tight and feels shredded, like a ball of glass is stuck in it. I want to cry and dislodge it, but the tears won't come.

The large glass doors open automatically with an audible "woosh" as I waddle into the lobby.

Alone.

CHAPTER 20

Labor Pains: Definitely

Everything is so bright and white in the hospital, like the set of a sci-fi movie. My nose crinkles at the smell of antiseptic and urine, and I hesitate in the doorway, not knowing what to do.

"Miss?" a female voice asks from behind a large reception desk that I have failed to notice. "Miss, do you need help?"

"I think I'm in labor. I'm pregnant."

"Yes, I can see that," she says, unamused. "Do you need a wheelchair, or can you walk over here?"

It dawns on me that I'm still standing at the door. I force myself to walk to the desk and repeat, "I think I'm in labor."

"How far apart are your contractions?"

"Contractions?"

"Yes, contractions. Your labor pains. How often are you having them?"

"I don't know. There was blood. I came here."

I sound like Tarzan of the Jungle before he learned how to speak English.

"Blood? You mean the mucous plug?"

"No, I don't think so. I mean, I don't know. There was just a lot of blood." I am stammering now, ashamed of my ignorance.

"Did you bring a maxi pad that you can show me?" The tone of her voice tells me she is becoming annoyed at this game we seem to be playing.

"No. It was more than I could —"

"Miss, is there somebody here with you?" She interrupts me, her voice drowning out mine. It's clear she's done with any attempt at courtesy.

"No ma'am." My cheeks are now burning, and I keep my eyes focused on the floor.

"How old are you?" she asks, softening her tone.

"I'm eighteen, ma'am."

I hear a heavy sigh and a clipboard dropping onto the reception desk. My eyes are still glued to the floor.

"Fill out these forms and bring them back to me with your insurance card."

There are so many forms, and they ask the same questions over and over. I fill in the answers I know and leave the others blank. Thirty minutes later, I am back at the reception desk with her pen and clipboard. She says nothing while she scans the pages, barely pausing at the blank areas. I chew my lip as I wait for her to give some kind of "next steps."

"Would you prefer a natural childbirth experience?" she asks, looking up at me.

I have no idea what that means, and I don't want to display my ignorance again. A natural childbirth must be better than an unnatural one, so I nod my head up and down.

"Sign here." She pushes another form across the counter, along with her pen again.

Almost as soon as I finish signing my name, a wheelchair appears and I am whisked away to the labor room, a cinderblock bunker located in the hospital basement.

For the next three days, I don't know if it is noon or midnight. My back pain is so intense that I can't feel anything else, including contractions. I'm outfitted with what looks like a double wide seat belt across my belly. It prints out a sheet to tell the nurses when I'm having a contraction and for how long.

There are two beds in the room. Six women come and go in the other one while I writhe away in agony. By the end of day two, I beg every nurse on duty to just cut me open. It turns out that natural childbirth means no C-section or pain medications — not even Advil.

I am permitted one visitor at a time, and Mac and Mom take turns sitting with me. When neither one is there, I gaze at the beige concrete walls. There are no windows, no artwork and no music, only the howls of other women in labor.

By day three, the staff are becoming concerned. It is now Thursday afternoon, and two interns take turns inserting their gloved hands into my birth canal. Years ago, I witnessed a calf being born on my uncle's farm. My cousins stood around the heaving cow, exchanging ideas on how to speed things up. All that's missing right now for me is some straw.

"It's been too long," Intern No. 1 says.

"Yeah, it's been...fifty hours!" Intern No. 2 exclaims as he flips through my chart. "Should we break her water?"

"It's worth a shot," Intern No. 1 replies.

Without a word to me, they insert what looks like a giant crochet hook between my legs, and I hear a subtle "pop." Hot liquid expels onto the absorbent pad beneath me, and I have an urgent need to push.

"Wow, that was fast!" Intern No. 2 says, and they exit the room almost running.

Three nurses materialize and start to push my bed out the door. They sprinkle me with calming phrases, like "You're doing great," "It won't be long now" and "Just listen to my voice," but I am panicking. One nurse holds my hand as we travel through a long hallway until the foot of my bed slams into the double doors of the delivery room, punching them wide open.

Lights blind me from every direction. My eyes ping-pong around the room, searching for someone familiar, but everybody is wearing masks, gowns and gloves. A fabric screen is draped across my midsection, preventing me from seeing anything below my breasts. It strikes me that a kidney transplant is probably more intimate than this "natural childbirth experience."

I push when I'm told to push and look to the nurse at my side for updates on what's going on. She asks me for one more big push, and when I comply, there is a collective sigh in the room. I see the doctor hand my child off to a different nurse.

"It's a girl," the nurse at my side says.

I watch the other nurse walk across the room where my daughter is weighed on a metal scale. The nurse charts her weight and then slaps the bottom of her feet. She has not made a sound so far, but this brings a roar out of her. Only then does the nurse bring her over to me for a quick kiss before whisking her off to a bath and the nursery.

I am moved to a hospital room with an actual window where I fall into the deep sleep of exhaustion. Newborns are kept down the hall in a nursery. They are wheeled into their mother's room for regimented feeding times throughout the day, which means I don't hold my daughter until she is brought to my room several hours later.

I marvel at how content she is after such a traumatic and terrifying event. Her bald head accentuates pointy ears, and this earns her the nickname of "Yoda" from the nurses. It is perfect for her because she seems wise and self-assured, even at day one.

In 1982, unwed teen mothers like me are either pitied or shunned. The future is bleak, with little hope for happiness, stability or career. And yet, somehow, my teen pregnancy begins to propel me towards all these things. My unplanned daughter has arrived in time to show me just how strong I am.

CHAPTER 21

Purgatory

Nurses bring my daughter to me only for bottle feedings. I have not completed a single feeding without falling fast asleep with her in my arms, and yet my pent-up exhaustion and anxiety melt away in these quiet moments.

Three days after my delivery, a nurse brings the blank birth certificate. She has presented it to me every day, asking me to fill in the baby's name, and every day I have asked her to please bring it back later. I never considered any girls' names because I was certain this baby was a boy.

"You're going home tomorrow," the nurse says. "Your daughter will be named Jane Doe if you don't do this today."

I decide on Tara, a Celtic name meaning "tower" or "sacred ground." I print it on the form along with my own information under "mother."

Mac will not even look at the birth certificate the next time he visits. He starts checking over his shoulder when I mention it, saying it's none of his business because he's just a family friend. He behaves as if every nurse, visitor, or doctor is a spy planted by social services to track him down as the father. He refuses to sign his name and leaves the spaces blank where the father's information should be.

I am discharged after four days and wheeled out of the hospital to Mac and the Cutlass Supreme. A nurse helps me into the passenger seat, places Tara in my lap, and waves as we pull away from the curb. I smush Tara into my chest, afraid she is going to slip to the floor, and then panic about suffocating her. I release my grip, only to clamp down again when we hit a pothole.

My anxiety grows as we get closer to home. I don't even know how to change a diaper. How am I going to figure out bottle feedings and diapers on top of school lunches, laundry, and cooking? Before we even reach the driveway, I'm overwhelmed.

"Mary and Donna are keeping the kids a few extra days," Mac says, to my relief. "They said it was fine for them to stay a while longer."

I send a silent *Thank You* to the couple in a cramped trailer who always make room for more at their table.

Mac opens the front door for me, and I am impressed by how clean and tidy everything is. I hand Tara to Mac while I pull off my jacket, and he keeps her tucked into the crook of his arm well into late afternoon. It is clear he is smitten with her.

Together we figure out how to use the bottle warmer. Mac insists that Tara be fed formula because he believes "only hippies breastfeed their kids" and "nothing but the best for my daughter." He refuses to place Tara in the crib at the foot of our bed until the sun sets and then checks on her every fifteen minutes until he falls asleep himself.

The hourly feedings from midnight until 6:00 a.m., however, are all mine. Mac surprises me by taking over in the morning so I can rest, and by the time Ian and Tyan return home a few days later, I feel my strength returning.

They are excited about the new baby and take turns holding Tara. Tyan wants to know when she will be able to walk and play games. Ian holds her close to his chest and stares into her eyes. "She's my little sister!" he says, beaming with pride, and I know he has found a container for all that excess love spilling from his heart.

Tara's arrival casts a spell over the house, bringing relative peace for an entire year. Mac doesn't disappear on drinking binges, and he doesn't keep a six-pack in the fridge anymore. Darlene's name has not been mentioned, nor has she been seen, and it crosses my mind that Mac's terror campaign might have focused her attention on baby Carl's safety as well as her own.

We move out of the Schoenherr Rd house and rent a tidy three-bedroom home in New Haven, just down the street from Bob and DeeDee. The house sits on a corner lot with the volunteer fire department on the opposite corner. Mac reasons that we should be closer to people and resources now that we have a newborn, and for once, we're in complete agreement.

PURGATORY

• • •

New Haven is a small, low-income town built around the foundry where nearly every resident works. Mac walks to and from his job each day, cutting his former forty-minute commute down to four minutes. The town and everything in it are dusted with black powder, and yet I am elated

to have a gas station with a payphone and a tiny grocer just a few streets away.

Summer weekends are spent fishing for catfish and perch. I fry them in cornmeal for dinner just about every night. The supply of squirrels in our freezer has not dwindled, however, because winter lasts an eternity in Michigan, so they are still a staple when the fish runs out.

The small allotment of food stamps helps tremendously, and I stock a new makeshift pantry in the creepy partial basement with its dirt floor and three-foot opening in the cobblestone wall for access to plumbing. I keep non-perishables in this crawl space, knowing Mac will never venture into it.

There are still occasions when Mac becomes angry. His jaw clenches, and all of us tense as we wait for him to release that anger. Lately it is Ian who gets the brunt of it, sometimes me. A verbal assault or a quick shove against the wall, followed by Mac slamming the back door as he walks to Bob's house to cool off. I remain on high alert, waiting for the ticking bomb to explode.

Tara is nearly two when the fuse is lit. Mac begins to stop at the gas station for a quart of beer on his way home from work. First it is once a week, then every couple of days. My heart drops into my stomach the day I open the fridge to find a case of beer.

Tara's magic spell is broken, and we are now headed back to square one.

• • •

I am washing dinner dishes while Mac sits on the couch and watches TV. He sends Ian into the kitchen for a beer. Ten minutes later, Ian is back for another. I keep Tara in the kitchen with me and take my time drying each plate, waiting.

"What the fuck is this?" Mac yells.

"A baseball," Ian replies.

"I can see that, you idiot. What's it doing on the couch?"

"Sorry, Daddy. I'll put it away."

I hear a clunk, and Ian begins to wail. He's standing in the living room with a large red welt on his cheek, the baseball at his feet. Mac has the front of Ian's shirt bunched into his fist and starts to push him against the wall.

Tara shoots out of the kitchen and throws herself at Mac's leg, wrapping herself around it and screaming, "No, Daddy! No!" Mac releases his grip and shoves Ian to the floor. Tara toddles over and kneels beside his crumpled body.

"Poor Ian," she says, stroking his hair. "My poor Ian."

"Go cry in your room," Mac says. Ian pulls himself up, takes Tara's tiny hand in his, and they walk toward his room.

"Keep that in your room while you're at it!" Mac yells as he throws the baseball, hitting Ian in the back. He then turns his attention to me.

"You got a problem?"

"It's just a baseball, Mac."

"The couch is where I relax after busting my ass all day. Is it too much to ask for me not to get a ball in my crotch when I sit down?"

"All I'm saying is —"

"Don't tell me how to raise my kids!" Mac pushes me into the wall, forearm against my throat. I can't breathe. I feel saliva running from the corners of my mouth, and my vision goes dark around the edges.

A piercing shriek startles us both. He drops his arm from my throat and backs away. Tara is standing in the living room, screaming with all her might. Her face is purple, and she looks like she may explode.

Mac rushes to her and she runs from him, hiding behind my legs. I pick her up and she buries her face in my chest, sobbing nonstop.

"Look what you've done," I say. "She's afraid of you now."

Nothing comes out of Mac's mouth. He is red-faced and visibly shaken. Without a word, he walks out the front door and down the street.

Mac does not come home all night, and I am determined to leave before he returns. I send Ian and Tyan off to school that morning and begin packing. With Tara on my hip, I drag the garbage bag of clothing to the gas station where I call collect to my parents' house. I don't care who answers the phone; I am going to beg, plead and cry until someone agrees to pick us up. Guilt stabs at my heart when I think of leaving Ian and Tyan behind, but my parents don't have room for all of us. Besides, I don't have any legal right to take them.

The phone rings three times before Mom's voice comes on the line. She says hello, but I don't say anything. I twirl the phone cord so tight around my finger that it turns purple.

"Hello?" she repeats.

"Mom?"

"Deborah? What is it? What's wrong?"

"Can you pick us up? We're at the gas station."

"I'll be right there."

Her red station wagon pulls into the parking lot fifteen minutes later, and I hoist the garbage bag into the backseat before climbing into the passenger side and pulling the seat belt across Tara in my lap. I'm like an escaped convict, my eyes searching the streets for Mac, as if he's a police officer who could drag me back to house arrest.

I don't relax until we pull onto Bellaire Street. Mom plants Tara in front of the TV with a cup of dry Cheerios before joining me at the kitchen table.

"So, Mac's back to his old ways, is he?"

"He choked me last night."

"Aye, you'll never change a leopard's spots."

"Tara saw it, Mom."

"Bloody hell! In front of wee Tara? You did the right thing," she says, patting my hand. "Put your things in the unfinished room. We'll talk about what comes next later."

Her words reassure me, and yet I still watch the clock all day, imagining the series of events taking place in New Haven. At 3:00 p.m. Ian and Tyan will walk into an empty house. I hope they see my note telling them to go to DeeDee's house. At 5:00 p.m. Mac will walk into the same empty house, and it won't take him long to figure out that I've left.

I am glued to the upstairs window that looks out over the garage and onto Bellaire Street, waiting for Mac to storm the house and drag me out, but the phone never rings and the Cutlass Supreme never pulls up.

As the sun goes down, I start to relax. Maybe it's really this easy. Maybe I can leave with Tara. Maybe it's all over, just like that. Maybe.

And maybe I'll keep Tara within arm's reach for the next few days, just in case.

CHAPTER 22

Path of Least Resistance

I wake up when the sun hits me in the eyes through the blinds. Tara is sitting in bed next to me, studying an upside-down children's book. She looks so serious, as if she is concentrating on memorizing an encyclopedia, despite not being able to read yet. She has always entertained herself, not crying much as a baby and preferring to play with her toes or gurgle at the animals dangling from the mobile in her crib.

I hike Tara onto my hip and go downstairs to the kitchen. The house is so quiet now, compared to just a couple of years ago.

Mark is stationed at Edwards Air Force base in California — he joined right after high school, his sights set on becoming a pilot. Steve now works full-time in the kitchen at Mt. Clemens General Hospital. Dad is working long hours for General Motors, and MaryAnne is in school all day.

"I'm in here," Mom says from the family room.

I set Tara down and go find Mom watering and pruning her plants. She has a green thumb, and the family room looks like a magical jungle with all the vines and greenery lining the walls. The shriveled, three-inch twig I threw out five years ago is now an eight-foot-tall rubber tree, bending at the ceiling.

"There is a bowl of Cheerios on the stool for Tara," she says, her attention still focused on the plants. "Help yourself to whatever you like."

"Thanks, Mom."

"We have an appointment at 1:00 p.m. with Social Services today."

"For what?"

"To get you an apartment, of course. You did'nae think you were going to live here, did you?"

I'm stunned. I did, indeed, think I was going to live there. All the safety and reassurance I felt yesterday evaporates, and the familiar sensation of having swallowed ground glass expands in my throat, preventing any words from escaping.

Mom stops plucking dead leaves from a creeping vine and turns to face me, hands on hips.

"Well?" she asks.

I say nothing.

"Go on and get your breakfast," she says, waving me off as she returns to her plants.

I head back toward the kitchen, trying to keep tears at bay. Tara sits on the step stool next to the table, eating her cup of dry Cheerios. She watches me as I walk past her into the powder room and close the door.

The tears come, despite my best efforts not to cry. I sob into a hand towel until the tears run out, and then I pull myself together for what lies ahead.

At 1:00 p.m. Mom, Dad, Tara and I are seated across a metal desk from a social worker. She's distracted, and it's obvious that she has little time between her appointments, judging by how often she flicks her wrist to check the time.

Dad has left work at lunch to join us, so I know this is serious business. With the Detroit auto industry taking a beating from the influx of Japanese imports and layoffs becoming more widespread, he doesn't miss work.

While I'm praying that Dad doesn't lose his job over me, Mom takes charge of the conversation, laying out the solution as she sees it.

"Her father and I will help pay for an apartment. Deborah will work, of course. We just need help with food and childcare until she's on her feet."

"I'm sorry, but it doesn't work like that," replies the social worker. "We don't subsidize your contributions. If you provide any financial help, it must be reported, and that will disqualify her from assistance."

"I thought you were supposed to help people," Mom says in a clipped voice, her frustration rising.

"We do help people, Mrs. Brannigan. If your daughter would like a housing stipend, we can provide an apartment at The Victory Gardens in Mt. Clemens."

"Isn't that where the young mother was burned alive?" Dad asks.

He, Tara and I have been quiet observers so far, but the mention of the housing project stirs him to life. A few weeks ago, all the local newspapers carried headlines of a young mother of two who had been raped, rolled up in an area rug, and set on fire. She was burned alive on the playground of the Victory Gardens housing project, and there were no leads on who did it.

"There was an incident there, yes, but it is being investigated—"

"No daughter of mine is going to live in such a place!"

"Hughie, calm doon," Mom says, putting a hand on his arm.

"I'll nae calm doon! She'll nae bloody live there."

Dad's Glaswegian accent becomes harder to understand as his temper flares. The social worker gestures with her hands, palms down, for everybody to calm down.

"Look, I've got another appointment in about ten minutes. Why don't I figure out how much help we can provide, and you can think about it? If you decide to move forward, just call my number and we can set it up then."

We wait while she runs numbers, and the numbers are grim. The monthly stipend equates to a full-time, minimum wage job. I ask if they will provide any childcare assistance when I find a job. The social worker tells me that any money I make from a job will be deducted from the assistance.

"Why would anybody want to work then?" Mom says, asking exactly what I am thinking.

"I can't answer that, Mrs. Brannigan."

"Can you not see how this system keeps the poor from succeeding?"

"Again, I can't answer that. I just process the applications. If you'd like to proceed, call my number."

The social worker stands to signal the end of our allotted time. Mom picks up the application and leads our small procession out of the building. Tara and I trail behind my parents through the parking lot, and I catch snippets of their heated debate as we walk.

"I won't have it," Dad says. "A bloody apartment in the same place where another woman died. And forget about her making any money because she has to give it back."

"I don't like it either, Hughie, but I can't take this on. It's just too much."

We reach the red station wagon and part ways. Dad returns to his job, and we return to Bellaire Street. I look straight ahead, watching cars braking or turning in front of us, not quite registering the lecture Mom is giving me.

Words like *responsibility*, *hard work* and *obligation* bounce off my eardrums. My mind is too busy chewing on what the "It" in "It's just too much" must be.

Mom has not sugar coated the extra burden Tara and I have brought to their already strained household finances. Yesterday she shook the half empty box of Cheerios and frowned, lamenting that she would need to buy two boxes each week now. Today's disappointment at Social Services only amplifies my feelings of guilt and worthlessness.

The phone is ringing as we open the front door and stops as we reach the kitchen table. I pull bread from the pantry to make Tara a peanut butter and jelly sandwich when it begins to ring again. Mom picks it up on the third ring.

"Hello? Yes, she is…Yes, I bet you've got a lot to say." She holds the receiver out to me. "It's Mac."

"What do I tell him?"

"Whatever the hell you like. I've got laundry to do."

She opens the basement door and heads to the washing machine. I stand with the receiver buried in my chest, terrified to put it to my ear. I close my eyes, take a deep breath and try to answer Mac's voice repeating "hello," but my throat is too tight, and only a choked hiss comes out.

"Debbie? Please don't hang up!"

"What do you want, Mac?"

"Debbie, I'm sorry. I'll never forgive myself for what happened, and I don't expect you will either."

I listen to the same apology I've heard dozens of times before. He is always sincere, his words punctuated with remorseful tears. He makes lavish vows and promises that are always broken. He is nearing the climax of his apology when I cut him off.

"Tara saw you, Mac." Those three short words sum up where my line in the sand is.

"I know. I hate myself for that. I promise she will never see anything like that again."

I say nothing.

"Can you put Tara on the phone? Not for me, for Ian. He hasn't stopped crying since you left. You know he's attached to her."

My silence signals compliance, and Mac calls for Ian to come to the phone. His steady sniffles tell me that he has been crying. I tell Tara somebody wants to talk to her and hand her the receiver. She uses both of her tiny hands to hold it to her ear.

"Hewow?" A gigantic smile spreads across her face, and she turns to me, still beaming. "It's my Ian!"

I drag out negotiations with Mac for two more days, just to buy myself some time. I knew the minute I took that phone call that I'd be returning to New Haven. That my parents, Mac, Tara, Ian — everybody will be happier that way.

Everybody except me.

I won't pretend that things will get better for me, but at least I *probably* won't be rolled into a carpet and set on fire.

CHAPTER 23

Night School

The brief escape to my parents' house was a mere skip in the record of my life. Weeks after my return, the needle drops into the same groove and plays the same song all over again.

Mac keeps his word to some extent — Tara never witnesses his abuse toward me again. Instead, he waits until she is asleep or out in the yard with Ian before twisting my arm behind my back, yanking my hair, or pushing my face into the wall.

Reuniting the kids almost makes it worthwhile. Tyan adores Tara, and Ian is on the worship level of that adoration. He and Tara are inseparable — they spend countless hours in the backyard playing. Ian teaches her important skills like how to make spitballs and how to ride a bike.

Mac is also enamored of Tara, taking her to the gas station after work every day to buy a cream soda and some peanut M&Ms. Neither Tyan nor Ian seems to resent Tara's special status with their father, probably because Tara is always happy to share her bounty.

I am in the kitchen frying fresh catfish for dinner when Mac calls me into the dining room. He has a pile of mail in front of him. Unopened mail sits in one pile, opened in another. He motions for me to sit down across from him.

"What does this mean?" he asks, sliding an opened letter across the table to me. I hesitate because Mac never allows me to open any mail, and this is a notice from the welfare office that was addressed to me. I pick it up and read, *Please contact us regarding your benefits. A response is required within 10 business days.*

"I don't know, Mac."

"Did you forget to do something? Are they cutting off benefits?"

"I really don't know. You've seen everything they've sent to me and everything I've sent to them."

"Well, you're going to call them tomorrow when I get home. You better not have fucked this up."

Mac is already convinced that his bar-hopping income will run dry. Each month I am taken to the local convenience store, where I sign over my check. The cashier gives Mac the cash, minus a fee. I never get to touch any of it, and Mac usually disappears for a few days afterward.

I barely sleep that night, afraid that I am going to be thrown in jail by the state or beaten senseless by Mac. Maybe both. The next day I just stare out the back door, waiting for Mac's blackened face and yellow helmet to appear. Just after 4:00 he turns the corner and comes into view.

"Hi Daddy!" Tara yells through the screen door, waving and jumping. But Mac doesn't approach the back steps; instead, he motions for me to come outside. I hitch Tara up on my hip and head down. She wriggles herself free and runs to Mac, curls bouncing. He clasps her hand, and his smile cuts a white gash across his soot-covered face. This is their daily ritual, and it never fails to make him grin.

"Are you coming too, Mommy?" Tara asks me.

"Mommy needs to make a phone call," Mac says, "but you and me are gonna get some cream soda and M&Ms." They swing clasped hands back and forth as we walk toward the gas station.

Mac inserts two dimes in the payphone and dials the number from the letter. When it begins to ring, he hands the receiver to me with a look that says, "Watch it." I give my case number and the reference number from the letter, and then I'm put on hold.

It's all I can do to keep from hyperventilating, so much anxiety is stuffed in my chest. Tara tugs at Mac's arm, impatient to go inside and get her candy. He places a small stack of coins on the payphone and says, "Make it short and sweet." They leave me in the parking lot, and I exhale loudly at the same moment a voice comes on the line.

"Oh, I'm so glad you called, Miss Brannigan." The female voice reminds me of a kindergarten teacher at snack time. "It looks like you qualify for our night school education program. There's no obligation to attend, but it is completely free."

"Really?" I reply, not sure what it means.

"Yes, really. You can get your diploma, GED, or both if you like. Is this something you'd like to take advantage of?"

School? I imagine being out in the world for a few hours with no kids and no warden. My heart skips a beat at the thought. I need to pull this off, but how?

"How long is the program?"

"Well, it is three nights a week for twelve weeks to get a diploma. If that's not possible, you could just take the GED prep class. That would be two nights a week for two weeks. Then you can schedule the GED test, which is a two-day test."

Somehow she fits all this detail into one breath, as if she's worried I might hang up and lose her.

"No, no, I'd prefer the twelve-week classes. What do I need to do?" I ask this question with my eyes on the door of the gas station.

"Excellent! We can fill everything out while I have you on the phone, or I can mail the form and you can fill it out and return it before March 1st."

"Can you mail them, please?"

The door to the station's mini-mart swings open, and Mac is striding back to me with Tara at his side, swinging her pouch of M&Ms while he twists off the cap to her Faygo cream soda.

"That will be just fine, Miss Brannigan. I'll get those out to you today. Just be sure you have them back to me before March 1st so we can get you enrolled."

I wait a few seconds until Mac is close enough to hear me say, "Yes ma'am, I will be sure to comply." I hang up the phone and turn toward Mac, my face a mask of feigned disappointment.

"Well, this sucks! I have to go to night school, or they're going to cancel all benefits."

"What? All of them? Even the WIC coupons?"

"I don't know, Mac. She just said 'all benefits'."

I say a silent prayer, hoping he will believe me and doing my best to look outraged by the injustice of it all, while my stomach churns on the inside.

"Son of a bitch!" Mac mutters, looking down at Tara. "Another one of Reagan's great ideas. Some president he is, taking food right from a baby's mouth."

I resist the urge to point out that he has spent every dime of our welfare benefits at a bar, leaving us without food on many occasions. Instead, I commiserate and agree with him, relieved he has bought my story.

The paperwork arrives and I fill it out, then spend the next two weeks with my stomach tied in knots. I am convinced that Mac will discover that my attendance in this program is voluntary. Four weeks after the letter arrives, however, he pulls the car into the parking lot of Richmond High School.

"I'll be back in three hours, Debbie. Right here. Don't be late."

I nod and hold my breath until I open the large double doors and walk inside the school.

Four years ago, I quit high school, convinced it was a prison. Today I recognize it as my only chance at freedom. The hope rising in my chest almost makes me cry as I walk down the hallway, touching every locker door on my way to Creative Writing 101.

CHAPTER 24

Drop In

Six weeks roll by in a flash. Homework is done at the dining room table after the kids are in bed, and I find myself looking forward to these final hours of the day.

I am sitting bleary-eyed at the table, surrounded by handwritten papers, when Mac stops on his way to the couch. He picks up one sheet and begins to read it.

"You spelled something wrong."

"I did?"

"Yeah, you wrote 'eventuate' instead of eventually."

"Oh, I meant that."

"That's not a real word."

"I think it is."

He pulls a dictionary from our small bookcase and begins leafing through it. His finger runs the length of a page and stops, then moves from side to side. He closes the dictionary and puts it back on the shelf without a word. I don't dare smile until the couch springs squeak in the other room.

The following night, I am trotting past the front office on my way to class when the school principal calls out to me. I stop and point a finger to my chest as if to ask, "Me?" and he nods, gesturing for me to come inside the office.

"Hello, Miss Brannigan."

"Hey, Mr. Thompson. What's up?"

"Your assessment results have come back."

Every student completes an assessment test on the first day of night school, and he now holds mine in his hands. I forget to breathe for a moment, afraid I have failed to meet a basic requirement and will be kicked out of the program.

"You scored 98 percent!"

"Is that good?"

"Yes, it means you scored higher than 98 percent of college level students," Mr. Thompson replies, his voice rising with excitement.

"Okay."

"Okay? This means you should be taking college courses. College courses!"

We stare at each other for a few seconds, and I wait for him to tell me what to do. Smiling, he hands over the test results and says for me to think about it.

I know there's really nothing for me to think about because when I'm eating squirrel pies for dinner, college is not something within my reach. I fold the paper and tuck it into my back pocket, content in that moment to have proof that I am not a bubble-headed blonde, as Mac so often tells me I am.

We finish the last class of the evening a little early, and three other students approach me in the main hallway, just inside the double doors at the entrance. It is Tony from my Creative Writing class, flanked by Pete and Sandy, a young couple that can't seem to keep their hands off each other.

"Hey Debbie, we're going to find a place for a nightcap. Want to come along?"

Tony is handsome and a little younger than me. He attends class in the blue cargo pants and striped shirt of a car mechanic, his name embroidered on a patch at his left shoulder. Each week, he arrives fifteen minutes late for class, presumably coming right from work. Without fail, Pete and Sandy save him a seat alongside them in the front row.

I have noticed Tony before — he's caught me stealing glances several times in class. I blush at this encounter, partly because I am attracted to him and partly because I'm anxious that Mac may see us through the glass doors from the parking lot.

"No, thanks. I mean, thanks but I can't."

"We won't be out late," Tony says. "Come with us, even if it's just for a little while."

"I really can't. I've got a... a babysitter waiting for me."

"You have a baby?" Tony and the couple are surprised at this news.

"Yeah, I do, a daughter. She's three now, so not really a baby."

"Are you married?"

"No. Her father lives in West Virginia."

I tell myself that this lie is simply me sticking to the story Mac created. In reality I just want to keep Tony interested because it feels good to be noticed by him, to enjoy the flutter in my stomach he gives me three days a week.

"Okay, well, maybe next time."

Tony and the couple wave goodbye as they exit the building. I take a couple of deep breaths, then follow them outside. The orange Cutlass Supreme is parked a few yards from the front door and I get in the passenger side, putting my books on the floor. I'm still closing the door when Mac starts the interrogation.

"Who was that?"

"Who was who?"

"You know who. Who was that guy talking to you?"

"Oh, him? I don't know his name. He's in my writing class."

"Why is he talking to you?"

"He asked if he could borrow my book. He lost his and wanted to borrow mine to do homework. I told him no, he couldn't."

"He's probably hitting on you and you're just too dense to notice."

"You really think so?"

"Maybe not. You've got a mom body now."

He puts the car in gear and pulls out of the parking lot. The remark about my body barely registers because Mac makes comments like that on a regular basis. I consider them argument bait, and since he always wins the argument one way or another, I never bite the hook.

"I got the results from my assessment test today," I say, steering the topic away from Tony.

"Let me guess...You're being sent to junior high night school."

"No. Actually, I scored higher than 98 percent of college students."

"That should tell you something about our education system."

"The principal thinks I should be going to college."

"And what ass did he say to pull money from to pay for it?"

I look out the window at the telephone poles marching by in perfect staccato time, imagining I'm in a virtual film strip and these are the frame breaks. Will the movie ending be happy, tragic, or unremarkable?

Happy seems optimistic and unlikely, while tragic implies something sudden and unforeseen. That fits better than unremarkable, which hints at long, drawn-out misery. I am not interested in that. Once Tara is grown and on her own, I'd welcome a car crash. Maybe cancer, but the fast kind, like pancreatic or….

"Are you listening to me?" Mac asks.

"Sorry, what?"

"I asked you how much longer you need to take these dumb ass classes. I'm getting tired of driving you back and forth."

"Thanks to my test scores, I just need to pass the GED exam next week and not fail my current classes to qualify for my diploma."

"So one semester? You're done in June, then?"

"Yeah, I guess so."

"Good. I'll be glad when life goes back to normal."

I look out the passenger window again and contemplate a brain aneurysm. Those are quick, right?

• • •

Steve drops by the next day, knocking three times before letting himself in the back door, as he does most Tuesday afternoons. He pulls two bottles from the six-pack he's carrying and puts the other four in the refrigerator, then plops down on the couch. He tosses me a Chunky bar before pulling the tab on his PBR.

Steve has brought me a Chunky bar every week since December, when he filled three Christmas stockings with miniature candies for the kids as gifts. I grabbed a mini-Chunky bar from Tara's stocking, lamenting how long it had been since I had one. Two weeks later, the Chunky bar ritual began.

DROP IN

This has always been Steve's superpower. He listens to obscure, offhand comments, makes mental notes, and gives sincere gifts. When I asked him once how he knew just what to get me, he just shrugged and said, "You mentioned it two years ago."

We stare at the TV screen, watching music videos on MTV and not saying much, as usual. When Steve pops open his second beer, I grab his attention before the "Money for Nothing" video from Dire Straits can steal it away from me.

"Hey, that scholarship to CCS you got. Are you ever going to use it?"

With Ms. Sorenson's encouragement, Steve entered and won second place in an art competition that awarded scholarship prizes to the Center for Creative Studies in Detroit. This private art college carries clout — it is the school that elite automotive designers hope to attend, and the name opens many doors.

"It pays for one semester, then I have to buy all the materials and books. Why bother going for one semester when I can't pay for anything after that?"

"You're working at the hospital now, though. Can't you save enough to go?"

"Have you seen tuition prices for CCS? There's no way my shitty job is gonna let me save enough to pay for it."

"But what if you ask Mom and —"

"Deb, they're not gonna help. Where is all this coming from, anyway? You're bumming me out."

He returns his attention to his beer and the TV. I know Steve's right. Our parents never went to college — they left school at fifteen to learn a trade, and their parents did the same, so the topic of college was never even mentioned growing up.

Mark, Steve and I all had jobs by age fourteen, and by the time we hit junior high, buying clothes, yearbooks, cars, and even school lunches became our responsibility. When I imagine asking my parents for tuition to community college, I can almost recite their lecture about pulling myself up by my bootstraps. Besides, Mac would never allow me to attend college, so who am I kidding?

155

"Need anything from the kitchen?"

Steve shakes his head without moving his eyes from the TV. I pour myself a glass of cherry Kool-Aid from the fridge, then pull the folded paper from my back pocket. I read my test score one last time before crumpling it into a tight ball and tossing it into the trash can.

CHAPTER 25

Spilled Milk

I complete the eight-hour GED test in under four hours, passing with flying colors. The milestone is bittersweet, as it means this will be my one and only semester of night school. There will be no more short stories to write, no accounting balances to calculate, and no peers to laugh with.

It is a Friday night with only two weeks of class left when Tony, along with Pete and Sandy, approach me once again.

"We're going out to celebrate on the last night of class," Tony says. "We thought you might join us if you had enough notice to get a babysitter."

He is so handsome with his dark hair and single dimple that indents his cheek when he smiles! I want to say yes, but before I can utter a single word, the whooshing sound of the school's double doors gets our attention.

Mac strides in, his long hair let loose from its usual ponytail. The heels of his motorcycle boots clash with the tile floors, and he is at my side in just four determined steps. He drapes an arm across my shoulders in a way that broadcasts ownership, not affection. The smell of beer oozes from his pores.

"How about you introduce me to your friends, Deb?"

I stare at my armload of books, unable to make eye contact with him or anyone else. Tony steps forward and extends his hand.

"I'm Tony, and these are my friends Pete and Sandy."

Mac shakes his hand warily. It's clear he was expecting a confrontation, not a friendly gesture.

"Well, I'm Debbie's husband, Mac, and we need to get home to our children. Ain't that right?" he says in my direction, squeezing my shoulders. I nod my head without looking up, and he pulls me behind him out the double doors and to the Cutlass.

157

He grips my arm with one hand and opens the passenger door with the other. The shove intended to push me into the car only sends my armload of books tumbling to the ground.

"Pick that shit up," Mac growls before rounding the car and getting in the driver's seat.

I glimpse Tony at the other end of the parking lot, opening the door to his restored Mustang, and I mentally will him to look over at me. I want him to pull me from the car and save me from the next twenty minutes, the next twenty years. Instead, he drives out of the lot without so much as a glance my way.

We are barely out of the parking lot when the ritual begins. Part of me wishes we could skip the warm-up — the taunts, the humiliation, and the baited questions with no right answer. Let's just get right to the punches, the kicks, and the end. Unfortunately, tonight looks like it is going to be a full production.

"Nice to meet you, I'm Tony," Mac says in a high falsetto voice that sounds like Mickey Mouse. "How old is he, fourteen? That little fucker almost pissed his pants when I walked in."

I say nothing while Mac continues his rant, waiting for my cue.

"Why were you talking to him again? And don't tell me he wanted to borrow your book again, either, because that was total bullshit, wasn't it?"

That's my cue — the question with no right answer. No matter how I respond, I am a lying bitch. I'm not in the mood to perform tonight, so I continue to say nothing.

"I'm talking to you!"

I shrug and stare off into the distance.

Mac's right hand leaves the steering wheel and is behind my head before I can even flinch, shoving me forward. He's trying to bounce my face off the dashboard, but I'm short so my nose hovers above my thighs instead.

I don't struggle or resist, just wait until Mac pulls me back up with a fistful of my hair. I stare straight ahead as he releases me, then punches my left ear. He hurls verbal insults for the remainder of the trip home, but I don't respond.

"I'm gonna wait for you in the lobby from now on," Mac says as we pull into the driveway.

My heart sinks, and I remember how one hour ago, I was heartbroken that night school was coming to an end. Now, I'm filled with dread at the thought of going back.

• • •

Mac keeps his word and waits in the lobby for me every night for the last two weeks of school. I keep my head bowed and eyes averted in every class, avoiding all social interactions.

On the last day, I am only a few feet away from Mac when I hear giggles and cheers coming from a small group of students in the hall and turn to look.

"We did it!" Pete cheers with a fist in the air as he and the other students head toward the double doors. I see Tony trailing at the back of the pack, and our eyes meet.

I have avoided Tony since Mac introduced himself as my husband, not wanting to see contempt in his eyes. Today, however, his soft brown eyes are flooded with what looks like pity, and I turn away, unable to bear the reflected image of my pathetic self.

My new diploma shares drawer space with the underwear and socks. By September my life has returned to laundry, cleaning, and cooking — nothing but the heavy weight of responsibility — and before long the monotonous days blur into each other.

Mac resumes drinking every day, and I no longer pack sandwiches for a day of fishing with the kids on Saturdays. Instead, Graham shows up at our back door on Fridays to whisk Mac off for a weekend of bar hopping. Sometimes they disappear for a few hours, sometimes for a few days.

It is a Tuesday night in February when the sun sets once again with no sign of Mac. I wonder how many days of work he can miss before being fired and retreat to bed early. Tara is excited to sleep in the "big bed" with me for a third night, and we fall into a deep sleep curled up together.

I'm still asleep when a meteor shower of lights explodes behind my eyes. My face jerks to one side, then the other. It takes several seconds for me to realize I am being punched in the face. Mac's silhouette hovers above me in the darkness. His knees straddle me, and in his blind rage he seems oblivious to Tara's presence in the bed. She begins to cry, and he pauses the assault, confused.

"Mac, Tara's hungry," I say, trying to reach him through his drunken fog. "She wants some milk."

Without a word, he dismounts from the bed and wanders out of the room. I sit up and pull Tara close, rocking her in one arm while feeling my face for damage with the other. Mac returns to the bedroom, swaying from side to side.

"She wants milk? Well, I got milk."

He pours the gallon jug over Tara's head, and she begins to sputter and choke.

I do not recall getting out of bed or opening the dresser drawer, and yet somehow Mac's revolver is in my hand and pressed against his forehead. Click. Click. Four more times, four more clicks.

I pull the trigger again, but the gun is empty. It dawns on me that it has always been empty. I stand firmly planted between Mac and Tara. He is slack-jawed and motionless, blinking as we stare at each other, but I do not look away.

"You're such an idiot," he says, leaving the room without turning his back to me.

Tara sits shivering in a puddle of milk on the bed, her gold curls now flat against her cheeks. The implications of what just happened begin to develop a little at a time in my brain, like a Polaroid picture. What if the gun had been loaded? What if Mac's fists had landed on Tara tonight? It's only a matter of time.

Calm and clarity replace my questions. I pull Tara's wet pajamas over her head and toss them to the floor. She does not complain — Tara never complains — and I dress her in a warm onesie, squeezing her beloved Lucky Bear to her chest. She wraps her arms around it and sits cross-legged on the floor, somehow knowing to be quiet as I open drawers and dump their contents onto the floor.

It seems like an eternity for me to unroll a garbage bag without making noise. Different colors and textures of clothing are swallowed by its gaping black mouth, and I turn to Tara, putting my forefinger on my lips. She mimics the gesture back to me and watches me creep out of the bedroom.

Mac is slumped on the love seat, his boots and jacket still on, with one leg stretched out on the floor and the other dangling over the armrest. I focus on his wallet, snug in his back pocket. The chain snakes up from it to his front beltloop. He replaced the original leather belt snap with an oversized industrial safety pin to keep his car keys handy.

I hold my breath and crawl across the carpet toward him. Every muscle in my body is wound like a steel spring, expecting him to bolt upright and grab me by the hair. My hands tremble as I push the catch of the safety pin open and slide the car keys up. The sharp end of the pin catches the key ring as I lift it over, and the keys fall to the carpet.

I brace myself for impact, and Mac's low rumble snore skips a beat, but he does not move. I stuff the keys into my bra and crawl back to the bedroom. Tara has not moved an inch, and a streetlamp eclipses the bedroom window shade, casting a perfect rectangle of light around her. I pause to take in the scene and am comforted, viewing it as a sign of divine protection.

Clasping Tara's hand, we tiptoe to the kitchen and out the back door to the Cutlass sleeping in the gravel driveway. I strap Tara into the passenger seat, throw the garbage bag into the back and slide myself behind the wheel. I glance at the back door of the house, certain that Mac will barrel out of it. My heart starts to skip as I put the key into the ignition, and I hesitate.

I don't know how to drive.

I could walk to my parents' house, but I dismiss that idea right away. It would be a five-mile trek with a three-year-old at 4:00 a.m., so I turn the key forward in the ignition. The radio powers on, and I tap the gas pedal, but nothing happens. I start to crank the key backward and forward in the ignition, each time becoming a little more panicked.

Finally, I bulldoze the key all the way forward, and the car roars to life. I move the gear shift to the R position and push the gas pedal while easing up on the brake. We hopscotch out of the driveway, jumping the curb as I spin the steering wheel wildly in every direction. The car stutters along the asphalt streets for at least a half mile before I locate the headlights and switch them on.

I have a white-knuckle grip on the steering wheel, my chin grazing it as I crane forward to see over the dash. I drive all five miles with my left foot on the brake and my right foot on the gas, our pace like a Sunday stroll. Nearly an hour later, I park at a thirty-degree angle in front of my parents' house.

The sun begins to yawn as I shift Tara on my hip, wipe the sweat from my palm, and ring the doorbell. It takes a few minutes for Dad to open the door. He is wearing pajama bottoms with a plain white T-shirt and is still maneuvering his Coke-bottle glasses into position over his disheveled hair. Mom appears behind him, dressed in a full-length nightgown with a messy ponytail over one shoulder. She seems confused and maybe a little afraid until she sees me.

"Oche! Not again," she mutters, her hands flying up in agitation before turning toward the kitchen.

A bucket of ice water over my head would have been a warmer reception, and for a minute I consider running into the woods behind the house.

"Come on in, honey," Dad says, opening the door wide. "She's just in a mood."

I drag the garbage bag across the threshold, still balancing Tara on my hip. I close the door behind me and stand in the foyer with my dad. Neither one of us knows what to do next.

"Honey, where should Debbie, where would you like…" he calls out. We hold our breath, waiting for an answer from the kitchen.

"The spare room," Mom says, sounding defeated. "Put your things in the spare room and get some sleep. We'll talk about this later."

Tara and I climb the stairs to the spare room, the same spare room that provided sanctuary when I fled from Mac's rage nearly one year ago. I open the door, and cold air wafts across my bruised face.

There is no insulation or drywall in the large room, so it is much cooler than the rest of the house. One half is occupied by Christmas decorations, seasonal clothing, and boxes marked *Goodwill*. The other half contains an antique queen bed, two nightstands, and a dresser. It's like a quaint bed and breakfast inside a storage unit.

The bed is warm and inviting, and Tara and I fall into an exhausted sleep. A room at the Four Seasons hotel could not feel better than the spare room does right now.

Mac snuggling with Tara

Debbie, Melody, and Cheryl going to a school dance

Debbie, Mark, and Steve with Santa

Debbie at age seventeen with Tyan and Ian

GALLERY

Tyan and Ian with mom's Easter gifts

Ian teaching Tara how to ride his bike

Steve with Tara on his Tueday visit

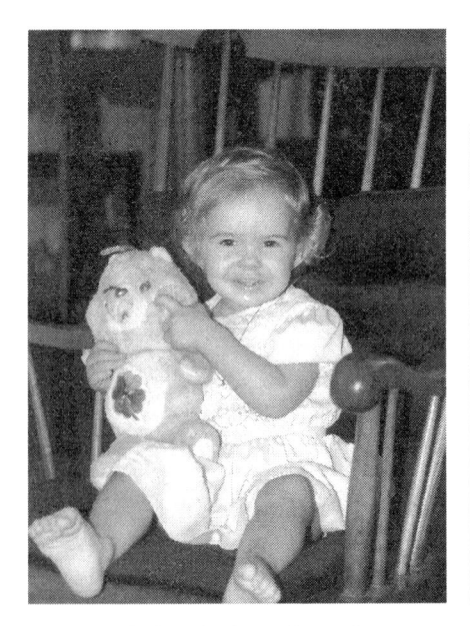

Tara with her beloved Lucky Bear

Tara in her navy dress just before I take her to the police station

GALLERY

Jan and James with Tara

Young Hugh receiving his
first place wrestling trophy

Mac and Tara

Bridget with her brother
Alex just before his death

167

CHAPTER 26

A Leopard's Spots

Mac waits two days before calling. This time when Mom hands me the phone, I take the receiver and hang it back on the cradle. She almost looks impressed but then shrugs and says, "You'll have to talk to him eventually. He's the father of your child."

The following morning, Tara and I are seated at the kitchen table with my parents when the doorbell rings. Dad leans back in his chair for a clear view of the front door at the end of the hallway. "It's Mac," he says.

We spring into action. Dad moves toward the front door, waiting to answer while I hurry Tara into the living room and tell her not to come out. Mom runs to grab a 12-gauge shotgun from their bedroom upstairs. It is almost as tall as she is, and she trips over the barrel coming back down as it scrapes the carpeting on the steps. I return to the kitchen and grab the phone from the wall, stretching the cord across the dinette table into the hallway, ready to call the police.

Dad steps out onto the stoop and closes the door behind him. Through the narrow glass panels on the door I see him, hands on hips, staring up at Mac, who is a good foot taller than he is.

I can't hear what is being said, but I know Mac is not getting past Dad, and if he somehow does, there is a loaded shotgun to contend with. After a short exchange, Dad reaches behind him and opens the door about two inches without turning his back to Mac.

"Bridie, bring the keys for the Cutlass."

Mac just wants his car back! I scramble for my purse and pull out the keys, more than happy to let him drive away in it. I toss them to Mom who hands them to Dad through the crack in the door. Mac disappears from the stoop, boots clacking down the driveway, and the Cutlass roars to life. Dad stands guard at the front door until Mac turns out of the subdivision.

I exhale a huge sigh of relief that I didn't know I'd been holding. Dad enters the house and nearly collides with Mom, still clinging to the shotgun.

"Bloody hell, Bridie! Do you even know how to use that?"

"I'll bloody well figure it out if I need to!"

"This is for you," Dad says, handing me an envelope. My name is written across it in Mac's handwriting.

"Deborah, before you read that, you need to think about something," Mom says, looking sideways at Dad, then directly at me. "This is the last time we open our door to you. If you go back, we'll nae take you in again."

"Bridie, do'nae start —" Dad begins, but Mom's hand goes up to silence him.

"Weesht, Hughie! I'm serious, Deborah. We'll have nae more, understand?"

I nod my head before slipping into the living room with the envelope. Tara sits on the couch with a cup of dry Cheerios between her legs. Her left arm is wrapped around the neck of Lucky Bear, and she inspects each Cheerio with her free hand before eating it. Every third or fourth Cheerio is offered to Lucky Bear, who only stares ahead and grins.

I open the envelope and begin to read, expecting the usual pleas for mercy and the empty promises to stop drinking. Instead, resignation is all over the paper. There are new phrases like *I know it is too late for me to change* and *I don't expect you to come back. I only hope that you will allow me to see my daughter again.* Mac closes with a request to sit down next Saturday at noon to talk about Tara's future without him.

My parents do not bother trying to engage with social services again once they hear this latest appeal. This time, they tell me I have two weeks to find a full-time job. Steve says there is a *Help Wanted* sign in the window of Hardees, right across the street from the Burger King he worked at last year. He drives me there and waits in the parking lot while I fill out an application.

I hand the completed application back to the day shift manager and turn to leave, but she asks me to have a seat in the nearest booth.

I am hired halfway through the interview and walk out beaming with pride, unaware that fast food jobs are generally given to anybody who asks for one.

Cash register training begins the next day, and it feels so good to work, even in an orange plaid polyester uniform and a visor.

• • •

I have three full days of employment under my belt when Saturday arrives. It gives me just enough confidence to keep my stomach out of my throat when Steve drives us to the rental home in New Haven. Ian runs to the passenger side window where Tara is waving nonstop.

"I'll be back in one hour," Steve says.

"Thanks for doing this."

"Whatever, Deb. If you're not here when I come back in one hour, I go to the police."

"Whatever, Steve," I mimic back.

"I'm serious! I'd go in there, but then I'd have to beat his sorry ass."

This makes me laugh because Steve is half the size of Mac and is so soft-spoken and calm now that violence seems foreign to who he is. As he reverses out of the driveway, he raises his index finger and mouths "one hour."

I enter through the back door with Tara on my hip. Ian has tethered himself to her, gripping her hand in his. When I set her down in the kitchen, he lifts her in a bear hug and swings her around. Mac strides into the kitchen and my chest tightens.

His hair is loose, the long waves cascading over his shoulders and down his back. He crouches down and opens his arms wide.

"I thought I heard my little Tara Belle in here."

Tara hesitates, burying her face in Ian's belly.

"Daddy's got a surprise."

Tara slides over to him a few inches at a time, and he scoops her up. I follow them into the dining room, marveling at how clean and tidy the house is. A teapot with an English garden scene and two matching cups sits on the dining table, surrounded by assorted cookies.

Mac is handing Tara a bag of peanut M&Ms and a bottle of cream soda when a woman I hadn't noticed rises from the couch in the adjoining living room. She gathers up her sweatshirt and purse, then stands there, waiting. Her bottled black hair is teased into a thorny crown. She is likely no more than thirty years old, but her heavy black eyeliner makes her look harsh and much older. I imagine her keeping pet rats or snakes which she names Hansel and Gretel.

Mac goes into the living room, and they mumble a few words to each other. She stares over his shoulder at me before turning and walking out the front door.

"Who was that?" I ask.

"Oh that's Gina, a guard at the foundry. She's been babysitting for me."

"She didn't look too happy."

"Oh, she always looks that way," Mac says, trying to laugh. "Ian, take your sisters and go out back to play. We need to talk about grown-up things in here."

The screen door slams shut as the kids head into the backyard. I sit across from Mac at the large oak dining table while he makes a big production of pouring tea into the cup in front of him.

"I didn't know this stuff was so good," he says, motioning for me to hand my cup over. "The key is you can't steep the bag too long."

"No thanks. My parents have been drinking tea for decades and it never caught on for me."

"It's all I drink now."

I say nothing, waiting.

"I know you don't believe me, and I don't blame you," he says, "but it doesn't matter anymore."

I remain quiet, unwilling to engage in a story I've heard far too many times. Mac hesitates, then leans toward me and lifts his long hair up, away from his right ear. There is a precise, three-inch square of bare skin behind his ear, and in the center of the shaved area is a small, distinct red hole.

"What's that?" I ask, frowning.

"I had a procedure done a few weeks ago. The results weren't good, and that's why I went out drinking that night. That's why I was so… Well, never mind, it doesn't matter now."

I bite the hook. "What were the results?"

"I have brain cancer. They tell me I have four to six months to live."

I don't know what to say. Part of me thinks I should say something consoling, but I'm not convinced that his story is true, so I just nod my head to let him know I heard. Mac kneels at my feet and puts his head on my knees.

"I can't face God without your forgiveness, Debbie."

"I can forgive you, Mac, but I'm not coming back."

"I don't expect you to. I just want to make sure Tara is taken care of when I'm gone. I want her to get my Social Security benefits. That will help you out, too."

Mac goes on to explain that I need to fill out an affidavit of parentage since he never signed Tara's birth certificate. It will be the legal proof needed to claim his Social Security benefits. At that moment, we hear Steve's Delta 88 pull into the gravel drive.

"I'll think about it," I say, gathering up my purse and heading to the back yard to extract Tara from her siblings.

In the backseat, Tara rolls one of Ian's beloved Hot Wheels along her thighs while telling Steve and me about all the fun things she did. She asks if she can see her Ian tomorrow, but I barely register any of it. My head is still sorting out how much I should believe of Mac's story, and my body is heavy from the weight of what just happened. I don't feel much in my heart except numbness.

I find Mom in her usual spot at the kitchen table, working on a crossword. I relay everything that Mac said and describe the shaved hair and red hole behind his ear.

"I don't know," she says. "The man is no stranger to lies. I'm going to call Judy."

Judy is a friend who also happens to be a nurse. She confirms that a hole behind the ear can be indicative of a brain biopsy procedure.

Mom remains suspicious. However, it isn't long before I start to beat myself up for my lack of empathy. Mac wants to take care of Tara, and me too, after he's gone.

It is the least he can do.

• • •

Two weeks later, my parents and I meet Mac and his lawyer at the Macomb County Courthouse to sign an affidavit of parentage, legally naming Mac as Tara's father. The following week I am putting cheeseburgers and shakes on a tray at Hardees when a heavyset woman clutching a large yellow envelope steps up to the counter.

"Are you Deborah Brannigan?" she asks.

"Yes. Who are you?"

"You've been served." She thrusts the envelope into my chest and hesitates for a moment, looking into my confused eyes. "Sorry."

I tear open the envelope and find a petition and summons to appear in court. Mac is suing me for full custody of Tara.

CHAPTER 27

The Gloves Come Off

I clutch the summons to my abdomen, legs trembling the entire three-mile walk home from work. I do a decent job of keeping my composure, but the minute I see my parents after opening the front door, I fall to pieces.

"What is it? What's wrong?" Mom asks.

I hand her the crumpled papers and wait, trying not to cry, while she flips through the pages. Dad looks over her shoulder, his face darkening with growing anger.

"That son of a bitch!" he shouts, swinging a fist at an imaginary Mac.

"Is it bad, Mom? Can he take Tara?"

"Over my dead body," she says, locking eyes with Dad.

"What do I do? It says I have to go to the courthouse!"

"I don'nae know, but we'll find out."

Mom says she will make a few calls and talk to some people, and Dad reassures me with a big hug. I feel better right away, thinking there's no way Mac will be able to get full custody.

Still, that night when Tara and I climb into bed together, I hold her a bit tighter.

• • •

The phone begins ringing the next morning before anybody is out of their pajamas. I am brushing my teeth when Mom yells up the stairwell for me to pick up the phone. I go to the unfinished room and lift the receiver beside the bed. She is still on the other line in the kitchen.

"Be careful, Deborah," she says. "He's a snake, so he is."

"It's not like that…" Mac begins, but Mom has hung up.

"Mac? What is this court thing about?"

"That's why I'm calling, Debbie. I got a copy of the summons yesterday, and it's not what I wanted at all."

"Why does it say you want full custody? Are you trying to take Tara from me?"

"No! You know I would never do that! My lawyer wrote all that up. These lawyers always ask for everything and hope for something a little less because they're not used to having clients that get along and work things out together."

"Why did you get your lawyer involved anyway? We already agreed to every other weekend."

"I wanted to have it legally recorded to build Tara's case for my Social Security benefits. I don't know why my lawyer asked for full custody because I don't even think I'll be able to see Tara every other weekend with my cancer treatments."

Mac promises we will straighten everything out next month and then goes on to explain that we aren't appearing before a judge. We are going to "Friend of the Court," a mediation process where disputes are — hopefully — worked out amicably without the need for a judge. This alleviates my fear of standing before a black-robed judge in a courtroom full of people, and I relax a bit.

Mom's lips form a straight line as I explain all this to her. She's not buying any of it.

"I would'nae trust the man, Deborah. Something's not right, you mark my words."

Over the following weeks, Mac calls regularly to talk to Tara and me. He tells me that he is no longer able to drive because the brain cancer deteriorates his vision and balance. Steve agrees to drive me over to the house once more but insists on waiting in the yard.

I find Mac in the living room, languishing on the couch. He claims the loss of balance forces him to spend several days and nights in the same spot. He also says he has trouble walking to the gas station for our calls and asks that I send a few letters by mail instead to liven his spirits and the kids', too.

I write letters in a booth at Hardee's during my break. One for Mac, encouraging him to stay strong and telling him that he is not alone. I also send short notes to Ian and Tyan, explaining that I still love them and will do my best to see them when I can, but my heart knows our paths are diverging.

Last week DeeDee called me at Hardees, begging me to *do something about those children*. Ian was seen riding his bike at two in the morning on a school night, and her concern was compelling. I sighed into the phone and told her there was simply nothing more I could do. Part of me had known that all structure and support for them would crumble when I left, but I have no legal right to Ian and Tyan, and my love for Tara and need to protect her is stronger than everything else.

• • •

Our appointed day with Friend of the Court finally arrives. I exit the elevator on the second floor of the Macomb County Building and scan the room full of people in folding chairs, all waiting for their names to be called.

I see Mac on the far side of the room, sitting with his lawyer. He glances over and I wave, but he turns away. Maybe he didn't see me? I take a seat close to the hallway entrance and wait, like everyone else.

"Charles McCall and Deborah Brannigan" calls out a man in a sport coat and tie, reading our names from a clipboard. Mac and his lawyer reach him first and are directed to a room in the hallway right behind him. They are already closing the door when I approach.

"Miss Brannigan?" the man asks.

"Yes, sir."

"Right this way, please."

I follow him a few steps down the hallway, and he swings open the door to a room next to the one Mac and his lawyer disappeared into.

"Why are we in separate rooms?"

"It's not uncommon in these types of cases," he says. "Please, have a seat."

I take one of four seats at a round table, and he takes the one directly opposite me.

"Would you like something to drink?"

My mouth is suddenly dry, and I gladly accept a paper cup of water from the cooler in the corner. He pours himself a cup of coffee before resuming his station across the table.

"Miss Brannigan, my name is Alex, and I'm here to help you and Mr. McCall come to a custody agreement. You have the right to legal counsel at any time throughout this process. It is my hope that we can create an arrangement that works for both parties. Do you understand?"

"Yes. We have already talked about this and have an agreement."

"Well, that will make my job much easier today." He opens a binder and clicks his pen, ready to start writing. "Alright then, please tell me what terms you are willing to agree to."

"We already decided on visitation every other weekend."

"Visitation for you?" he asks, beginning to write.

"No, for Mac. I mean, Mr. McCall."

"I see, and what about holidays?"

I tell him we had not talked about those details, so I'm not sure what he should write down. He offers suggestions about rotating holidays, Father's Day, and birthdays. I tell him that all seems reasonable to me. He writes in his ledger, making bullet points for each holiday, then closes it and stands up.

"Alright, I'm going to step next door and present this to Mr. McCall. Please stay here until I return."

I fidget for a minute or two, then decide to get another cup of water from the cooler. Alex opens the door as water plunges into my cup. I am surprised by how quickly he has returned. Through the open door behind him, I see Mac and his lawyer on their way out. Mac is looking at me with a sinister grin, his middle finger raised.

"What's going on?"

Alex asks me to sit down, but alarm bells are going off in my head.

"I don't want to sit down, just tell me what's going on!"

"Mr. McCall's demands are for full custody of your daughter with no visitation rights for you."

I am dumbfounded, unable to find any words to respond to what Alex just said. He asks me again to please sit down so he can explain what happens next, and I collapse into the closest chair.

"Mr. McCall is refusing mediation, Miss Brannigan, which means you will need to appear before a judge. You will be receiving an order to appear in court. You have the right to obtain legal counsel, and I would encourage you to do so prior to your court appearance."

Numb, I head home to explain the turn of events to my parents. Their response is to curse and bang their fists on the table. They start running through a list of friends and neighbors that may know a good attorney.

I say nothing. It seems like I'm not in my own body, just hovering above it as an observer. I know my parents are right, that we need to get an attorney and fight back. Yet part of me still wants to believe that Mac will call tomorrow and explain away this silly miscommunication.

The next day comes and goes with no phone call. Then three more days with no phone call. On day five I find myself waiting in the law offices of John D. Burtch, wondering how I could have been such a damn fool.

CHAPTER 28

Will Work for Money

I have never met a lawyer before, and I imagine an arrogant man in a pin-striped suit who intentionally uses words outside of my vocabulary. John Burtch, however, is nothing like I imagined. His smile is warm, and he welcomes my parents and me into his office like he has all the time in the world just for us.

My parents explain the predicament, becoming angrier the longer they speak. Mr. Burtch turns to me several times to interpret their words because the angrier they are, the more pronounced their Scottish accents. Mostly, I just wait. He listens quietly, writing notes on a legal pad atop his large desk. When they finish, Mr. Burtch leans back in his chair, bringing the fingertips of both hands together at his chest.

"Well, I can definitely help you with this situation."

My parents and I release a collective sigh of relief.

"There is a $300 retainer fee to get started, and my bill rate is $75 per hour, which will be invoiced monthly."

Our relief is hijacked by awkward discomfort. We shift in our seats, uneasy about the amount of money this could cost.

"Don't worry," Mr. Burtch says. "I've successfully navigated many of these custody cases, and I'm confident we will have a very good outcome in a short amount of time."

Dad pulls a checkbook from his coat pocket, and my face starts to burn from the guilt of him paying the retainer and the shame of my being somehow unable to get my life together. This is a lot of money for my parents.

"Debbie, from this day forward you do not speak to Mr. McCall," Mr. Burtch says, turning to look at me. "Not on the phone, not in person, not at all. All communication will be between his lawyer and me. Do you understand?"

I nod my agreement.

"My first order of business will be to file a motion to delay the court appearance. I need some time to research Mr. McCall's background. You'll be hearing from me soon."

We all stand and shake hands with Mr. Burtch as we leave the office, feeling better than we did when we arrived. Back in the station wagon, we process the meeting.

"That went well," Mom says.

"Yes, it did," Dad replies. "Burtch seems like a right nice chap."

"For that kind of money, he'd better be more than nice."

I squirm in the backseat at my mom's comment, consumed again by guilt and shame.

"Thank you for the retainer," I say. "I'm going to pay you back."

"Too right you are, and those monthly invoices are all on you," Mom replies. "Looks like a second job is in order."

She's right. I work full-time at Hardees, but my $130 paycheck doesn't go very far. After paying sixty dollars in room and board fees to my parents every week, I am left with seventy dollars. This will not be enough to pay for even one hour of my legal fees.

• • •

My cousin Erica sits blowing smoke out of the corner of her mouth at our kitchen table a few days later. She is Mom's favorite niece and little more than a decade younger, so they behave more like siblings. I am barely through the front door, still in my Hardee's uniform, when they call me into the kitchen.

"I hear you're looking for a job," Erica says. "You should apply where I work."

"Are they hiring?"

"They're always hiring."

"I don't have any experience. What kind of job could I get?"

"You could start as an illustrator, something entry level."

I have no idea what my cousin Erica does for work, only that she works in a design shop. Visions of colored markers, watercolors, and sketch pads fill my head. I imagine an entire room full of artists designing posters, logos, or magazine ads.

"Do you really think I could get hired?"

"Sure. My boss likes to hire women. He says they work twice as hard for half the pay," Erica laugh-coughs out lumps of smoke. "I'll tell him about you."

Two weeks later I pull open the lobby doors of EWS & Co., lugging my high school art portfolio behind me. The receptionist ushers me through an office door, and I take a seat in front of the hiring manager, Tom Cooke, at his desk. I try to balance my portfolio on the floor between my knees.

Tom is in his early forties, with eyes like melting chocolate and a bushy black moustache that has overtaken his upper lip. He clasps his hands in front of him and waits for me to settle in before speaking.

"So, you're Erica's cousin. She's told me a bit about you, says you're a real hard worker."

"Yes sir, I am."

"I see you've brought a few things to show me," he says, motioning toward the portfolio.

"Yes, yes, I have!"

I unzip my portfolio and pull out my best work: an ink illustration of a koala bear, another of a goldfish in a champagne glass, and a penciled rendering of an old Victorian house. Tom looks them over with a puzzled expression.

"We don't really do drawings like this here. This is an automotive design shop. We do technical drawings and engineering layouts."

"Oh, okay." I begin sweeping the drawings haphazardly back into the portfolio. "Thank you for your time." My cheeks are red-hot, and my lower lip begins to quiver. I knew this opportunity was too good to be true.

"Now, now, wait a minute."

I sit still at the edge of my seat. Tom seems to be having an internal debate with himself, looking up to the ceiling then down into his interlaced fingers. He lets out a heavy sigh and runs both hands through his thick Ricky Ricardo hair.

"I suppose we could use another technical illustrator."

"Really?"

I know in my heart that he does not *need* another illustrator, that he simply feels sorry for me. Oddly, I am okay with pity if it gets me a job that doesn't require a polyester uniform and a visor.

"Yes, but I can only pay you five dollars an hour."

My heart skips a beat. *Five dollars an hour?* I can't believe what I'm hearing. That's almost two dollars an hour more than Hardees, and I get to draw all day? I accept the job on the spot, my heart filled with joy and gratitude, and leave with a start date in two weeks.

I break the news to Val, my Hardees manager, that I landed a job as a technical illustrator and can no longer work full-time for her. She is happy for my good fortune and even happier to learn that I wish to stay on the schedule part-time for the dinner shift.

Erica connects me with one of my soon-to-be coworkers, Lori, who drives in from Algonac and passes right through New Baltimore. She agrees to pick me up each morning, and I agree to pay her $20 every Friday for gas.

Sleep is impossible the night before my first day on the job. I am terrified of missing the alarm and being fired before I even start and am dressed and watching through the window of the front door an hour early. My heart pounds when Lori pulls into the driveway, right on time at 5:15.

I climb into her small coupe, and she welcomes me with a cheery "Good morning" and a cup of black coffee from the gas station. Lori has a helmet of untamed dark curls, with metal barrettes at each temple creating beaver dam pileups of hair on her head. The wire rims of her eyeglass frames seem too thin to hold her thick lenses in place.

During our thirty-minute drive, Lori gives me the rundown on everybody at the office—what their quirks are and who can help with what.

"Glen will be training you," she says. "He's our main illustrator, but he also owns a body building gym. A big 'ol teddy bear, he is."

By the time we pull into the dark parking lot of EWS & Co., any anxiety I may have had has turned into enthusiasm.

Lori leads me into the building through a back door. The room is enormous and wide open, with bare steel rafters thirty feet above. There are no windows or walls of any kind, just rows and rows of ten-foot-long drafting tables covered with sheets of seafoam green protective paper. Three-legged metal stools sit in pairs at each table.

A few tables have duct tape boundaries at the center. Most of them resemble a flea market booth littered with triangles, slide rules, tracing paper, ash trays, and coffee mugs. Two filing cabinets sit near the center of the room with Playboy centerfolds taped on every side.

We are the first employees to arrive. Lori scans the metal rack of timecards and plucks one out. "This is yours," she says, and I clock in for my first day as an illustrator.

Lori walks me to the last row of drafting boards and pulls out one of the three-legged stools. "Here's your seat. You and Erica will share this board," she says, then continues to the back wall where a coffee pot sits on a folding table. While she scoops coffee into the filter, I settle in at "my" drafting table, awestruck.

"Here are some supplies to get you started." Lori puts a paper cup of hot coffee in front of me, along with a fistful of pencils and pens and sheets of graph paper. She tells me to go ahead and draw my name on the green paper because it's my workstation now.

My workstation.

For the next hour I practice my name in several artistic renditions on graph paper before committing anything to my drafting table. The time clock *ka-chunks* more often as people trickle in. I glance up each time, looking for Glen. Lori says I will know him when I see him.

Sometime after eight o'clock, I begin inking "Debbie" at the corner of my drafting table, with an old English "D" and big plans for a whimsical daisy to dot the "i." Halfway through the second "b," my desk is eclipsed by a massive shadow. I look up to find a man who can only be Glen smiling down at me.

"You must be Debbie," he says, leaning down to examine my handiwork.

"Not bad. Of course, this means you have to stick around, or we have to find another Debbie to sit here."

Glen's smile paralyzes me. He is a tower of lean muscle, well over six and a half feet tall, with shoulders and biceps that look like cannon balls stuffed under his shirt. His olive skin, hazel eyes, and thick black hair give the impression of a Roman gladiator. He is so gorgeous, I cannot speak.

"I'm going to tidy up a few things before we get started," he says. "It'll give you some time to finish your masterpiece. Unless you're done?" He nods at my hand, pen still posed upright at the letter "b."

I shake my head and manage a weak smile. Glen seems amused by my awkward muteness but somehow not surprised. He must get this reaction all the time. I watch him walk down the aisle toward his drafting table near the front of the room, his buttocks a pair of coconuts in jeans.

Shifting on my stool, I wipe my sweaty palms along the thighs of my jeans. Once my hand is steady again, I ink in the remaining letters on my table.

Forget the daisy! I draw a four-leaf clover above the "i" instead because I must be the luckiest person alive.

CHAPTER 29

A Leg to Stand On

I spend three full weeks just printing the alphabet in block letters and sketching small parts on onion skin paper before Glen shows me how to draw on plastic mylar sheets, using expensive Rapidograph ink pens.

I'm intimidated because there is no room for error with the sheets. I start a line but stop halfway. Glen pulls my hand upward, off the sheet, before the ink can pool.

"Linework must be done in one smooth motion, Debbie. Here, let me show you."

Glen stands behind me, his body pressed against my back. He cups my hand in his and guides it effortlessly across the mylar, creating a pristine, perfect black arch. Several heartbeats pound in my ears while he remains pressed against me. I hold my breath, wanting him to stay there.

Before he moves away, his thumb sweeps along my wrist. My stomach summersaults at the simple touch, and I begin to sweat.

"Go ahead and practice on scraps of mylar for the rest of the day," Glen says, coughing a bit. There is a dark pool of sweat at his collar, and as he walks back to his desk, he holds a manila folder in front of his groin.

• • •

The following morning, Glen shows me how to use a tiny fiberglass brush to erase small imperfections of ink. My first attempt with the brush burns a hole right through the mylar.

"Here, let me show you," he says, cupping my hand in his. Only this time he smiles and winks, letting me know the pretense of work is purely for those around us.

"Can I take you out one night this week?"

"I work at Hardees every night this week."

"That's okay. I put in a few hours at the gym every night. Do you get a dinner break?"

"Yes, at eight o'clock."

"Would you mind if I come visit you on break tonight?"

"If you don't mind sitting with me in my orange plaid uniform."

"I think you look sexy in that uniform."

I blush, forgetting that everybody here has seen me in that awful outfit. I change clothes in the bathroom at the end of each day, and Lori drops me off in the Hardees parking lot on her way home to Algonac. I walk the last three miles home in the dark at the end of each shift.

Glen strides into Hardees that night at eight o'clock sharp. Every head turns at the sight of this hulking man clutching a fistful of dainty wildflowers.

My coworkers are a mix of envious and incredulous, asking if he plays professional football or has an available brother. Even Val loses her no-nonsense, managerial persona and becomes flustered when I introduce her. When she takes his order, she drops the tray, spills his drink, and flutters her hands in all directions.

Glen becomes a regular at Hardee's, arriving for my dinner break nearly every night. He is nicknamed "Hugo" by my coworkers for his huge size, and they chant "Hu-go! Hu-go!" whenever he steps into the restaurant. They pile free cookies onto his tray, and it is clear from the grin on his face that he loves the attention.

My work weeks are long, usually fifty-five hours or more between my two jobs. I don't mind it because I really like both jobs. I am learning so much about drafting and illustration, and my "regulars" at Hardees call me by name and share their family photos.

After six years of isolation and dependency, I feel more than happy now. I feel empowered.

• • •

The legal drama with Mac went quiet once we left John Burtch's law office. As promised, Mr. Burtch was able to delay the court appearance. I was just beginning to relax and think it might all fade away when he calls with an update.

"We've definitely got his attention," Burtch says. "I don't think he expected you to hire a lawyer."

"Is he willing to talk about visitation?"

"No, he seems to think he can win full custody because he was granted custody of the other two children."

"Can he do that? I mean, if he did it before, maybe…." My voice starts to break as panic swirls in my chest at the thought of losing Tara.

"It's not likely. The court almost never removes a minor child from its current environment. Mr. McCall was granted custody of Ian and Tyan because his wife left them when she fled."

"So, we still have to go to court?"

"I'm afraid so. He's going to do his best to portray you as an unfit parent."

"I'm a high school dropout working two jobs and living with my parents! Won't the judge think I'm unfit?"

To my surprise, Mr. Burtch laughs heartily.

"No, none of that is relevant. Mr. McCall, however, has had so many DUIs that his license is now suspended. He's also got a police record and a job that pays about as much as your fast-food job does."

"What do you think he's up to?"

"The only way he could win custody is to prove that Tara is in danger with you, which is exactly the strategy they're taking."

"Danger? What kind of danger?"

"He is requesting the court to order a psychological evaluation of you."

"What? A psychological evaluation? Can he do that?"

"We could fight it, but I actually think it's a great idea."

"Why?"

"Because he will be subjected to the same evaluation, and I'd bet money it won't go well for him."

I take Mr. Burtch's advice and arrive at the court-appointed psychologist's office for my evaluation, which involves an hour-long friendly chat and a two-page questionnaire. Two weeks later, we receive the psychological analysis. It states that I am naïve and immature but intelligent. The final opinion is that I am a caring and competent mother.

The assessment of Mac is also succinct and to the point: "Mr. McCall has sociopathic tendencies." The recommendation is that he have only restricted or supervised visitation with Tara.

• • •

Mr. Burtch and I have barely finished our legal slam dunk victory dance when a letter arrives in the mail the next day from the district attorney's office. I have an appointment to talk about allegations of welfare fraud.

"This is Mr. McCall's handiwork, I guarantee it," Mr. Burtch says when I tell him. "He's pulling out all the stops now."

I decline to have him accompany me to the DA's office. I want to prove that I can accept responsibility and get this blemish cleared from my conscience.

I tell the DA that I applied for benefits out of fear but knew it was wrong. I also tell her that Mac refused to sign the birth certificate at the hospital before we took Tara home. This surprises her.

"Are you telling me that Charles McCall lived with you while claiming benefits?"

"Yes ma'am."

"That sounds like a clear case of fraud to me."

"Yes ma'am."

I sign papers, admitting to my guilt. I apologize, explaining to the DA that I am working two jobs now, trying to change my life. Her face remains rigid and business-like, but her voice softens when she walks me to the door.

"You'll get a judgment in the mail with repayment instructions, Miss Brannigan. I truly hope it all works out for you."

Later that same week, there is a legal envelope from the DA's office propped up on the dinette table when I arrive home from Hardee's at 11:00 p.m., soaked to the skin through my polyester uniform because it rained the entire three-mile walk home.

I debate opening the envelope for a minute because I'm just so tired and don't want to think about how I'm going to pay all that money back. Then, like a Band Aid, I rip it open in one swift tear.

I am puzzled by the repayment amount. It is a lot of money, but far less than I expected. On the second page, I see why the amount is reduced — I am ordered to pay back half, while Mac has to pay back the other half!

Mr. Burtch is thoroughly entertained when I share the news with him.

"That's twice his plans have backfired on him, Debbie! Mr. McCall sure likes to shoot at his own feet. At this rate, he won't have a leg to stand on in court next week."

• • •

My day in court arrives all too soon. I borrow a floral dress from Mom's closet. As I hoped, it looks matronly, even on my twenty-two-year-old body. Mr. Burtch is waiting for me outside the courtroom and sees the fear in my eyes as I approach.

"Relax. I'll do all the talking," he says, patting my shoulder.

The stakes are high. Today the judge determines who will have temporary custody of Tara throughout the months of legal battle ahead. According to Mr. Burtch, whomever the judge assigns custody to today is almost certain to win permanent custody in the end.

Mac and his lawyer are already in the courtroom. It is the first time I've seen him in nearly three months. He sneers at us as we take our seats, as if we don't stand a chance.

Mac's lawyer speaks first. As expected, he tells the judge that I dropped out of high school at sixteen, I was a teen runaway, and my fast-food job will never be enough to support Tara.

Mr. Burtch stands and clarifies that I dropped out of school to run away with Mr. McCall, which was statutory rape at the time. He also explains that I completed night school with above average grades and recently gained employment at an engineering firm. Mac's head swivels to look at me at this news. It's obvious he did not know about my new job.

In the end, it is the psychological evaluation that carries the most weight. The judge grants temporary custody of Tara to me and weekly visitation to Mac. He is allotted three hours a week with her and not a minute more.

CHAPTER 30

Deja Voodoo

The court grants me thirty days to comply with the visitation order. Mr. Burtch says he will negotiate a day and time through Mac's lawyer.

"Go home and celebrate," he says. "You'll hear from me soon."

Several days of blissful quiet go by. I sit at the kitchen table with Mom, enjoying warm afternoon sun that floods through the sliding glass doors that look out to the backyard. Tara sits in my lap eating Cheez Whiz on toast, her new favorite, and Mom sips tea and nibbles at digestive biscuits while pondering the clues to a new crossword puzzle.

"Do you hear that?" she asks, halting the teacup halfway to her mouth.

"Hear what?"

A split second later, I hear it: police sirens. Through the sliding glass doors, we see a plume of kicked up gravel and dust growing larger and closer. Amid the grey dust cloud are red and blue flashing lights. Three police cars are barreling at high speed down Callens Road behind our house.

We open the doors and lean out for a better view. This is not something you'd expect to see near our tucked away subdivision. We assume the cars will continue beyond our neighborhood toward the more populated areas along 23-Mile Road.

Instead, tires squeal as the police wheel into our subdivision. We run to the front door and out onto the porch, just in time to see a shaggy-haired teenager backing out of the driveway across the street. He continues to reverse into our driveway, clearing the street for the police as they come down our road.

All three police cars come to a screeching halt in front of our house, one blocking the driveway. Officers surround the teen's car, guns drawn.

193

They order him out of the car and face down on our front lawn. Mom takes two steps toward the chaos when a police officer in full tactical gear yells at her to get inside the house immediately.

For once, she doesn't even think about arguing. We continue to watch the action through the living room window. Our neighbors peer out behind their curtains and blinds as well. We all suspected that young Paul across the street was selling small amounts of marijuana, but this situation seems more like a major drug cartel bust.

The shaggy-haired teen is handcuffed and lifted onto his feet. He sobs uncontrollably, the snot running down his chin. Two officers begin to search his vehicle while two others approach our front door. Mom opens the door before they reach it.

"What's going on here?"

"Ma'am, I need all of you to step out onto the porch," the older officer says. "And keep your hands where I can see them."

"Don't you tell me what to do in my own house!"

"Ma'am, I won't ask you again."

Mom grunts her displeasure but does as they ask, moving onto the porch. I follow on her heels, Tara on my hip.

"Is anyone else in the house?" the older officer asks.

"No, just us," Mom replies.

"You're sure there's nobody upstairs in the bedroom?"

"Are ye daft, man? I just told you —"

"Ma'am, please stand aside. We need to sweep the house."

Both officers draw their guns and begin to search our house. Several minutes later, they return to us on the front porch and yell out "All clear!" to their fellow officers in the driveway. Then they turn their attention to us.

"We had an anonymous call reporting a murder here," the older officer says.

"A murder?" Mom and I say at the same time.

"Yes, the caller stated that a woman by the name of Debbie Brannigan was shot in the head in the upstairs bedroom."

"That's me." I squeak the acknowledgement out as my stomach starts to knot into a ball.

"You're Debbie Brannigan?"

"It's that good for nothing McCall, so it is!" Mom shouts, shaking her finger in the air.

I take Tara into the house and turn on the TV for her, then retrieve my driver's license to prove my identity to the police. While I'm gone, Mom explains the custody battle and her suspicions that it is Mac who called in the false report. I know in my gut that she is right.

"Somebody could have been seriously hurt," the older officer says, with an edge to his voice that makes it sound like we called in the false report.

"Too right, but it's nae us that ye should be lecturing now, is it?" Mom replies. "'Tis that bloody snake ye should be after."

The traumatized teen is uncuffed in the front yard with muffled apologies from the officers. He climbs into his car and drives away, and I think that poor kid will never buy a ten-dollar bag of weed from Paul or anyone else again.

The police cars begin to leave one by one. The faces of neighbors quickly disappear from the windows, embarrassed to be caught snooping. Before they leave, the tall officer tells us they will write up their findings and note our suspicions about Mac, but they can't act on suspicion, so nothing will happen to him.

The remainder of the day is spent explaining the events to concerned neighbors who call or stop by. When Dad gets home from work that night, we relay the drama once more for him. His face turns bright red, and he releases a string of Scottish curses I've never heard before.

We all go to bed, weary and angry and more than a little frightened by the day's events. Our sleep is obliterated by the sound of fists pounding on the front door. It's 2:00 a.m., and I meet my parents in the hallway outside our bedrooms, all of us groggy and confused. The banging on the door continues, and there are bright red lights thrumming through every window.

Mom and I huddle halfway down the stairs while Dad intercepts Steve, who has come up from the basement to investigate with a baseball bat. Dad opens the front door to find three firefighters on the porch, with more in the firetruck parked on the street, its emergency lights flashing.

"Where's the fire, sir?"

"Fire? There's nae fire here," Dad replies.

"There was an anonymous call saying the upstairs bedroom was on fire."

There is an awkward silence before Dad explains the false police emergency earlier that day and how this is most likely another false alarm called in by the same person.

"This is a volunteer fire department, sir. All these men got out of bed to come here, and you're telling us this is some kind of sick joke?"

"I'm awfully sorry, mate."

The volunteers climb back onto the firetruck, shut off the lights, and drive away. Neighbors also turn off their lights and return to bed. It is almost 3:00 a.m. when our household does the same.

We sleep late that Saturday morning, waking only when the phone begins to ring. The dark hollows beneath Mom's eyes tell me she didn't sleep well. Neighbors start calling, one right after the other, and she spends the next few hours on the phone. She assures each of them that it's just Mac stirring up trouble, and now that he's had his fun, that will be the end of it.

By late afternoon, calm returns to the house and we resume our lives. Mom's pen scratches crossword answers in the paper, MaryAnne plucks away at the piano, Dad naps in front of the TV, and Steve does whatever he does in the basement. Tara and I sit cross-legged in the front room, weaving potholders.

We all jump at the sound of heavy knocking on the front door. I look out the front window and see an ambulance in the street and a police cruiser in the driveway. Mom beats me to the door and swings it open to reveal the two officers from the day before. Both stand erect, their hands resting on their holsters.

"Hello again," the older officer says. "I don't suppose there's been a murder here today?"

"Bloody hell!" Mom curses. "Again?"

The officers nod in unison.

"You might as well come inside," Dad says, joining us at the front door.

We congregate around the kitchen table. Today the officers are more interested in hearing who may be making these false reports. Mom begins her tirade against "that snake" again, but they cut her off.

"We record every incoming call, ma'am. The caller today was different from yesterday."

I tell the police about Mac's history of making false reports with Darlene, explaining that he recruits friends to help him, and they do it from a payphone so it can't be traced. Dad chimes in about the fire department showing up at 2:00 a.m.

The older officer nods his head and says they will contact the fire department for Chesterfield Township. The other officer continues to scribble in his notebook for a few moments, then looks up at his partner. They nod at each other, thank us for the information, and see themselves out.

"They'll nae do a damned thing," Mom says as soon as they're gone.

"Mac knows how to get around the law," I reply. "He won't stop."

"Even he knows better than to call in too many times," Dad says. "He's probably done for now."

We all nod in agreement, but nobody is convinced. Dad pulls on his jacket and calls out to MaryAnne and Tara, asking if they want to go to the hardware store. They're not interested until he promises a stop for ice cream on the way back.

"We'll be back in two ticks," he says, heading out the door holding both of their hands.

An hour later, Dad is installing a dead bolt on the front door. He is not a handyman, and after cursing for a while, he recruits the next-door neighbor to help him. The sun is threatening to disappear by the time they finish.

"There'll be nobody sneaking past this front door," Dad says with pride.

The deadbolt is a small comfort, but one that helps us sleep a little better that night. At least until 2:00 a.m. when the pounding on the front door returns, along with the firefighters on our front porch.

CHAPTER 31

Hope in a HoHo

Each day repeats the previous one, with police at our door in the late afternoon and firefighters in the early morning hours. Dad's belief that Mac will stop calling has yet to prove itself.

By day five, both departments shift to contacting us before sending out their resources. This alleviates the circus at our front door but does nothing to ease the growing anxiety under our roof. Every phone call is a reminder of Mac's relentless fear campaign.

It's no surprise when the same two police officers materialize on the front porch late one afternoon. Dad answers the door, telling them nobody has been murdered today and asking why they didn't call first.

"We're here for another matter, Mr. Brannigan. We need to talk to Debbie."

We congregate in the kitchen, and the officers decline Mom's offer of coffee. The older officer lays a piece of paper on the table and sighs, as if he doesn't want to say what he's about to tell me.

"Mr. McCall filed this police report today, claiming you punctured the tires of his girlfriend's car yesterday."

"What? That is a total lie!"

"He also claims that you have been harassing him, sending letters to him and the children. Are these from you?"

The officer produces the cards and letters I wrote a few months ago when Mac was supposedly dying from brain cancer.

"Yes, sir, but Mac begged me to write them. He said he was dying."

Saying all this out loud makes me realize just how absurd the whole situation sounds and how gullible I have been. Of course Mac has lied to me about his cancer! He's very much alive and knows how to stir up trouble. I shift in my chair while the officer makes a note of this information.

"Can you tell me where you were yesterday at 8:00 a.m.?"

"I worked the breakfast shift at Hardees. You can ask my manager."

"We'll confirm that. Thank you."

The officers tip their hats as they get up to leave but stop at the front door.

"We are obligated to follow through on every complaint," the older officer says, looking at me. "This is nothing, I'm sure."

His unspoken apology lingers as they tip their hats once more and close the door behind them.

Back in the kitchen, Mom has gathered up the letters and cards from the table. Her lips compress into a thin line of anger as she flips through each.

"Is that nae bloody awful?"

She says this to nobody in particular, and yet I think she is referring to me—how stupid and awful I was to send letters in the first place. But before I can say "I'm sorry," she tosses them all into the trash, the whole time muttering how Mac will answer for his cheek one day.

A quick read of the police report confirms my suspicions that Gina is Mac's new live-in girlfriend. This is not a big surprise to me. The supposed eyewitness to the crime, however, does surprise me. It is Larry from the adult foster care home on the same street.

New Haven's Adult Foster Care is on the opposite corner from the rental home. Ian often shoveled sidewalks there during winter months, and one afternoon Larry returned one of Ian's lost mittens. Mac invited him in for a beer, and soon after Larry became a regular visitor.

Larry suffers from advanced Parkinson's disease, rendering him dependent on others for daily care. His face is slanted, and his speech is a torturous string of stutters. It's no stretch to imagine Mac slinging an arm around Larry's shoulders, telling him that if he'll "just do this one thing," they can hang out and be buddies.

Even for Mac, this is a new low.

• • •

Despite the daily chaos, I work both of my jobs without interruption. Time with Tara shrinks to a few hours on weekends, and to better keep my connection to her, I routinely bring home a Big Cookie from Hardees, leaving a scavenger hunt for her to solve in the morning.

One night I arrive home at almost 1:00 a.m., frozen to the bone, only to find the Big Cookie inside my jacket pocket disintegrated into something like wet sawdust. I trudged three miles in sleeting rain with nothing more than a light windbreaker and my uniform. The cookie never stood a chance.

My wet Kmart shoes squish and squeak on the way to the kitchen sink where I turn my jacket pocket inside out, rinsing the sugary crumbs down the drain. A shadow grows on the blinds over the sink, and I turn without thinking, fists out front, ready for battle.

It's Dad.

He wears a plain white T-shirt with plaid pajama bottoms, and his face twitches with stabs of remorse and sadness. I've never seen him cry, but somewhere I know that this is what it would look like just before the tears.

"Dad, you scared me! Are you okay?"

He says nothing, his lower lip beginning to quiver.

"Dad, what's wrong?"

"Look at you, honey! You're soaked to the bleedin' bone, that's what's wrong."

He steps out into the hallway and retrieves a towel from the small powder room. Draping it around my shoulders, he kisses my forehead.

"I'm so sorry, honey."

"Sorry for what, Dad?"

"You should'nae be walking home like this. I've let you down and I'm sorry."

He wraps his arms around me, and it's only then that I realize how hard I'm shivering. The embrace lingers a heartbeat too long, until the unfamiliar intimacy begins to feel uncomfortable.

"Dad, why are you up so late?"

Releasing me from the hug, he steps back and starts to pat the pockets of his pajama bottoms, looking for something he'd forgotten until just now.

"Aye, here it is. This is for you."

He hands me a yellow sticky note with Tara's handwritten message: *It's really neat. It makes heat. So you can eat.* Tara has left me a scavenger hunt tonight.

Dad and I follow the trail of clues from the microwave to the piano to a teapot on the kitchen table. Inside is a pack of Ho Hos that have clearly spent time in a back pocket. The attached note has a pair of puckered lips drawn with *I LOVE YOU MOM* in all caps written above them.

"She's a clever wee thing, isn't she?" Dad says, smiling.

I nod my head and swallow the knot in my throat. This is a three-year-old reaching out to let me know she is paying attention. I forget the soggy shoes, the three-mile walks home in darkness, and the fact that I need to be up in four short hours for my next job. None of it matters compared to this. I just need to keep moving my daughter and me forward.

"I've got to get to bed, Dad. Thanks for waiting up for me."

I head to the staircase, expecting my dad to follow me up to his bedroom. Instead, he turns toward the living room.

"Aren't you going to bed?"

"I recorded the hockey game earlier. I'm just going to finish watching it. You go on off to bed, now."

I glance inside the living room and see the pillow and blanket on the couch. It's no secret Mom has banished him from the bedroom, but I play along to keep his dignity intact.

"Don't stay up too late, Dad."

He will still be on the couch in a few hours when Lori pulls into the driveway to pick me up for work.

CHAPTER 32

Yabba Dabba Doozie

The communal payphone at the back of the drafting room rings non-stop this morning. I sit near the back of the building, so I answer the phone more than most. But not today.

All last week I penciled a perfect rendition of an underbody brace for the Pontiac Fiero. Today will be my first solo attempt at finalizing an illustration in ink.

The plastic mylar sheet is rolled out, blue tape at each corner securing it to my table. I hover my ink pen, about to drop it onto the sheet, when the phone begins to ring again. I begin putting ink to mylar as Victor strides by my desk to answer the phone.

Victor is the backup receptionist when it comes to answering the community pay phone. Most of the incoming calls are about potential gigs for his fledgling band that plays local clubs during the week. It isn't until he raps his knuckles at the end of my board that I am brought out of my head.

"Phone call, Debbie."

I stare at him for a long minute before registering what he says. The payphone has never rung for me before, so I answer it with some trepidation.

"Hello?"

"Hello, honey! It's Papa Bear."

"Dad? Is everything okay?"

"Aye. Nothing to worry for. You're not working at Hardee's tonight, right?"

"That's right. Why are you asking?"

"Tell yer wee friend Lori that I'll be taking you home after work today. We've got some shopping to do."

He doesn't elaborate, and I don't ask because he sounds so excited.

SQUIRREL PIE

Sure enough, Dad is waiting for me in the employee parking lot as we trickle out the back door at the end of the day.

I climb into the red station wagon, and he pulls out of the lot, his face beaming.

We turn onto VanDyke Avenue, known for its miles of car dealerships. I don't dare hope until he pulls into the Chevrolet dealership and parks.

"Let's go pick out your car, honey."

"Really? Are you serious, Dad?"

"Yes, really. You've walked home in the dark too many times."

He explains that he can use his GM employee discount and co-sign the loan. The payments will be up to me. After talking to the finance department, we settle on what I can afford — a shiny red Sunbird, base model. It has no radio, no air conditioning, no power windows and a manual transmission. The car is one step above Fred Flintstone's car, and I love it.

We shake hands with the salesman, who agrees to call the minute that Dad's discount and insurance are verified, in about two or three days.

I take the color brochure from the dealership and show it to everyone at work the next day. Coworkers show their enthusiasm by pointing out the radio with cassette player or the custom seats shown in the images.

"Well, mine won't actually have that," I say, "but it *is* red."

Two days later I can't sit still at my drafting table. Today Dad and I pick up my new car, and it is all I can think or talk about. My heart feels light, and it seems like the entire universe is opening in front of me, offering me some much-needed breathing room.

I rush to the payphone every time it rings, hoping it's Dad confirming a pick-up time. Just after lunch, the phone rings, and I answer after the second ring. Dad's voice hesitates at the other end of the line.

"Hello, honey. Umm, hello."

"Hey, Dad! What time are you picking me up?"

"Umm, have you talked to your mother today?"

"No, I haven't. Is everything okay?"

"You should call your mother. She wants to talk to you."

"About what? And what about the car?"

"Just give her a call, honey."

Dad doesn't say goodbye or give me a chance to ask more questions. The dial tone hum of an empty line replaces his voice. I pluck two dimes from the perpetual pile of loose change on the phone shelf and call home. Mom answers on the first ring.

"Hey, Mom. Dad said you wanted to talk to me."

"Yes, Deborah, indeed I do. You should know that I am increasing your room and board."

"Uh, okay... How much?"

"One hundred and twenty dollars."

"So, an extra $30 per week?"

"No, Deborah. Your room and board is now $120 per week."

"But…but…Mom, that's double what it was."

"Yes, it sure is."

Her voice sounds distant and matter of fact. I fumble for words, but none come. I twist my finger into the coil of the phone cord as I do silent math in my head. I grip the wall of the phone cubby, my chest tightening as the realization hits me.

"I won't be able to afford my car!"

"No, you won't, so I guess you need to call the dealership and let them know."

The lump in my throat is so large and painful that I can't respond. Clearly, she is angry with me, but I don't know what I've done. I worked so hard to get my head above water, only to have her push me below the waves again. I want to ask her "why?" but I know she won't give me an answer. Tears begin to pool in my eyes, and the silence stretches until Mom breaks it again.

"Well, then, that's that. Perhaps you and your father will think twice before running off to buy a new car behind my back!"

There is a click followed by the familiar hum of a dial tone. All the joy, hope, and confidence that had taken root in my chest are yanked out, leaving a dark chasm behind. I keep the handset to my ear as tears cascade down my cheeks. I wipe them away, only to have them replaced by more.

It takes several minutes for me to pull it together enough that I can hang up the phone and dart to the restroom. I don't come out until I'm empty of tears.

I clock in at Hardee's and nearly collide with Val when she steps out of the side office. She has been waiting to present me with a bright red keychain, emblazoned with the Hardee's logo in gold lettering.

I stare at the floor when I tell her there is no new car: not today, not any day. She stuffs the keychain into my palm and says "Keep it" with a squeeze of my shoulder. She doesn't ask any questions, but her eyes tell me she cares.

That night, I barely notice the water seeping through a new hole in my cheap shoes, making them squeak the entire walk home. Dad isn't waiting up for me in the kitchen, and it is several days before we cross paths. He stops abruptly, startled to see me sitting at the table with Tara, and drops his gaze to the floor.

"I'm sorry, honey," he mumbles before grabbing his jacket from the chair and heading out the front door.

• • •

I work the breakfast shift Sunday morning at Hardees and walk home in my tattered shoes. I am so tired I almost walk right past the work boots and short legs splayed out underneath a rusted blue car parked on the street in front of the house.

"Dad?"

"Oh, hello, honey! You're just in time." He scoots out from under the car and stands, wiping his greasy hands on an old rag.

"For what?"

"Why, to take your car for a spin," he says, with a dramatic flourish of his arm toward the sad little Pontiac Astre. "I just replaced all the hoses."

"My car?"

"Aye, I know, she is'nae much to look at. But she's in better shape than those manky shoes of yours."

"Dad, did you buy me this car?"

"It's from Hank's yard. I did a wee bit of welding in exchange for it."

Hank owns a junk yard and gave Dad a job years ago when he was laid off from Chrysler. Since then, they have become good friends, and Hank's generosity has saved our family on numerous occasions. Although looking at this car right now, I do wonder who got the better end of the deal.

"Thanks for this, Dad."

"Oche, t'was the least I could do, honey."

He twists the rag in his hands even more, avoiding my eyes. He looks like he's about to cry, and it makes me want to join in.

"I love it, Dad! I really, really do."

"Let's take 'er for a spin, and I can show you how to drive."

I get in the driver's seat, and Dad begins to list all the defects of this car: no reverse gear, no air conditioning, no radio, and the windshield wipers have an electrical short, so they are on all the time. I have one foot on the gas pedal and the other on the brake.

"Just the right foot on the gas, honey. You only use one foot with an automatic transmission."

I put my left foot down on the car mat, and it goes straight through to the concrete below, taking the floor mat with it. The rusted-out hole is big enough to pass a bag of potatoes through it, and I drop my right foot down on the pavement as well.

"Bloody hell!"

"It's okay, Dad. We can just put some cardboard over it."

"No, honey, that's too big a hole for that. I'll get some sheet metal from Hank and tack it on this afternoon."

"Can we still take it around the block?"

"No, it's not safe."

"What if we put some brontosaurus ribs on the roof?" I ask, then shuffle my feet on the concrete in a running motion, yelling, "Yabba Dabba Do!"

In seconds, our giggles build to a roar, and we fall against each other. The invisible wall of disappointment, hurt, and frustration built over the previous days crumbles in an instant.

CHAPTER 33

Hood Ornament

The new deadbolt gives a satisfying thunk when I turn my key in the door behind me. I struggle with my lunch bag, Hardees uniform, keys, and purse while shuffling down the driveway in near darkness. I've been driving myself to work all week but can't seem to get myself out the door without a trail of chaos in my wake.

In the pre-dawn darkness, I can see a dark outline on the hood of my blue junkyard rescue. I creep closer, thinking it may be a sleeping cat, and jump when my foot kicks over an empty bottle of PBR, sending it spiraling down the sidewalk. At my feet I spot a pack of Kool menthol cigarettes, Mac's brand, placed upright on the sidewalk.

In a split second, my senses shift into hypervigilance. The beer bottle continues to skitter on cement, but it sounds as if it's in a tunnel far, far away. I scan the windows of neighboring homes, hoping for light in one of them. They all stare back with dark eyes.

Cold fear washes over me, sending cramps through my bowels, as I lean over the car hood and notice the long ears and cotton tail. A rabbit is stretched out near my windshield, front paws pulled above its head. The eyes are open but frozen in death. Its stomach is cut open and the intestines pulled out, the gore splayed across the entire hood.

The sight paralyzes me for several seconds, but my next thought sets me in motion: He's here. I am certain Mac is close by and watching.

Attempting to appear unfazed, I open the car door and toss my belongings inside. Then I take hold of the rabbit by its ears and slide it down the hood, onto the pavement, a slick trail of death in its wake. I get in my car and crank the ignition.

Halfway down the block, a car fires up and headlights turn on. It peels out of the subdivision, and once the taillights disappear around the bend of Callens Road, I turn off the engine, putting my forehead on the steering wheel and breathing to pull myself together.

My stomach does cartwheels on the drive to work. I keep checking my rearview mirror and worrying that someone is following me. I finally make it to work, locate my timecard, and punch in late for the first time ever. Somebody jokes that I must have forgotten how an alarm clock works, and I put on a weak smile, trying to laugh along.

For the next two hours, it is impossible to focus on anything but the clock and the community payphone. I wait until 8:00 a.m., then plug two dimes into the phone and call home. Mom answers on the second ring.

"Mom?" My voice wavers.

"Deborah? What is it?"

"There was a dead rabbit on my car this morning."

"A what?"

"A rabbit…." I pause to swivel my head around to be sure nobody is close enough to hear. "The stomach was cut open. There was a bottle of PBR and pack of Kools on the sidewalk too."

"That bloody snake!"

"What should I do?"

"Where is the rabbit?"

"It's in the big trash can in the garage. The one by the wheelbarrow."

"Aye. I'm calling Chief."

"Chief" is the Chesterfield Township chief of police, an older man who makes the hearts of women in our neighborhood race with his good looks and genuine concern. He made a house call soon after the false police and fire calls began, and all I could do was stare at his square jaw, blue eyes, and silver hair while he took notes and drank coffee.

"Mr. McCall is no stranger to law enforcement, Debbie," he said. "If you need anything or feel your concerns aren't being taken seriously, you call me directly."

We never resorted to using the business card he left on the kitchen table that day, but Mom uses it now. It takes her another two hours to call me back with an update, and it isn't very hopeful.

"Chief sent a squad car over."

"So, they're going to arrest Mac?"

"Pfft! They're nae going to do a damned thing."

"What do you mean?"

"They said you should'nae have tidied up. There was no crime scene for them to look at."

"I didn't think of that."

"Nae bother. We have no proof it was Mac."

"What about the beer bottle and pack of cigarettes?"

"They said that could be anybody's litter."

"So, they're doing nothing?"

"Chief says he'll have a cruiser make routine patrols of the subdivision this week. That's it."

I hang up, disappointed and also terrified. Mac has played this game before, but I haven't. He knows how to bend the rules and get away with anything. In my heart, I know the worst is yet to come.

As if on cue, Mr. Burtch calls me later that afternoon to let me know that Tara's visitations with Mac will begin Sunday from noon to 3:00 p.m.

"I'm afraid you'll need to drop her off and pick her up at his residence."

"Both ways? But that's not fair."

"It's the only way he would agree to your request for Sundays."

I relay the dead rabbit story to him, my voice breaking as I relive my terror from that morning. He peppers me with questions such as "Did anybody see him?" or "Do you have security cameras?" I answer "no" to all the questions that might place Mac at the scene, and Mr. Burtch sighs.

"I'm sure it's just posturing and nothing more, Debbie. I see this type of bad behavior all the time in custody battles, albeit not to this extent. He really cut the stomach open?"

• • •

Sunday arrives all too soon. Tara and MaryAnne start breakfast with a Cheerios war. They throw whole grain ammo at each other while ducking for cover behind cereal boxes, a teapot, or a napkin holder. Mom puts a stop to it by telling MaryAnne to get ready for church.

"Why do I have to go to church, but Tara doesn't?"

"Wheesht! That's enough out of you. Go get dressed."

"But it's not fair!"

"Tara is off to see her father today. Now go and get a move on."

"Can I go with her?" MaryAnne has moved behind Tara, arms encircling her with a protective embrace.

This is a big change from a year ago. MaryAnne did not welcome becoming an aunt at the age of six. Tara was the reason why her big sister no longer spent countless hours playing with her. Eventually, MaryAnne began treating Tara as a pesky little sister, making her eat mud pies and putting her in the dryer for quick spins. Today, however, she seems to be taking her auntie role seriously.

Mom puts her hands on her hips and begins counting backwards from five. MaryAnne takes Tara's hand and together they scramble up the stairs. Moments later, Tara returns to the kitchen with MaryAnne's miniature solid wood replica of a Louisville Slugger, a Detroit Tigers souvenir.

Steve has agreed to go with me for this first drop off at Mac's. He clips into his seatbelt while Tara choke-holds Lucky Bear with one arm and drums the ten-inch baseball bat on the backseat, singing *C is for cookie, that's good enough for me.* She is overjoyed to see her Ian today.

I pull my little blue Astre perpendicular to the gravel drive at the back of the house. Ian and Tyan are nowhere to be seen, and the back door is uncharacteristically closed. I decline Steve's offer to escort me and climb the three cement steps with Tara to the back door. Ian swings open the door with a toothy grin, and Tara squeals in delight. He drops to his knees and hugs her so hard that they look like Siamese twins.

They disappear into the house, and Mac's outline looms behind the screen of the storm door, which is propped open by his foot.

"You wanna come in?"

"No. I'll be back at 3:00."

He leans out the door, nods toward the car and waves at Steve in the passenger seat. Steve raises his middle finger in return.

"I never did like that piece of shit brother of yours."

I walk down the concrete steps, get in the car, and pull away without another word. We drive to Hardee's, where I pick up my check and treat us both to a burger with fries.

"You did good, Deb," Steve says, taking a swig of Coke.

I'm not sure if he's referring to me leaving Mac for good, me not engaging with Mac back at the house, or buying him the best burger he's ever had. But I do get that he's trying to let me know he cares.

"Thanks."

Three hours creep by. We return to the little rental house in New Haven to retrieve Tara. I expect to see the yard full of kids but there are none. I climb the cement steps again and peer through the screen door into the kitchen before knocking on the aluminum frame.

"Hello?"

"It's open," Mac says from the living room.

I hesitate at the sound of his voice, then crack open the door and step inside before calling again.

"Tara? Come on, it's time to go."

To my relief, she runs into the kitchen full of excitement. "Mummy! Look what I got!" She holds a plastic T-Rex in one hand and a stegosaurus in the other, clashing them together in a prehistoric battle. "Ian gimme these."

"You wanna come visit with Ian and Tyan?" Mac is now leaning against the kitchen doorway.

"No…well, I mean yes, but I can't right now. Steve is waiting for me."

"Okay, have it your way." Mac picks Tara up in a bear hug and kisses her forehead. "Daddy loves you, sweetums."

Ian and Tyan take their turns doing the same, and then Mac hands Tara a plastic bag, reminding her not to forget her presents.

I clasp her hand in mine, open the screen door, and step outside. I am tense as we walk down the cement steps, expecting Mac to pull my ponytail or kick me in the backside. Only when the car starts do I relax.

"That actually went pretty well," I say to Steve.

Tara pulls each item from her plastic bag to show her Uncle Steve while I drive. Her nails are painted a seashell pink, and Tyan gave her the half-empty bottle to take home. There are crayon drawings, a yo-yo, and a bag of peanut M&Ms.

"Mummy?"

"Yes, Punkin?"

"Daddy said this present is for you. You put your keys on it so you don't lose them."

I reach back, curious to see what peace offering Mac has sent with Tara, and I nearly swerve off the road as she drops a rabbit foot keychain into my palm.

CHAPTER 34

Legal Limbo

Glen puts his cheeseburger down and looks at me, disbelieving. We were only ten minutes into my dinner break at Hardee's when he sensed my unease and asked if something was troubling me. I blurt out that Mac put a mangled rabbit on my car last week.

"A rabbit? You mean like a real rabbit?"

"Yes, a real rabbit with real intestines and blood. It was horrible."

"What kind of Jack the Ripper shit is that? This guy is mental."

"I know. But I don't know what to do."

"I'll tell you what to do. Give me his address and I'll pay him a visit."

I have tried to keep Glen separate from the turmoil of my custody battle. Partly because I don't want my dysfunctional life to scare him off, but also because I'm afraid he might do something to Mac that would land him behind bars. His agitated response solidifies my fears.

"The cops are patrolling the neighborhood now, so I'm sure it won't happen again."

"I don't know, Deb. That's some messed up shit. If he gives you any more trouble, you need to tell me about it. I'll teach that pencil neck a lesson or two."

I nod my head and change the subject, regretting I ever mentioned the rabbit. In that moment, I make a silent vow never to speak of Mac again. Surely this custody battle will be resolved soon, and Mac will come to his senses so life can regain some semblance of normalcy.

• • •

Tara's second visit with Mac arrives all too soon. I drive to New Haven alone because Steve can't afford another day off work from the hospital.

215

Mac meets me at the back door, opening it wide enough for Ian to step out and take Tara's hand. They head into his bedroom, swinging clasped hands. Mac leans out the door to look at my car.

"Didn't bring your bodyguard today, eh?"

"He had to work."

"Whatever. I'll see you at 3:00."

He doesn't invite me in and lets the screen door smack shut behind him while he disappears into the house. I yell through the screen to Tara that I will be back at 3:00 and that I love her. She pokes her head out of Ian's bedroom door, a cowboy hat perched atop her curls, and blows me a kiss.

Well, that was easy, I think, walking back to the car. No threats, no intimidation, and no drama. Maybe normalcy has already begun to take shape. I don't expect a friendship between Mac and me, but for the first time, I allow myself to believe that we may settle things amicably.

There is plenty of time for my drive out to Richmond to meet my new friend, Carrie, for lunch. Carrie sits at the drafting table in front of me at work, and during my first few weeks I hadn't even said "good morning" to her.

I had not attempted to make friends at work, mostly because Glen was all I could see, but also because I felt out of practice, like I no longer knew how to make friends. It was Carrie who extended the olive branch of friendship after my team leader had a quiet conversation with me about dressing "more appropriately" at work.

I had only been working at EWS & Co. for a few weeks, and my heart sank at the thought of spending any amount of money on clothing. I owned two pairs of jeans and a handful of shirts, which were all showing wear and tear.

The next day Carrie brought in a garbage bag full of old clothes, claiming she no longer needed them. She never mentioned overhearing the conversation with my team lead, but I am certain she heard every word. I wanted to buy her lunch as a thank you.

Time flies with Carrie; she is funny, kind, and quirky. Not once do I feel awkward or self-conscious with her, and I am certain we will be the best of friends. We hug our goodbyes and I rush back to New Haven, humming and sure my life is finally turning a corner.

The yard is full of neighborhood kids when I pull the little blue Astre alongside the curb. Tara is half the size of most but manages to keep up in a game of frozen tag. I stand at the sidewalk watching the action and don't see Mac sitting on the back steps with a cooler until he calls to me.

"Welcome back. You want a Coke?"

"No thanks, I drank a jumbo-sized one at lunch."

He shrugs and opens the cooler, pulling out a sweaty can of generic cola. He peels the tab off and nods his head toward Tara in the yard.

"She's going to sleep well tonight."

"I hate to take her away from all the fun, but we should probably get going."

"Let her get in one more round. Come on inside for a minute. I gathered up some of your things for you."

"What things?"

"There were a bunch of shirts you left in the dryer, and then there's your camera gear and books."

I begin to interrupt, saying I don't want the shirts, but then stutter at the mention of camera gear. Mac purchased an SLR camera for me last Christmas. It was an extravagant gift, and one I used incessantly. I went through film faster than toilet paper. I expected never to see it again when I left this place.

I jump at the chance to reclaim it now.

Mac leads me through the screen door, past the kitchen and into the dining room. There is a white banker's box on the large oak table, the type with handles and a fitted top, only there is no top on this one. Mac lifts it from the table and hands it to me. "All yours," he says.

He deposits it into my arms with an odd sneer on his face. I look down to peer at the contents. There are strips of torn clothing that had once been shirts. The contents of a cat litter box are interspersed with my former wardrobe, and on top of it all are the glass shards, metal springs, and dented body of a destroyed SLR camera.

I am still trying to process what I'm seeing when Mac lifts the bottom of the box up with one hand and forces my head down into it with the other. "Eat shit!" he says.

My nose grazes a litter-coated cat turd, sending my stomach into convulsions. Instinctively, I knock the box away while kicking my feet wildly, hoping to catch Mac's shins. The box lands on its side, scattering debris across the dining room floor. I turn and make a break for the screen door.

I make it halfway through the kitchen when Mac grabs the back of my shirt and wraps his arm around my neck. He plows a knee into my backside with sledgehammer force.

"You think you can break up this family and have no consequences?"

Another knee to my backside.

"You want to be free and single, you whore?"

Another blow.

"You will be dead before I let you take Tara from me."

I don't wait for the next blow. I twist to one side, out of the way. He is momentarily knocked off balance and I kick backwards at his other leg. He stumbles and releases me. Sheer terror ejects me through the screen door, and I jump from the landing into the backyard.

A yard full of children stop to stare at me. I sweep Tara up onto my hip and run toward my car. I am opening the car door when Mac steps out onto the concrete landing, sipping a can of generic cola, and waves.

"Thanks for coming by. I'll see you next week."

• • •

I call Mr. Burtch first thing Monday morning and recount the whole incident to him.

"Did you file a police report?"

"No, all I could think about was getting the hell out of there."

"Were there any witnesses?"

"No, we were in the house."

He lets out a heavy sigh and I'm not sure if he is concerned or annoyed.

"I'll petition the judge for a change of venue. Is there a public place that Mac can walk to?"

His authoritative voice makes me feel at ease. He proposes the New Haven police station for future visitation exchanges and assures me the motion will be filed immediately.

The judge's response comes quickly and succinctly: motion denied.

"He won't consider a change after just two visits."

"What about him beating me up?"

"Accusations like this are common during custody battles. Without witnesses or a police report, he says it is only your word against Mac's. I'm afraid he's not going to take any action."

"I can't go back there!"

"I know. It's a bad situation. I'm sorry, Debbie, but you'll be held in contempt if you don't go back."

And just like that, I find myself driving back to the little white house the following Sunday. The sun is bright and the skies clear, yet the yard is devoid of children. In fact, it is devoid of anything: no bikes, no toy dump truck, no jump rope in the dusty patch below the tree. I knock on the screen door, hoping nobody is home.

The sound of heavy boots on linoleum clenches my stomach and I reflexively descend one step down off the landing. Mac swings open the door and steps out. I descend another step while releasing Tara onto the concrete landing. She senses something is off and hesitates, looking back to me.

"Mummy, where's my Ian?"

Mac scoops her up, opens the back door, and slams it behind him.

For the next three hours, I drive aimlessly through the streets of New Haven. I scan the neighboring yards for signs of Ian or Tyan playing at a friend's house. I circle the block at the little white rental several times, but the kids never appear, and the copper-colored Cutlass never moves. At 2:55 I knock at the screen door.

"You're early," Mac says from the living room at the front of the house. "I've got five more minutes. You gonna wait out there or come inside?"

SQUIRREL PIE

I peer through the screen to see Tara perched in his lap, sharing peanut M&Ms with him on the velvet couch.

"I'll wait in my car."

"Mummy's being silly, isn't she?"

Mac tickles Tara as he says this, and she giggles. I hear him whisper something in her ear, and she giggles again.

"Mummy, I got new cowboy boots."

I hesitate before opening the screen door. I tell myself that since Tara is with him, he won't do anything to me. I cross the kitchen into the dining room. The large oak table is gone, and lined up along the wall in its place are a half dozen garbage bags.

Tara leaps from Mac's lap and ushers me over to one of the bags, pulling out a pair of cheap plastic cowboy boots.

"See, Mummy? New boots!"

Mac rises from the couch with a can of PBR in his hand. Instinctively, I position Tara behind me.

"You're not supposed to drink when Tara is here, Mac."

"You're not supposed to be a bitch, so we're even."

"Where are Ian and Tyan?" I ask, suddenly aware of how empty the house is.

"I sent them ahead. We'll catch up with them next week."

"What are you talking about?"

"See those bags? Those are all new clothes for Tara. Everything is packed and next week when you drop her off, you can kiss her goodbye. You won't ever see her again."

In one motion, I scoop Tara onto my hip and stride toward the back door, ready to get out of here now. I have one foot out on the landing when my head jerks backward. Mac has a fist full of my hair.

I don't care if he pulls every hair out of my head, we are leaving. I plow forward, managing to get us clear of the kitchen and onto the landing. Mac holds on to my hair relentlessly, then punches the back of my head.

Tara begins to howl, "No Daddy, no!" and I tuck her head between my right ear and shoulder while Mac releases a series of punches to the left side of my face.

He stops abruptly when a police cruiser turns the corner and drives by. His fingers are still tangled with my hair when the taillights go red, and the cruiser backs up.

CHAPTER 35

Too Much To Lose

The officer who saved the day was on his way back to the station when he happened to glance in his rearview mirror. The incident is written up as a domestic dispute with no arrest made. At this point, I'm convinced only murder will get Mac into a pair of handcuffs.

Despite my frustration, I am elated to have an official police report with a bona fide officer of the law as my witness. John Burtch wastes no time filing a second motion, and the judge agrees to hear us out now that we have documented proof.

I am fidgeting on a bench outside the courtroom doors when I catch sight of Mr. Burtch approaching in his blue suit. He places a briefcase on the bench next to me and cinches his necktie. He has the confident smile of a cat with a cornered mouse.

"This police report is a game changer, Debbie. How are you feeling about seeing the judge?"

"Nervous. What is he going to ask me?"

"I'll do all the talking, so don't worry about that. Ready?"

Ready or not, I follow him when he opens the courtroom door, and we head down the aisle toward the front. We wait less than thirty minutes for our case to be called. I stay seated while Mr. Burtch stands and wastes no time with niceties.

"Your Honor, you may recall a prior motion that was filed on behalf of my client when she was assaulted while picking up the minor child from visitation?"

"Yes, I recall. Proceed."

"That motion was denied because my client's claims were deemed unsubstantiated. I have now provided the court with a police report from her most recent visitation to Mr. McCall's residence. This was witnessed by a New Haven police officer and confirms my client's claims of routine abuse. We request the court to order supervised visitations."

The judge peers at the papers on his desk through the bottom half of his glasses. His jowls sway like Jell-O molds with each nod of his head. He scowls, removes his glasses, and rubs the indentation at the bridge of his nose.

"Counsel, I will agree that a change in venue is reasonable. Supervised visitation, however, is for the safety of a minor child. I don't see any threat to the child."

"Your Honor, Mr. McCall has informed my client of his intention to abscond with the child to an unknown location at his next visitation."

The judge's facial expression evolves from annoyed to angry as Mr. Burtch lays out his case.

"That's enough, counselor. This court hears similar accusations in every custody battle. Mr. McCall has custody of two children, he has a job, he leases a home. This man isn't going anywhere. Petition for supervised visitation is denied. Hence forth, visitation exchange will take place at the New Haven police department. Next case!"

"Thank you, your Honor."

Mr. Burtch turns on his heels, scoops up his briefcase, and motions with his head toward the door. I trail behind him up the aisle and back out into the corridor. He sets his briefcase on the same bench to loosen his necktie.

"Well, that went smoothly."

"It did?"

"Sure! A police station is about as safe as you can get. Mac won't be able to harm you there."

"But I still have to leave Tara with him?"

"I'm afraid so. Supervised visitation was a long shot."

"He's going to disappear with her!"

"The judge made sense, Debbie. Kidnapping is a serious offense, and Mac has too much to lose. He's just trying to intimidate you."

I chew on these words for days, trying to swallow them. When Sunday arrives, we all begin our morning routine. Steve leaves for the hospital without breakfast or a word to anybody. Mom, Dad, and MaryAnne all head off to church. I pull Tara's curls into stubby ponytails and pour Cheerios into a bowl.

Lucky Bear faces Tara on the kitchen table, waiting for his share of breakfast. Instead, he battles a plastic T-Rex figurine. By the time Tara has emptied her bowl, Lucky Bear is declared the winner and tucked under her arm.

I am waging an internal debate about dropping her off at the New Haven police station. I don't know how much legal trouble I will land in if I don't take her for this scheduled visitation, but my gut tells me that Mac is serious with his threats.

"Mummy, can I go play with Nicole?"

"Sure, Punkinhead."

She slides off the kitchen chair and heads to the front door. I watch her lace up the tiny saddle oxfords, her tongue peeking out for added concentration.

My mental debate is over. Tara is not going for visitation today. Each time the phone rings, I expect Mac's angry voice to be at the other end, but he never calls.

She misses the following Sunday as well, with still no word from Mac. It is naïve, but I let myself believe that he packed up and left town without a word. Before long, I forget all about Sunday visitations.

CHAPTER 36

Mail Call

The front yard is overflowing with neighborhood children as I guide the little blue Astre to its usual spot along the curb, covering its expanding oil stain on Bellaire Street. The subdivision has become home to dozens of young families, and today it appears that every child has found their way to my parents' front yard for a game of tag.

It is not often that I can witness Tara's childhood taking place. I miss so much of it while working the dinner shift at Hardees, but today is a rare evening off. I sit in my car watching Tara and Nicole trying to keep up with the older kids until she catches sight of me and runs to the car. She clasps my hand before I am even out of the driver's seat.

"Mummy, did you see me? I tagged Joey!"

We pause at the end of the driveway to check the mailbox while Joey runs over to clarify, "No you didn't. You missed me by a mile!"

I swing the mailbox door down and attempt to retrieve Tara with my free hand. She is advancing on Joey with a red face and clenched fists.

"I did, too, Joey. I got you!"

"Okay, you two, that's enough. It's just a game."

"Is that a squirrel?"

Joey ignores Tara, craning his neck toward the mailbox. My hand is still holding the curled metal latch of the mailbox door, and I turn to follow his gaze. There, inside the metal dome, is a bushy squirrel tail atop a stack of mail.

A fucking squirrel.

I quickly slam the door shut, but not before a circle of kids have crowded around me. The boys are buzzing with excitement about a squirrel in the mailbox.

"What is it?" one of them asks.

"There's a squirrel in there," Joey says. "I saw it."

227

"Is it alive? Can I see it?"

I scan the circle of young faces and find MaryAnne. She is the only one that doesn't wear a look of curiosity because she knows something is wrong.

"Is Mom home?" I ask.

She nods and I tell her to go find her. Within moments the front door opens, and Mom is hurrying toward the mailbox. Her face is a combination of worry and absolute resolve.

The wall of children part like the Red Sea to let her through. She sees my death grip on the mailbox door and springs into action.

"Wheesht, children! The whole lot of you, into the backyard now."

"But we want to see the squirrel," Eric says.

"There'll be popsicles for those of you in the backyard and a bang on the ear for those of you who aren't. Now!"

The crowd funnels into the backyard. Joey and Eric are at the end of the line, looking back several times in hopes of seeing a live squirrel launch from the mailbox.

"Don'nae tell me there's a squirrel in there, Deborah."

"I only saw the tail."

"Well, let me have a look then."

She pulls the door down and sighs at the unmistakable sight of a bushy squirrel tail. I reach in to pull it out for a better look, and Mom grips my wrist to stop me.

"Aye, let's nae destroy the crime scene. I'll call Chief."

Mom distributes popsicles in the backyard while I stand guard at the mailbox. It takes thirty minutes for a police cruiser to arrive, and when it does, the same two officers emerge from the car.

They are the ones who brought me home as a runaway, followed up on the false fire and police calls, and confirmed my alibi when Mac accused me of puncturing his girlfriend's tire. They have spent so much time with our family that we now call them Officer Dan and Officer John. They, in turn, refer to my parents as Mrs. B. and Scotty, a nickname my father has always preferred.

"What have we got today?" Officer Dan asks.

I pull open the mailbox, and he bends forward to peer inside with the aid of a small flashlight. Without a word, he pulls the stack of mail toward him, inching the carcass out with it. Mom and I gasp at the sight of a headless little corpse.

The squirrel carcass is belly up, its appendages curled into a rigor mortis crouch as if it died while burying an acorn. Officer Dan moves a front paw with his flashlight and plucks a business card resting on its belly.

It is a simple white card with the image of a pitchfork and *Devil's Disciples Motorcycle Club* printed in blue lettering. There is no name, just a phone number on the front. On the back is a handwritten message that reads, *You want war, bitch? You got it!*

Officer Dan retrieves a Polaroid camera from the police car and begins taking photos of the squirrel at various angles. He takes a close-up of the calling card, capturing both sides before handing it to me. He then lifts the squirrel by its tail and removes the bed of mail, handing the stack to Mom. She backs up one step and I intercept, taking the stack instead.

"There's no blood," Officer Dan says, turning to Officer John. "It's odd, like he's had it for a long time."

I'm too embarrassed to mention that I'm sure it's from the half dozen squirrels we always kept in the freezer for meals.

"Let me guess, Officers," Mom says, now recovered. "There's nothing you can do about this?"

"The escalation is concerning, Mrs. B.," Officer John says. "This was done after mail delivery, which means in broad daylight."

"Anybody could have reached in there for the mail," I chime in. "That makes it worse."

"It appears you're not the sole target anymore, Debbie," Officer Dan says. "It's your entire family now."

Mom stifles a gasp with a hand to her mouth. I grip my stomach, trying to keep its contents in place. Officer Dan goes on to explain that they have been building a case against Mac for the false police and fire calls. They have been waiting to collect any further calls, but now he thinks it may be wise to act sooner rather than later.

"We'll need your help, Debbie."

An hour later, Mom and I are at the Chesterfield Police Department. Chief is now with us, and he takes us to a back room, one at a time, to identify voices from the phone recordings. Mom goes first, and when she returns, I am promptly whisked away because we are not permitted to talk. Chief sits me on a stool and gives me a pad of paper and a pencil. Somebody has numbered the notepaper from one to twelve.

"There are twelve calls, Debbie. After each one plays, I want you to write down a name if you can identify the voice. If not, just write "X." Do you understand?"

I nod my head and giant headphones are fitted over my ears. I give a thumbs up when I hear the dispatcher's voice then freeze when Mac's unmistakable voice comes on. My hand trembles as I write his name next to number one.

I identify Gina on one call, Larry on three, and Mac on the remaining eight. It is a relief to me that Graham's voice is not on any of them because I always liked Graham. Mom's list matches mine, and Chief smiles when he compares them.

"This is good. Please be patient, this will take some time. You can expect charges filed against Mr. McCall in a few weeks. We'll notify you when that happens."

• • •

Every night I rummage the pile of mail left for me on the kitchen table, searching for just such a notification. It has only been a few days, but I hope for a miracle. A week has slipped by when I return home to find a legal-sized envelope on top of the mail stack. Macomb County Court is printed as the return address.

My heart skips a beat, as I think this must have something to do with the charges against Mac. I pull out the paperwork and printed in bold letters is *Show Cause Hearing*. It takes me a moment to realize that I am being summoned to court. I haven't taken Tara to see her dad in four weeks, and the judge wants to know why.

I plead with John Burtch the next morning, hoping he can wave a business card and make it all go away.

"You are defying a court order, Debbie, and judges typically don't like that." He laughs lightly, trying to take the edge off and yet still convey the severity of my situation.

"Can we delay?"

"It's best to face this head on."

Ten days later we are in the Macomb County Courthouse, standing before the judge. It is obvious he is annoyed, and although Mr. Burtch does his best to reiterate my concerns about Mac disappearing with Tara, he is abruptly cut off.

"Do I really need to hear all this again, Counselor? Please remind your client that she is bound by a court order, not a court suggestion."

The judge then points his index finger at me, turning in his seat to face me directly.

"Miss Brannigan, if you fail to comply with this order, please bring a toothbrush when you return to this courtroom because you will be spending thirty days in county jail."

"Thank you, your Honor," Mr. Burtch says.

He touches my elbow and steers me toward the back doors. The entire proceeding took less than ten minutes. We clear the double doors of the courtroom, and Mr. Burtch lets out a heavy sigh when we reach the bench in the corridor.

"I'm sorry, Debbie."

"I don't understand what the judge said. What happens if I don't drop her off?"

"You'll be found in contempt of court and taken to county jail for thirty days. If that happens, Mac could be granted custody."

"I don't know what to do, Mr. Burtch."

"It's in your best interest to take her to the police station this Sunday. It's also in Mac's best interest to stay put and he knows that. I'm sure everything will be fine."

I am not so sure it will be fine. The next day I pick up a child ID kit from the police station and ink Tara's fingerprints onto the 3x5 card. I also teach her how to pick up a phone, dial zero, and ask the operator to call the police.

On Sunday morning, I dress Tara in a vibrant sailor dress. It has large blue lapels and a brilliant red neckerchief. It is an eye-catching outfit, one that people will remember seeing. I take photos of her from every angle, knowing they will come in handy for a police bulletin.

My intuitive fear is so profound and visceral that I have to shut it off to function. I become numb, opting to feel nothing in order to get through the day. I drive the little blue Astre to New Haven on auto pilot, making turns without even thinking.

The New Haven police station is small, with no parking spots available. I park down the street and take my time walking Tara to the front door. I squat down and hug her before going in, reminding her to dial zero on a phone if she doesn't see me before bedtime.

Mac is waiting inside, arms folded and brows knitted. A desk clerk waves me to the opposite end of the counter. She comes out from behind the counter and takes Tara's hand, leading her over to Mac. He shoots me a contemptuous look before closing the station door behind him.

I'm instructed to wait five minutes before leaving the building, but I have no intention of leaving the building. I plant myself in a plastic chair along the wall and wait. Even though the desk clerk gives me cups of bad coffee and tries to engage in polite conversation, I just sit and watch the clock.

I stand at 2:55 p.m. and go into the parking lot. I scan the street for signs of Mac returning with Tara, and there are none. I go back inside at 3:10 and implore the clerk to "do something." She tells me that he is only ten minutes late and has a thirty-minute grace period according to law.

At 3:30 p.m. I point out that he is now thirty minutes late and we need to send people out to look for them. She says she will note Mr. McCall's tardiness for the record and returns her attention to the papers on her desk.

At four o'clock I leave the police station without a word and get in my car. I drive over to the white rental house and park along the curb.

The driveway and yard are empty. The back door is locked, and so is the front door.

The windows along the side of the house are too high off the ground for me to see inside, even on tip toes. I roll an old tractor tire in the yard over to the house and stand on it. My nose grazes the windowsill as I stare into the dark living room. Every stick of furniture is gone.

The house is completely vacant.

CHAPTER 37

I Told You So

Mom is standing at the stove, stirring a pot when I walk through the front door. "You're late, Deborah. Dinner's almost ready." When I don't answer, she looks up.

"Where's the wee'an?"

"I don't know."

Her spoon falls to the floor, and the kitchen immediately swirls with activity. Mom pulls the phone from the wall and calls Chief. MaryAnne tugs at my shirt, asking if Tara is going to be okay. Steve emerges from the basement, bewildered by the noise. Dad stuffs his wallet into his back pocket and turns to me.

"Let's go, honey."

We drive for six hours, stopping only for gas. Dad is convinced that Mac is on his way to Trimble, Ohio, to see his parents and that somehow, we can intercept him.

We arrive at James and Jan McCall's ramshackle house well after 10:00 p.m. I am still fumbling with my seat belt as Dad marches to the front porch and bangs on the door. I catch up to him right as the front door opens.

James scowls at Dad and shifts his weight forward, as if readying for a fight—he has no idea who this stranger is. Then he sees me, and the brief wave of guilt that washes across his face makes it obvious he knows why we are here.

Jan appears out of thin air behind James, dressed in a night gown. She bats her husband's chest with the backside of her hand in reprimand for his poor manners.

"Come on in," she says, motioning us into the house.

Dad and I sit in worn wingback chairs that face Jan and James, who are seated on the sofa. James crosses his arms, still scowling, while Jan drapes a crocheted blanket across her lap.

"I think you both know why we are here," Dad says.

"Now, Mac ain't about to do no harm to his little girl—"

"We got no information for you," James interrupts, his eyes locking onto Dad.

"You can'nae sit there and tell me you have'nae heard from him."

"Maybe we have. Maybe we haven't," James replies. "Ain't none of your business either way."

"He's taken Tara away from her mother, for godsakes! Have ye no heart, man?"

James sets his jaw in a harder line than it already is, then nods his head toward me. "She knew what she was getting into with him! Don't start crying about it now."

"Just give Mac some time to cool down and it'll all smooth itself out, I'm sure," Jan says quickly, attempting to diffuse the growing tension in the room. "He's on his way to Arizona. Got some friends out there, I think."

"That's bloody bullshit!" Dad shouts, jumping to his feet with fists clenched.

James stands up, more than ready to oblige him with a fight. Jan and I step between them to intervene, and I push Dad out the front door while Jan does her best to keep James in the living room. The men are still trading insults and threats as we climb back into the station wagon.

"That bloody bastard!" Dad yells, punching the dashboard several times. "He knows damned well where they are and it sure in hell is'nae Arizona!"

We make the six-hour return trip in silence. The only sound is the hum of our tires on the pavement. The highway is nothing but a long stretch of black in the headlights, and weeks of stress, anxiety, and long workweeks suddenly catch up, threatening to overwhelm my body. I am succumbing to sleep when Dad breaks the silence.

"I'm sorry, honey."

"I know, Dad."

His voice is choked with helplessness, but I have no solace to offer because I'm drowning in the same ocean.

• • •

We pull onto Bellaire Street at almost 5:00 am. I fall into bed, worn out, as the sun climbs its first rung in the sky. I open my eyes a few hours later when Mom knocks on the bedroom door and says softly, "Chief is here."

I will myself out of bed and find Chief waiting at the kitchen table, his blue eyes brimming with compassion. "We are going to find her, Debbie."

Tears are shed and tempers flare as questions are asked, and calls are made over the next hour. I am numb in the eye of this emotional hurricane, repeating "I told you so" in my head. Mr. Burtch has very few words when I call.

"Tara is gone."

"Gone?"

"He took her. The house is empty."

Long moments of silence stretch out before he says, "Be at the courthouse tomorrow. 8:00 a.m."

• • •

The large glass doors of the county building are being unlocked from the inside as I reach the top step. Mr. Burtch is already there, and he escorts me into the polished marble entryway. Cleaning crews push their carts out of sight, and guards empty the last precious drops from paper coffee cups in preparation for another busy day.

The click-clack of Mr. Burtch's wingtips across the marble flooring halt without warning, and he turns to face me. His lips tighten, then part, but nothing comes out. He tries again, looking first to the floor then into my eyes.

"I am so incredibly sorry about this, Debbie."

I give a simple nod and his trajectory down the corridor continues, the wingtip staccato echoing in our wake. I follow him to the judge's private chambers, and he leaves a request to approach the bench before the day's docket gets underway.

From there, we take an elevator to the sixth floor, where he files paperwork and has it fast-tracked. He tries to explain it all to me with words like *motions, petitions,* and *parental rights*. I nod to let him know I heard the words, but I can't seem to grasp any of it.

At 9:00 a.m. sharp we stand before the judge in his courtroom. Recognition flashes across his eyes, and heavy lines form between his brows, signaling annoyance at seeing us before him yet again.

"Counselor, there better be a good reason for this urgency."

"Yes, your Honor, there is."

"Proceed."

"My client complied with your visitation order on Sunday."

"And?"

"Mr. McCall absconded with the child, your Honor. He has not been seen since my client dropped off the child for visitation. His home is vacant, and police are searching for them."

The air goes still. Several heartbeats of complete silence elapse while this information seeps in. I wait for apologies, remorse, perhaps even humility from the judge. Instead, I see redness congeal in his jowls. It rises to his cheeks, like mercury in a thermometer, and I jump when the heavy wooden gavel comes down with a thundering crash.

"Mr. McCall is to be stripped of all parental rights!"

Another crack of the gavel.

"Upon the child's return, he is to have no further contact with her. Not by phone, not by mail, and certainly not in person. Am I clear?"

The gavel comes down once more before Mr. Burtch can respond, and the judge sets it aside, as if extinguishing any further temptations to use it.

"This is outrageous, Counselor."

"Thank you, your Honor."

I struggle to keep up with Mr. Burtch as he makes a beeline to the large wooden double doors. He does not pause to adjust his tie outside the courtroom this time but marches to the elevators, pushing the button several times.

"Now what?" I ask.

"Now I get those petitions and motions signed by the judge before he cools off."

We exit on the sixth floor, and Mr. Burtch approaches the same clerk who helped us this morning. Her full cup of coffee still sits untouched at the corner of her desk. She drops several sheets of paper into a manila envelope and hands them over like a race baton, and we pause just long enough to say thank you.

We head to the elevators and step into the same car, still waiting for us. We return to the judge's chambers and leave the manila envelope with an aide, who promises to put the papers in the judge's hands the moment he returns from courtroom sessions.

Mr. Burtch lets out a sigh of relief when the chamber door closes, and I realize that he knew exactly what to file before we even entered the courtroom that morning.

"How are you holding up, Debbie?"

"Okay, I guess. What happens now?"

"The judge will sign these into order today, I'm certain of that."

"What does that do?"

"Mac will not be allowed visitation or custody. He will not be permitted to contact you or Tara in any way. There will be a restraining order to keep him away from your entire family."

"That only works if we find him."

"*When.* *When* we find him, Debbie. The police will catch up to him soon."

I look away, trying to disguise my look of frustration combined with resignation. I know Mac, and I know he has planned this for a long time. If he wants to disappear, he will leave no trace behind.

"I'm sorry, Debbie, but I have to appear in another courtroom. I'll call you when we have everything signed, and I'll also get an update from the police. But please let me know if you hear anything first."

I clock in at work just before 10:30 a.m., but there are no wisecracks today. People avert their eyes as I walk the long aisle to my drafting table at the back of the building. My cousin Erica gives me a hug when I take my seat next to her.

She tells me that nobody expects me to be here today, and I should go home in case the police call. I want to ask her who will pay my lawyer fees if I lose my job, but instead I tell her Mom is home to take any calls. Then I lay out my drafting tools.

Glen appears at the edge of my drafting board, and his brown eyes are brimming with compassion. I look away, unable to hold his gaze because it will cause a wall of uncontrollable tears to rush out.

"Hey, Deb. I'm here for you. Please tell me what I can —"

"Not now. I can't do this at work. I'm sorry."

He retreats to his drafting table, and I roll out a fresh sheet of mylar. I skip lunch and work until the lead in my mechanical pencil whittles down to nothing, and then I replace it with a fresh one and work some more. Coworkers begin lining up at the time clock, ready to go home. I am unrolling another sheet of mylar, ready to start another illustration, when the payphone begins to ring.

The time clock thwacks rhythmically as my coworkers exit to the parking lot. Nobody is going to walk back here to answer this phone. After it rings for what must be the fiftieth time, I pick up the receiver.

"Debbie? Is that you?"

It's John Burtch, his voice a mix of relief, excitement and panic.

"What's wrong?"

"I think Mac may be staying in Alger with Tara. I have an address and we can be there by 9:00 p.m. if I pick you up now."

"Pick me up?"

"Yes, I'll be at your office in fifteen minutes."

• • •

I wait in an empty parking lot, wondering if I misinterpreted the conversation. Is my lawyer really driving us three hours north to follow a lead? Surely I'm mistaken? I'm about to jump into the Astre and head home when his Oldsmobile turns into the lot.

The cream-colored leather melts around my backside as I settle into the passenger seat. I pull the seat belt across my chest, and we turn out of the lot into traffic. Mr. Burtch wears the same blue suit and black wingtip shoes from this morning. He hasn't been home yet.

"I contacted the local sheriff up in Alger. He's going to escort us to the address when we arrive."

"Did the police give you this address?"

"No, I found it."

"Where?"

"I went through the trash bags along the curb at Mac's house."

He continues talking about what he found, but the information barely registers. I am picturing him exiting the pristine marble county building and driving thirty minutes into soot-covered New Haven. The sight of him combing through Hefty bags in his navy-blue suit and wingtips must have raised many eyebrows in the neighborhood.

"Are you hungry, Debbie?"

I'm suddenly aware of the sedan pulling into a McDonald's drive-thru. I reach for my purse, then stop, because I know there is no money in it.

"No thanks."

"How about I order an assortment of things? If you get hungry, you can pick from it."

Two large paper bags are soon laid flat on the seat between us. The smell of fries, burgers, and pies causes my stomach to groan with hunger.

"Please, help yourself."

I pull a few fries from their greasy paper pouch. Mr. Burtch smiles, then scoots a cheeseburger over toward my thigh. I pick it up, and he sheds his blue suit jacket and red necktie, tossing both into the backseat. With a paper napkin across his lap and a burger in one hand, he resumes our journey north.

"Thank you for not going to Hardee's, Mr. Burtch."

"There's nothing wrong with Hardees."

"I feel like I'm going to wear that plaid uniform the rest of my life."

"It won't be forever."

"It sure feels like it will be."

"Well, not so long ago I worked at McDonald's flipping burgers. In fact, I stayed so long they made me manager and were ready to send me to Hamburger School. Did you know there was such a thing?"

I laugh, not sure if he is pulling my leg or not.

"Seriously. McDonald's has Hamburger School where they teach business and management classes. I was on the fast track to becoming a district manager."

"What happened?"

"I thought about my future and realized I didn't want a life in fast food. I quit that job and went to law school."

"Just like that?"

"The law degree took several years, but yes. My point is you can chart your own course, too. You have it in you to be whomever you want to be."

We ride in silence, eating our burgers and fries. His words cause the gears in my mind to churn. *Who do I want to be?* is a question I've never asked, and it scares me to realize I have no answer. I close my eyes in quiet contemplation and fall dead asleep.

"We're here, Debbie."

Mr. Burtch is shaking my shoulder. My eyelids feel like I'm wearing lead mascara, and I am having trouble forcing them to stay open. The dashboard clock shows 8:42 p.m., and I apologize for sleeping throughout the entirety of the trip.

"No apologies. You needed it. I'm going to let the sheriff know we are here."

The fog in my head begins to lift as I watch Mr. Burtch disappear into a small white building. Within minutes the door opens, and he re-emerges with a stocky officer trailing behind him. They shake hands in the beam of the Oldsmobile's headlights, and the sheriff turns toward a police car across the lot.

"We're going to follow him over to the house now," Mr. Burtch says as he resumes his post behind the wheel. He asks me if I'm okay, but he's the one who looks anxious. I nod, and he puts the car in gear.

We turn into the empty street, following the police car through several turns and down a gravel road. The sheriff pulls into a front yard littered with derelict cars. The Oldsmobile rolls to a halt several yards behind his bumper.

I unfasten my seatbelt to get out, but Mr. Burtch tells me to wait. He meets the sheriff at the front of his cruiser, and after a brief conversation, the sheriff turns to walk toward the front door while Mr. Burtch stays back. He knocks multiple times before the door opens, and it is several minutes later before he steps inside the home.

Mr. Burtch returns to the Oldsmobile and locks the doors, and we wait together silently. As the minutes tick by, the tension builds and my worry grows.

What if there is a shootout?

The front door of the small house cracks open, and I am ready to duck for cover when it swings wide. There is no gun fight, though. Just the sheriff shaking hands and tipping his hat to a haggard-looking couple.

He walks to the driver's side of the Oldsmobile. Mr. Burtch lowers the window and the sheriff leans in with one arm on the hood to prop himself up.

"We just missed him."

"He was here?"

"Sure enough. Folks inside say they had no idea that little girl was kidnapped. They put him up for a night, some sort of favor for a friend of a friend. He left this afternoon saying he was headed for Arizona, but they think he was lying about that."

Mr. Burtch then asks about getting a statement from the couple about Mac going to Arizona, and the sheriff assures him it won't be a problem to fax one over in a day or two. They shake hands through the window, and we thank him for all his help.

When the driver's side window slides back up, Mr. Burtch turns sideways to face me directly.

"It's okay if you want to cry."

I lean my forehead on the cool glass of the passenger side window. I probably should cry — it's what any other mother would do — but I can't summon the tears.

I had not expected this address to mean anything. Not for a minute did I think Mac was careless enough to leave a trail behind, and yet Tara was right here just a few hours ago. Equally surprising, it was my lawyer who picked up on the trail by digging through garbage for answers.

I don't want to cry. I want to smile.

For the first time in years, hope takes root within me.

CHAPTER 38

Starsky & Hutch

The next two weeks pass at a frenetic pace. Mr. Burtch meets me at the county building twice and zips from floor to floor like a hummingbird. I am an anchor around his neck as I try to keep up. I sign papers, and they turn into court orders a few days later. What they are for, I have no idea.

Within days of Tara's abduction, my parents and I hire a husband-and-wife private investigator team recommended by one of Mom's friends. Mom and Dad pay the $2000 retainer fee, but all expenses and hourly fees are my responsibility.

I am officially hemorrhaging more money than I earn. Steve pulls some strings at the hospital and lands me a part-time job delivering food trays to patients. Each day, I leave EWS by 3:45 and race to the hospital to clock in for my 4:00 to 8:00 p.m. shift. Val moves me to the late-night shift at Hardee's, which means I now get home sometime around 2 o'clock in the morning.

I shuffle police visits and phone calls around these eighteen-hour workdays. The days meld together in sheer chaos. It's only when I go to bed at night do the minutes stretch into eternity. I sit with lingering imprints of Tara: her plastic dinosaurs on the nightstand, a multi-colored potholder half-finished in its plastic loom on the floor, a Care Bear T-shirt rumpled on the bed. I move none of it, hoping she will materialize into the scene through sheer will.

Eventually, sleep overtakes me. The alarm reminds me, just a few hours later, that it is time to repeat the whole cycle.

I fall asleep on my feet as my drafting team leader attempts to teach me something new. He wakes me with a gentle hand on the shoulder, saying I need to take better care of myself.

I know he is right, and I call Val from the payphone to tell her I will be in two hours late tonight. She doesn't ask why and tells me not to think twice about it, that I need to do what I need to do.

What I need to do is sleep. My brain decides we are close enough to start napping when I turn onto Callens Road and I have to roll the window down for the last mile to help me stay awake.

Annoyance prickles my skin when I turn onto Bellaire Street and find that somebody has parked in my spot along the curb. I park behind them, inspecting the car as I walk toward the driveway.

It is a blue Chrysler sedan with unusual side view mirrors and headlights. In a flash it hits me that it is an unmarked police car, and I run up the driveway, my heart beating hard enough to break out of my chest. They've brought Tara home!

Mom swings open the door when I reach the front porch.

"Did they find her?" I ask, gasping.

"No, love, but the FBI are here."

"The FBI?"

"Yes, they're handling the case now."

Mom leads me into the kitchen where two agents sit with file folders and cups of coffee. Ant hills of cookie crumbs surround the last remaining square of Dad's homemade shortbread in the center of the table. They wipe their lips and stand to greet me.

"Hello, Debbie. I'm Special Agent Michaels and this is Special Agent Berkman."

Agent Michaels has a slighter build than his partner. His tightly wound dark curls and silver wire-rimmed glasses make him handsome in a bookish kind of way. Agent Berkman looks younger, with broad shoulders and sandy blonde hair. Both wear sport coats and pocket protectors. An image of TV detectives Starsky and Hutch working at IT jobs pops into my imagination, and I extinguish the urge to laugh.

"You're FBI?"

"Yes, we'll be handling your daughter's abduction case."

"Why is the FBI involved?"

"We have a statement from an acquaintance of Mr. McCall saying the child was being taken to Arizona. Interstate abduction is a federal case and that's when we get called in."

I flash back to Mr. Burtch shaking hands with the sheriff through the window of his Oldsmobile in Alger, asking him if he could get a statement from the couple about Mac going to Arizona.

Mom pulls out a chair so I can join them at the table. She refills their coffee cups and puts a cold Tab cola in front of me before sitting back down.

Agent Michaels peppers us with questions. Most of them we expect, like "Who does Mac associate with?" while others seem irrelevant, such as "What brand of cigarettes does he smoke?"

I'm surprised to learn they have already visited the New Haven foundry to question his coworkers. They have also canvassed the neighborhood and taken statements from several neighbors. Agent Michaels believes a few of the leads are credible and worthy of following up.

"Do you think he really went to Arizona?" I ask him.

"It's not likely, but we do believe he has crossed state lines. We will contact field offices in the locations identified by the more credible leads."

"What locations?"

"We'd rather not say at this time."

He asks for the phone number of our private investigators, and Mom retrieves a business card from the living room, telling him to keep it. Agent Berkman wants to know if the couple has provided us with any useful information, and we are forced to admit that they have not.

I don't mention that I have signed over my last two paychecks to them, and that all I have gotten in return is a short phone call with a recommendation for a restaurant serving "the best seafood in North Carolina," which I was billed for.

The agents are about to leave when Mom asks if they'd like the Devil's Disciples calling card that was left in the mailbox. Agent Michaels declines, saying they have a photocopy from Chief and have already called the number, leaving several voice messages.

When the front door closes behind them, Mom and I fall into each other's arms, jumping up and down like schoolgirls.

"God Almighty, Deborah! The FBI!"

"I can't believe it, Mom."

"Aye, he'll nae be able to outrun the likes of the FBI, the snake."

I am so energized by the FBI's involvement that I forego my nap and head into Hardee's, filled to the brim with optimism. Val hugs me after I update her on this latest development.

I don't share the saga of my life with the high school kids I work alongside, but I do with Val. She has become more than a manager to me, more like an auntie. I suspect she is not quite forty, although her competent demeanor projects an older image. When I told her about Tara's abduction, her usual fluttering hands went still, and tears perched upon her lower lids.

"Whatever you need, I'm here for you, Debbie."

And I knew she truly meant it.

• • •

I return from a bathroom break at Hardee's to find Glen in the lobby with flowers and a shopping bag. I forgot he was coming today, and the surprised look on my face shows it. This is our first dinner break together since Tara was taken.

I have made no effort to pull Glen into the churn of police inquiry, private eye calls and courtroom appearances. I also made no effort to update him on my new work schedule until yesterday. To be honest, I have made no effort to include him in anything. Whenever he visited my drafting table to ask for updates and offer support, I would busy my hands and tell him, "Later. Not here at work." But later would never come. I was desperate to manage the circus that my life had become without letting Glen see just how out of control it was. I thought that if he saw the chaos, he would leave.

My gaze drops to the floor, and he mistakes my guilt for reluctance. He hesitates before thrusting the small bouquet of carnations toward me.

"Hey, umm, Deb. It's okay if, you know, like, if you don't want...."

I wrap him in a full body hug, and the cashiers heckle us with wolf whistles.

"Take it to the back of the dining room," Val says in mock disapproval.

We go to our usual corner booth at the back of the dining room. I slide in first, and Glen squeezes his linebacker body in next to me. I apologize for keeping him pushed to the outside of my life, and he apologizes for not knowing what to do or how to fix it. In ten short minutes, we manage to find our way back to each other.

"So, do the police have any leads?"

"Oh my God, Glen! I haven't even told you. The FBI are on the case."

"The FBI? That's a big deal."

"They've already been to Mac's job and talked to all the neighbors. They said there were some credible leads they were going to follow up on."

"So maybe Tara will be able to use these pretty soon then." Glen slides the shopping bag over to me. Inside is a one-hundred-and-fifty-piece Lego set. "I thought we should start acting like she's back. You know, positive thinking and all that."

"She's going to love this."

"I know she's not into Barbie dolls, but I didn't want to get her a bucket of newts, either."

We laugh for the first time in weeks. Val lets my thirty-minute break stretch into forty-five before sending the fry cook out to tell us that the honeymoon is over.

I go to bed that night more hopeful than the night before. I leave the dinosaurs and potholders on the floor where they are, but I curl the Care Bear T-shirt to my chest before drifting off to sleep.

When the digital alarm clock starts buzzing, I slap the snooze button, but it keeps sounding the alarm, no matter how many times I slap it. Rolling over, I see the LED display reads 3:18 a.m.

It dawns on me that it is not the alarm clock making such a racket but the phone. I sit up and lift the receiver to my ear.

"Mummy?"

CHAPTER 39

Tapped Out

I spring out of bed, my bare feet hitting the floor with a hard thump. It takes a moment for me to find my breath, to speak without falling to pieces.

"Tara! It's Mummy. Where are you?"

She coughs, and I hear the dreaded accordion wheeze of asthma in her lungs when she takes a breath in to reply.

"Mummy, I need med-sin."

"Tell me where you are!"

I hear a shuffling sound like slippers on a dirty floor, followed by muffled voices, then nothing.

"Tara! Tara, can you hear me?"

"You're a stupid bitch," Mac's voice slurs as he speaks.

"Mac, where are you? Tara's having an asthma attack!"

"Yeah, no shit."

"She needs to go to the hospital."

"Yeah, she does, but I can't do that now, can I? All because you called the fuckin' FBI on me!"

"Mac, I didn't call anybody. You told some people you were going to Arizona, and—"

"Just shut the fuck up. You're gonna tell your fancy lawyer to write up an order giving me full custody, understand?"

"I don't know if I —"

"Shut up! You're gonna do it and get the fuckin' FBI off my ass or your whole family is gonna be sorry. I can wipe you all out with one phone call."

"But Mac, I —"

"I'm gonna call you in a few days. That custody order better be done by then."

The hum of a dial tone in my ear confirms the connection is severed. I stare at the heavy receiver in my hand, watching it shake. My legs begin to tremble, and I realize it is my body doing the shaking, not the phone, and collapse into a heap on the floor next to the bed.

A wave of cool air chills my sweat-soaked skin. Dad stands in the doorway, clutching at his shirt, Mom directly behind him. The air-conditioned jetstream from the main house surges into the attic, and I have to fight the urge to put my head down and go to sleep.

"What's all the racket?" Dad asks. "Did you fall out of bed, honey?"

"Tara called."

Mom gasps, cupping her cheeks with her hands. Dad remains frozen in the doorway.

"Mac knows the FBI are looking for him."

I attempt to pull myself up from the floor, but my legs are unsteady, and I sink back down. My parents help me onto the edge of the bed, and Mom sits beside me, somehow finding the wherewithal to retrieve a pen and paper. She makes notes of the phone conversation as I relay it to them. They both wince when I tell them about Tara coughing.

Tara's chronic asthma started early, just before her first birthday. It crept into her lungs one day and never left. Most of the time it seems to sleep, dormant in her small chest. Then she will cough, and the subtle rattle when she breathes in signals an impending two-week battle against bronchitis.

She is too young for an inhaler and must rely on a nebulizer, a shoebox-sized machine that delivers medicine in vapor form through a breathing tube. Sometimes her asthma is so severe that antibiotics or even steroids are used in conjunction with the nebulizer to help clear her airways.

Tara has none of this with her.

TAPPED OUT

• • •

The following day, I take a long lunch hour to meet Agents Berkman and Michaels at a local Ram's Horn restaurant. They request a corner booth on a deserted side of the restaurant, and we slide along the molded bench seats to face each other across the Formica tabletop.

"Your mom isn't coming?" Agent Michaels asks.

"Is she supposed to?"

Before he can reply, Mom materializes out of thin air and hefts her oversized handbag onto the table. She huffs, out of breath, when she slides in next to me.

"Sorry I'm late."

Agent Michaels asks me to relay the phone conversation with Mac first. Mom then fills in details from her notes about the call time and Mac's demand for a court order to give him full custody of Tara.

"He said he would call you again?" Agent Berkman asks.

"Yes, in a few days."

"This could lead to something significant," Agent Michaels says before turning to Mom. "Will you grant permission for us to place wire taps on your home phone?"

"You want to record our phone calls?"

"It is more involved than recording conversations, Mrs. Brannigan. It allows us to track where a phone call is coming from."

Mom and I turn toward each other, wearing identical smiles of hope, mixed with relief.

"Damned right I'll grant permission!"

Agent Michaels retrieves multiple forms from his leather satchel and explains the implications of consenting to a federal wiretap, as well as our rights and protections.

"Do you understand these forms as I've explained them to you?"

"Aye, I do. Where do I sign?"

Mom signs her name at the bottom of several forms, giving permission as the homeowner to have our phones monitored by the FBI. Agent Michaels tucks the signed forms back into his satchel, promising to

253

SQUIRREL PIE

fast-track them so they can begin monitoring calls as soon as tomorrow.

"I need you to keep Mac on the phone as long as possible, Debbie," he says. "The longer the connection, the better our chances are of locating him."

I nod my head but say nothing. The call last night was only a few minutes and left me crumpled on the floor. How am I going to endure anything longer when terror is gnawing at my gut and blocking my voice?

"Let's make a list," Agent Michaels says as he puts a blank piece of paper on the table and pulls a pen from his pocket protector. It's as if he intuited my fears.

Thirty minutes later, we walk out of the restaurant with a bullet-pointed list of questions to ask Mac. On the flip side is a list of credible answers to give when asked about filing a change in custody. I place the list on my bedside table, next to the phone, and we wait.

• • •

For the next three days, anytime the phone rings, we all jump out of our skins. Mom's conversations with her friends are not as lighthearted, knowing they are no longer private. Her brief responses sound like the choppy format of a morse code telegram — "Yes, no, okay."

At 10:00 p.m. on the fourth day, the phone rings. When Mom picks up the line in her bedroom and says hello, there's nothing but silence. She doesn't hang up but listens, hearing the faint sound of a TV in the background. She tells the silence that I'll be home from work at 1:00 a.m. and is answered by a soft click and then the dial tone.

Mom is waiting for me in the kitchen when I walk through the door in my wretched Hardee's uniform just after 1:00. She is certain that it was Mac who called and that he will call back soon. The list of questions and answers is in front of her on the table, and we wait together in tense silence. Shortly after 1:30 we give up, retreating to our bedrooms upstairs.

It is just after 2:00 a.m. when the phone wakes me from a shallow slumber.

"Hello?"

There is a long silence. The sound of weight shifting in a chair. More silence.

"Mac, is that you?"

"Who the fuck else is calling you at this time of night? Only a whore would have to ask who this is."

My body reacts to his verbal abuse with sweating palms and quickening heartbeat. I try to focus but start to panic when I realize the list with all my talking points is still on the kitchen table downstairs. I scan my memory, desperate to recall what I'm supposed to talk about.

Weather? Was weather on the list? No, but Agent Berkman did say that if Mac talked about a recent storm or if I heard heavy rain in the background, I should write it down.

"It's raining here," I blurt out, not thinking. "Is it raining where you are?"

"I didn't call to give you a fuckin' weather report, you idiot. Who told you to ask that?"

I am sinking fast with nothing to grab onto when I catch sight of my bedroom door inching open. Mom tiptoes to my side, placing the list of bullet points on the table next to me. The hollow of my chest starts to fill with confidence.

"Nobody. It's just that Tara's asthma gets worse when it's rainy, and I'm worried about her."

"She's fine! Right now, the only conversation I want to have is about the FBI and that goddamned custody order!"

I remember Agent Michaels' advice to use simple, one-word responses to make Mac talk more in order to get the answers he really wants.

"Okay."

"Okay, what?"

"What do you want to know?"

"What do I want to know? I want to know when the court order will happen! I want to know when the fuckin' FBI will pack up and go home. How about that for starters?"

I share the phone's earpiece with Mom, our foreheads touching. She points to the digital clock, and we share a small smile at Mac's long-winded tirade.

"My lawyer says it's not that simple, Mac."

"Tell your lawyer he'd better make it simple! I want something written up this week, you understand me?"

I scan the list of talking points and find the right response.

"How do I get the paperwork to you for a signature?"

"Well, uh, I'll —"

"Maybe a post office box?"

"Just get the paperwork going and I'll tell you how later."

"Okay."

"And the FBI, I want them off my ass now."

"Okay, I'll try."

Mac lets loose a long string of expletives, stitched together with insults and demands. Mom and I watch the red LED display of the alarm clock on the bedside table change from one number to the next.

"When I call you again, that custody paperwork had better be typed up or you will never see Tara again!"

"Is she still wheezing?"

The phone clicks, and the familiar dial tone hums.

Mom records the call time in her pocket-sized notepad, purchased specifically for this purpose, and we grin at the total. I managed to keep Mac on the line for seventeen minutes! With the FBI tracing this call, Mac will be in handcuffs before we know it, and then Tara will be safe at home again.

CHAPTER 40

On The Clock

Agent Michaels sits at our kitchen table, reviewing the phone record of Mac's seventeen-minute call. It has taken three days for the FBI to update us with their findings. I half-expected Tara to be with him today, sure they must have located and arrested Mac by now.

"It's a good start," he says.

"What do you mean 'a good start'?" Mom asks.

He continues shuffling pages of the report back and forth, marking certain line items with a red pen. I am about to repeat Mom's question to him when he lifts his eyes to look at us.

"Yes, it's a very good start."

"Do you know where Mac is?"

"Oh no. No, Debbie. We're just getting started."

I stare back at Agent Michaels, my disappointment obvious. I don't know what to say, and I look toward Mom.

"Are you saying seventeen minutes was'nae long enough?"

"It was a very good effort, Mrs. Brannigan, but you'll need to keep him on the line longer next time he calls."

"We thought you could trace where the calls came from." Mom's voice is steady, and her directness inspires me to chime back in.

"And why haven't you arrested Mac?" I ask.

"I'm sorry, I should have explained the process better. This isn't like what you see on TV."

Agent Michaels peels a sheet of lined paper from a legal pad and draws a crude map that encompasses New Baltimore and the south end of Detroit. He explains that the wiretap traces a call going from one Bell Telephone Company tower to the next.

"When you pick up the phone, the trace begins here." He colors a red circle on the makeshift map where New Baltimore is shown. "And the next tower is here." He colors another circle around Chesterfield. "And then it moves to the tower in Warren, onward to Detroit, before terminating here in Southgate."

"So he's in Southgate?" I ask.

"No, that's as far as the trace got before the call was terminated."

"Seventeen bleedin' minutes, and we did'nae get any further than Detroit? Is that what I'm hearing?"

"I'm afraid so, Mrs. Brannigan. Each tower requires several minutes to coordinate to the next one. Depending on how far away he is, it could take anywhere from thirty to sixty minutes to locate the call."

Mom pushes her chair away from the table and gets up. She paces the length of the kitchen, shaking her head and muttering "bloody waste of time." I am hollowed out by the realization that Tara has been gone for over a month now and will not be coming home anytime soon. I stare at my lap, forcing the knot in my chest down into my stomach.

I have learned to slip on an invisible suit of armor at times like this. Nothing penetrates the armor — no fear, no anxiety, no hollowed-out loss. Other emotions, like joy and hope, are forsaken too, but the numbness the armor provides allows me to move forward day after day, so I consider it a fair trade. Agent Michaels, however, seems confused by our reactions. He tells us that the phone record still reveals a lot of pertinent information, such as they now know that Mac hasn't traveled north into Canada.

Mom returns to her seat at the table, looking a little less defeated. Agent Michaels encourages us to watch the clock each time Mac calls and try to keep him engaged for at least thirty minutes.

Keeping my hand engulfed in flames for thirty minutes sounds less painful to me, and that night I lay atop my unmade bed, staring at the ceiling. The phone begins to ring at 1:22 am, and I record the time in Mom's mini notebook before picking up on the third ring.

"Hello?"

"Guess who."

I drop the phone to the floor and take my time picking it back up, a delay tactic Agent Berkman had suggested.

"Hello, Mac?"

"What the fuck was that?"

"I'm sorry. I fell out of bed trying to turn the lamp on."

"Pull your shit together! I'm not wasting any time."

"Okay, sorry."

Two minutes on the clock...

"Did you do what I told you?"

"You told me to do a few things, Mac. Which one are you asking about?"

"Jesus Christ! Are you really this stupid?"

"You mean the custody agreement?"

"Yes, you idiot, the custody agreement! And when will the FBI get called off?"

Four minutes on the clock...

I stick to the elaborate storyline fabricated by Agent Michaels, telling Mac that the papers are being drafted and will be finalized next week. I also ask him what I should do with them when they're ready, and the line goes quiet while he thinks.

"I want them mailed to my lawyer's office."

"Okay, do you have his address?"

"No, I don't have his fuckin' address. Jesus, your lawyer will have it! Stop dicking around."

Ten minutes on the clock...

"Okay, I'll make sure to ask —"

"Just shut up and listen! What have you done about the FBI?"

I play dumb and tell him I don't even know how to contact the FBI, that they are dealing with the police, not me. Mac lets loose a torrent of angry names, calling me a lying whore, a manipulative bitch, and a piece of shit mother.

"I don't know why I am even wasting time with you! I have people standing by, just waiting for me to give the word."

"What people?"

"They left a little white calling card in your mailbox. Maybe I'll give them a call tomorrow and have them start picking off your family, one by one. Who should go first? That piece of shit brother, or your spoiled brat sister?"

"You don't mean that!"

"Like hell I don't! Get the FBI off my ass and those papers to my lawyer now!"

Click. Dial tone. Sixteen minutes on the clock.

My hand trembles as pent-up emotion now avalanches through my nervous system. It takes several attempts for me to get the handset back in its cradle properly.

I lie back on my bed and stare at the ceiling, repeating all of Mac's words in my head. My insides feel shattered, and this call was shorter than the previous one. How much longer can I do this? What will he do with Tara? What will he do to my family?

I am still staring at the ceiling when the alarm goes off three hours later. The bed feels magnetized, pulling me into it. I peel my body up, change my shirt, and start another long workday.

• • •

There is not enough bad coffee to focus my eyes or clear my head at work. A third cup is half gone when Glen walks back to my drafting table.

"You look exhausted, Deb."

"I didn't sleep at all last night."

"You're not going to work tonight, are you?"

"I need the money, so yes."

"You need sleep more than money."

I'm about to list all the reasons why he is wrong when Victor passes by and wraps his knuckles on my table.

"Phone call, Debbie."

I look apologetically at Glen, who gives me a half smile and steps aside.

"Hello?"

"Hello, Debbie," Agent Michaels says. "I see there was another call logged early this morning. I haven't retrieved the transcript yet but thought I'd do a quick follow-up with you while it is fresh in your memory."

"Yes, Mac called around 1:30. It was only sixteen minutes long; I couldn't keep him talking."

"That's okay, just keep trying. Did you tell him the custody order is being drawn up?"

"I did, but I think he knows I'm lying. He seems to be more afraid of the FBI finding him."

"That's good. People make mistakes when they're afraid."

"But he said he was going to call the Devil's Disciples and have them kill my family!"

"You don't need to worry about that."

"But he said it would just take one phone call…"

"We've been in contact with them. A high-ranking member of their organization called to say they have no affiliation with Mr. McCall. They have never heard of him."

"Do you believe them?"

"Yes, I do. They don't get involved with child kidnappings and are quite agitated that Mr. McCall has lied about being a part of their organization and put them under the scrutiny of the FBI."

"So, none of it is true?"

"None of it. Mr. McCall should be more concerned about them finding him before we do!"

We talk for a few minutes about how I might keep Mac on the phone for longer durations. Agent Michaels emphasizes that, while these phone calls are hard, they are also a stroke of good luck. He jokes how the calls make their job a whole lot easier.

"One more thing, Debbie… About your private investigators."

"Have they been helping?"

"That's what I want to talk about. Can you take them off the case, please?"

"You mean fire them?"

"Call it what you will. But we need them off the case, as soon as possible."

"Why?"

"We have a very methodical approach to our investigations, and let's just say they hinder our efforts by riding bareback into town carrying a neon banner. They blow everybody's cover."

Anger stirs in my belly when I think of how many paychecks have been handed over to this couple. And then I realize it will be one less debt to carry on my back, so I feel a little lighter. I hang up the phone and walk to Glen's drafting board near the front of the room.

"Everything okay?" he asks.

"Oh, just an FBI manhunt and some kidnapping stuff. You know, the usual."

"I'm worried about you with all of this, Deb. It's too much."

"I know, and you're right about me needing more sleep. I'm going to call Val and have her put somebody else on my shift tonight."

"How about a night in? I can bring a movie and some carryout to the house?"

"It's a date."

That evening, Glen and I sit on the blue corduroy couch of our family room, eating pressed duck and lo mein noodles from cartons, our legs tangled beneath the velour blanket. He brings me up to date on how his fledgling body building gym is doing, then impersonates a few of our coworkers, causing Tab to shoot from my nose with a sudden burst of laughter.

The phone doesn't ring. There are no police knocking at the front door. No fire truck lights are beaming through the windows.

Glen wraps his massive arm around my shoulders, and I lay my head on his chest as the opening credits of *Back to the Future* play across the TV screen. My eyelids immediately begin to droop.

I awake to the morning alarm, in my bed, with Glen's blue hoodie draped across me. I linger in its warmth and musky scent, remembering last night's playfulness and sense of safety.

Will life ever get to be a series of only these simple moments?

I put my feet to the floor and begin another unpredictable day, with sincere hope that it will.

CHAPTER 41

Unlikely Ally

Unfortunately, pressed duck and a musk-scented hoodie prove to be no match against Mac's relentless phone campaign. My pit of despair digs deeper each day.

Over the next several weeks, the calls escalate in violence and occurrence but not in duration. He calls nearly every day, always around 1:00 or 2:00 a.m., and he always hangs up before the twenty-minute mark. Always.

"He knows we are closing in on him, Debbie," Agent Michaels says, attempting to reassure me. "It won't be long before we find him, or he gives himself up. Just keep doing what you're doing."

It has been over three months since I last saw Tara. The hope that had bubbled into my chest while sitting in Mr. Burtch's car now gurgles low in my belly, unable to breach the distance to my heart. The sense of loss suffocates me, along with the weight of staggering financial bills and primal terror every time the phone rings.

When the phone begins ringing at 3:20 on a Thursday morning, I put the receiver to my ear and brace for the verbal assault, but there is nothing. I say hello but get no response. Music plays softly at the other end, perhaps in a nearby room. Somebody is breathing into the phone, so I try again.

"Mac, can you hear me?"

"I can hear you alright."

His words stretch and wobble, slurred by far too much alcohol. I wait for him to launch into a new list of demands, but he remains silent. I watch the digital clock shift to another minute, hoping he has fallen asleep with the phone in his lap. I can barely hear him when he mumbles into the phone.

"I'm done fucking around with you."

"What do you mean?"

"I know your phones are tapped. I know you're not getting custody papers for me."

"Mac, I'm trying —"

"Just be quiet. I've decided to send Tara home."

Blind hope ignites before reason can extinguish it. Agent Michaels was right! Mac is giving up. I spring to my feet, locking the phone between my chin and shoulder so I can write down the pickup location for Tara.

"Thank you, Mac. Where can I pick her up?"

"I'm sending her to your front door."

"But, how —"

"She'll be in a box."

The sound of gunfire is so loud, I drop the phone.

When I return it to my ear, there is only a dial tone. I nest the receiver back into its plastic molded resting place and sit on the edge of the bed with my hands in my lap. I remain motionless until the alarm goes off an hour later, then get up and go to work.

I don't think about the call, and I don't talk about it. If I say the words out loud, then it will become real, and my psyche refuses to even consider that. Instead, I float somewhere above my body, tethered by some invisible string.

Detaching my mind from my body is a protective strategy I developed over years of violent beatings. It is a reflex, and quickly severs any emotions that become too hard to cope with. The detachment usually lasts just long enough to survive whatever is happening and its immediate aftermath, but this time, I don't think I will ever be able to reconnect my mind and body.

For three days, there are no phone calls.

My subconscious claws at me for acknowledgement. Three days without contact is surely confirmation that Mac shot Tara, and probably himself too. I am teetering on the brink of emotional collapse when the phone rings on Sunday afternoon.

"Debbie, it's Mary McCarty. Do you remember me?"

It takes just a moment for her name and face to register in my foggy brain. She is Mac's friend from Algonac, the woman who watched Ian and Tyan when I returned from the hospital after Tara's birth.

"Yes, I remember you."

"Mac called me this morning. He wants you to take a phone call from him at my place."

"He's alive?"

"Umm, yeah, he's alive."

"What about Tara? Did he…hurt her?"

"I don't think so. I heard her asking for a popsicle and she sounded just fine."

Something breaks free inside me, and an emotional eddy pulls me back into my body. A moan escapes my throat that doesn't sound human.

"Debbie, I don't know what in the hell Mac has been putting you through, but it's not right."

"He said he was sending Tara home in a box, and then he fired off a gun!"

"I'm so sorry. No parent should ever hear something like that."

Mary sits quietly while I sob awhile longer, then my breath finally evens out.

"Debbie, Mac said the FBI has your phone tapped. Is this true?"

I say nothing, unsure if I am permitted to reveal this information. I clear my throat then just sigh into the phone.

"I understand you probably can't talk about it. But please let the FBI know that I am willing to have my phone line tapped."

"Really? You would do that?"

"Yes, really. Mac sounds unstable and irrational. That child needs to come home."

• • •

Agent Michaels drops all professional decorum and lets out an uncharacteristic "Hell, yes!" when I give him the news. It takes a few days for him and Agent Berkman to meet with Mary and get the phone tap in place. Mac grows impatient and begins to call Mary every day, asking about arrangements. She does her best to placate him, saying she has been playing phone tag with me but is certain she will have a day and time for our call soon.

Mac isn't the only one growing impatient. I pester Agent Michaels daily about the new phone tap at Mary's and how much longer it will take. After four months of dead-end leads and tracing pointless calls, hope seems futile. But hope is all I have, and I'm betting it all on this new arrangement with Mary.

The following Sunday, Mary's tiny living room is packed with me, my parents, two special agents, and a suitcase that opens to reveal a reel-to-reel recording device. Mac said he would call at 1:00 p.m. and it is now 1:15.

We sit with our knees nearly touching, like sardines in a can, shifting awkwardly and making small talk. A large clock is visible in the adjoining kitchen, and we all take turns looking from it to the silent phone.

At 1:20 it begins to ring, and Agent Berkman slips on a headset as he pushes a button to begin recording. Agent Michaels motions for everyone to be quiet and then signals Mary to answer the phone.

"Hello, Mac? Yes, she's here. No, she came by herself, just like you asked."

Mary hands the phone receiver to me with a look that says, "You can do this."

"Hello?"

"How many times did you shit your pants after that last phone call?"

"I thought…I thought it was real."

"That was just a preview. Next time it will be real."

Mac speaks with renewed authority, demanding that I have all police charges against him dropped and get a judge to sign a new order that gives him full custody of Tara. He makes no attempt to hang up at the twenty-minute mark, certain that this call is not being traced.

He begins wrapping up his demands and insults after thirty minutes. Agent Michaels signals for me to keep him talking.

"Can I talk to Tara?"

"What for?"

"I'm not going to do anything for you until I know she is okay."

"Alright, hang on a minute."

The phone rustles, then is quiet. I look to Agent Michaels, and he gives me a thumbs-up. There is a shuffling at the other end of the phone and then Tara's sweet voice says, "Helwo."

"Tara, it's Mummy!"

"Are you coming to pick me up?"

"I'm trying, Tara."

"Okay, that's enough," Mac says, taking back the phone.

"I didn't even get to tell her I love her."

"You wanted to know she's okay, and now you know. You have one week to get everything I asked for or else!"

The line disconnects. Everyone in the room lets out a collective breath. Agent Michaels turns to Agent Berkman and asks how long the call lasted. Thirty-three minutes is his answer.

We all look to Agent Michaels hopefully, and he gives us the truth — the call still probably wasn't long enough to get an exact location.

"This can'nae continue," Mom says, putting into words what we are all thinking. "There must be another way."

For the next hour, we brainstorm ideas. Agent Berkman is wrapping the headset cord for the reel-to-reel, getting ready to pack it all up, when Mary's phone begins to ring. All eyes turn to Mary, who shrugs and says, "No idea." Agent Berkman reconnects the reel-to-reel and puts the headset back on. The room falls silent as she picks up the receiver.

"Hello?"

"Hey, it's me."

Mac's voice plays over the recorder. Berkman turns a knob to lower the volume while adjusting the headset cord. Agent Michaels waves him off, signaling for him to stop moving, and we all huddle around the suitcase, straining to hear Mac's end of the conversation.

"Hey, Mac. I wasn't expecting you to call back so soon."

"Did she leave?"

"Yeah, she didn't stick around. She seemed pretty shook up."

"Good! Maybe that will light a fire under her ass and get the Feds off mine. I swear to God, Mary, if they get any closer, they'll be dragging two dead bodies out of here."

"You've said that before, Mac, and I don't want to hear it again, understand?"

"Yeah, okay. Sorry. Look, I called to ask a favor. I'm in a real bind."

"What do you need?"

"This piece of shit car broke down, and I have no money. I mean like *no* money—we're eating cereal for dinner."

"I can give you some money, Mac. Do you want me to wire it?"

"No, that'll leave a trail. Besides, I need a ride too. I know it's a lot to ask, but could you bring it to me tomorrow?"

"Sure, Mac. Just tell me where you are and I'll be there."

"Okay, do you have a pencil?"

"I sure do."

CHAPTER 42

Joy Ride

Mary hangs up and tears a sheet from her small memo pad beside the phone. She presents it to Agent Michaels. Scrawled in pencil is *1009 Marietta Street, Zanesville, Ohio.* "That should help things," she says with a wry grin.

Mary has just accomplished what months of FBI surveillance, private investigators, and phone taps had failed to do — get an exact address. The cramped living room erupts with cheers and hugs all around. Tears threaten to spill over, but I blink them back, determined not to feel hope again until Tara is safe at home.

Agent Michaels tempers our celebratory mood with his stereotypical seriousness. He wants to formulate a detailed plan, right now.

"He's expecting you to arrive in your car tomorrow," he says, gazing directly at Mary. "Are you willing to make that trip with federal agents tailing you?"

In a millisecond I compile the reasons why she wouldn't agree to such a heavy request. For starters, she is Mac's friend, not mine. I also consider the many times she helped with Ian and Tyan, yet I cannot summon a single memory where we repaid the favor.

Time hangs suspended while Mary stares at the floor, considering the request. When she looks up, it is me her eyes fall on, and my stomach clenches, certain she is going to decline.

"You bet your ass I am. That child needs to be at home with her mother."

Only Mary will accompany the agents to the Marietta Street address. One civilian is more than enough for the FBI to worry about. My parents and I are told to go home and stay close to the phone.

SQUIRREL PIE

• • •

The six-hour drive begins at 9:00 the following morning. Agent Michaels leads the way across the Ohio state line in an unmarked vehicle. They reach Zanesville just after 3:00 p.m. and rendezvous with federal agents from the Cincinnati field office, along with local police officers.

Mary is briefed on how to proceed. Federal agents will go first, parking on Marietta Street in unmarked cars. Zanesville police cars will be on the next block, waiting to be called to the scene. Mary will wait fifteen minutes before driving down the street and arriving at the address Mac gave her.

Everyone is in place when Mary rolls her beat-up Chevy down Marietta Street and parks along the curb at #1009. Mac appears in the doorway of the house as she exits the car. He lingers behind the screen door, hesitant to step outside, but Mary draws him out by holding up several grocery bags and signaling that there are more in the backseat.

He meets her in the middle of the front yard, and federal agents erupt from several cars, encircling them with guns drawn and yelling for them to get down on the ground with their hands behind their heads.

Mac and Mary are handcuffed by local police who are now on the scene with lights flashing. Uniformed officers outnumber federal agents as they keep neighbors off the property and reroute traffic.

A female officer sweeps the house and finds Tara hiding under a kitchen table. She coaxes her out with a stuffed bear and the words, "Your mom has been looking for you."

Agent Michaels slides into the passenger seat of an unmarked federal vehicle while an agent from the Cincinnati field office radios an update from the driver's seat. Mac slouches in the backseat, but as Agent Michaels closes the door and slides into the front of the car, Mac sees Mary being pushed into a police cruiser, her hands cuffed behind her back.

"What's going to happen to her?" he asks.

Agent Michaels ignores the question and turns sideways in his seat to face Mac and advise him of his rights.

"Would you like to make a statement?"

"No."

"Alright, you will now be taken to Columbus and arraigned on federal charges of kidnapping."

"I just want to know what you're going to do to my friend."

"We haven't decided what to charge her with yet."

"She didn't know about any of this, I swear it."

"I guess we'll find that out when we talk to her."

Agent Michaels shakes hands with the agent in the driver's seat, congratulating him on the successfully executed plan, and then exits the vehicle. With a nod and a wave, the driver pulls the car away from the curb and heads toward Franklin County Jail with Mac.

Mary is transported to the local Hilton hotel, where she enjoys a night of champagne toasts with federal agents in the penthouse suite.

• • •

Mom, Dad, and I have been sitting at the kitchen table for hours, anxious and not saying much. Mom has kept a close watch on the clock, giving vague updates throughout the day.

"Nine o'clock. Mary should be in Mt. Clemens soon..."

"Eleven o'clock. They'll be crossing the Ohio border about now..."

"Three o'clock. We should be hearing something soon..."

At 4:30 p.m. the phone begins to ring. We stare at each other, afraid to move.

"Go on, love," Mom says. "That'll be for you."

"Hello?"

"Debbie, we got him!" Agent Michaels's voice crackles with excitement. "Mr. McCall is on his way to jail."

"What about Tara? Where is she?"

"She is with Child Protective Services in Zanesville. You can pick her up anytime."

I look at my parents, and they look back at me, eager for information, but I can't speak. Tears cascade down my cheeks, and I simply nod my head.

"Praise Jesus!" Mom shouts.

"Debbie? Are you still there?"

All the emotions I've buried over the last few weeks, months, and even years, decide it's time to attempt an escape. They get tangled in my throat, and when words will not come, I hand the phone over to Dad. Mom puts an arm around my shoulders, and I bury my face into her neck, allowing everything out in uncontrolled sobs.

"There, there, love. It's all over now."

Thirty minutes later, Dad and I back the car out of the driveway. We arrive in Zanesville close to midnight and get a room at a local hotel. First thing in the morning we drive to the Child Protective Services facility.

The brick building has no features other than the long narrow windows that run vertically beside the glass entry doors. The small lobby is equally unremarkable, with its six feet of tile floor ending at a reception window. Next to the window is a sturdy metal door with no doorknob.

For a moment, I wonder if Agent Michaels mistakenly gave me the address to Franklin County Jail, but then a pony-tailed young woman wearing tortoise shell glasses slides the shatterproof heavy glass window open with an audible woosh.

"Good morning! Can I help you?"

"I'm here to pick up Tara Brannigan. She was brought in yesterday."

"You must be "Mummy" then?" she replies with a wink.

"That's me. I'm her mom."

"I'll need to photocopy your driver's license, please."

I dig through my purse in a panic. *Is it with my Hardees uniform? Have I really come all this way and now I won't be able to leave with Tara?* I'm about to break into tears when my fingertips brush the smooth square of plastic, flat against an inside pocket. I hand it to her through the glass partition.

She flips the license from front to back. "Michigan, huh?" she says to nobody, then turns to make a copy before handing it back to me.

"Tara's been asking for you. We love that she calls you 'Mummy'."

"It's a Scottish thing, I guess."

Dad steps forward, ready to cut these pleasantries short.

"Is there a form to fill out? We'd like to get the wee'an home as soon as possible."

The woman practically squeals at the sound of Dad's heavy accent. She hands me a form with a clipboard and pen while giving Dad a full account of her own Scottish ancestry.

I fill out the short form, irritated that I am writing down all the same information that appears on my driver's license. She looks it over and smiles, telling us that Tara will be out in just a few moments. Then she slides the glass pane closed and picks up the phone.

There are no chairs to sit on and only public service posters on the walls. The Food Pyramid is the only one with actual art to look at, with its familiar loaves of bread, plates of spaghetti, and homemade pies. Dad and I stare at it for what seems like forever and then begin to pace.

Time moves so slowly that it seems to be going backwards, and I begin to think that something is wrong. Maybe Tara isn't even here. Maybe she is lost in the system. Maybe she is at some other facility and it will take weeks to locate her.

Finally, we hear multiple latches click from the other side of the metal door, and then the door creaks open. A heavy-set woman with streaks of premature gray hair steps into the lobby. A curled-up child sits perched atop her bent forearm. The child's face is buried in the woman's neck, revealing only the dark brown shadow of a boy's crew cut hairstyle. Dirty Keds sneakers dangle below red Toughskins jeans.

I glance at Dad and see the look of disbelief on his face. He's probably thinking the same thing I am, that they've brought the wrong child out. My emotions begin to teeter between anger and utter helplessness.

"Look, Tara, who is that?" the woman asks.

The child is clutching a small police teddy bear to its chest and looks up with uncertainty at the woman. Our eyes meet, and I see her. It's Tara.

"Mummy, did you come to get me?"

I try not to cry but Dad beats me to it, "greeting like a wee wane" behind me. The social worker places Tara into my outstretched arms, and I hug her a little too tightly. Dad embraces us both, pressing his forehead to mine.

We cry tears of joy and relief until Tara wriggles between us, protesting that we are squishing her. She looks from Dad to me with a puzzled expression.

"Mummy, are you crying because you missed me too much?"

"Yes, Punkinhead, I missed you so much."

"Can we go home now?"

"We sure can. Let's go."

CHAPTER 43

Karma Bus

Within days, Mac is extradited to Michigan and held in county jail. Although I'm not required to appear at his arraignment hearing, I take a day off work to attend. I'm not about to miss the sword of justice finally swinging down on Mac.

I take a seat near the front of the courtroom, next to Mr. Burtch. He has a full day of court appearances scheduled, but like me, he wouldn't miss this day for anything. I may have hired him to be my lawyer, but he is a caring advocate and my biggest cheerleader.

"What did I miss, Mr. Burtch?"

"Nothing yet. They'll be bringing him out soon. How do you feel about seeing him?"

Before I can respond there is a shuffle in the courtroom and a door opens. Mac is led in by a uniformed officer. His orange jumpsuit is too large, giving him the appearance of a child in its father's pajamas. Handcuffs bind his wrists together at the waist.

His thick mane of wavy brown hair was cut off while he was on the run, and now blunt, uneven ends hang just below his ears. The bushy beard that occupied most of his face is gone, too, revealing a weak chin and slight overbite.

"Is that really him?"

"Not quite how you remember him, eh, Debbie?"

I stare at this version of Mac in disbelief. This can't be the man who terrorized me for six years, not this fragile creature. I silently chide myself for not seeing beyond the motorcycle bad ass disguise he wore all those years.

Mac scans the courtroom while his handcuffs are removed. His eyes land on me for a split second, then fall back to the floor. He looks ashamed, and empathy starts to swell inside me, but recedes when I recall him saying Tara was coming home in a box.

He stands mute, invoking his Fifth Amendment right, pleading neither guilty nor innocent. The judge sets bond at twenty-five thousand dollars and Mac is led out the same door he entered in. There are no cries for mercy and not a single reprimand from the judge. Everything is handled with perfunctory efficiency, leaving me a bit disappointed.

"That was uneventful," I say as Mr. Burtch and I exit the courtroom.

"These hearings usually are."

"Well, at least he was slapped with a twenty-five-thousand-dollar bond. I know Mac doesn't have that kind of money."

"You should know that he only needs to come up with ten percent of that amount, Debbie." Mr. Burtch has come to a full-stop and is facing me.

"Ten percent? You mean he only needs twenty-five-*hundred*-dollars?"

"I'm afraid so. Mac will probably be out on bond today or in the next couple of days."

My jaw drops open, and Mr. Burtch tries to reassure me that the conditions of his bond forbid Mac from making any contact with me, my family, or Tara. He has mistaken my reaction as fear when, in fact, it is my indignation that the sword of justice is nothing more than a butter knife.

• • •

Tara's fourth birthday arrives just three days after Mac's release from jail. We host a small celebration at the kitchen table with homemade birthday cake and a few neighborhood kids. I keep one eye on the backyard as I hand out cake and ice cream.

Steve sits on the garden swing with his boom box cassette player and a baseball bat at his side. Dad paces up and down the hallway to the front door, looking out to the street. Mom watches him, biting her lower lip.

We are all on high alert, waiting for Mac to crash the party, but Mac never appears.

A week goes by, then two. When Thanksgiving comes and goes without incident, we begin to relax. I still jump whenever the phone rings, but I have stopped constantly checking my rear-view mirror while driving to work.

The dinner rush is in full swing at Hardees when Val comes to the front line and puts a hand on my shoulder.

"There's a call for you, Debbie."

"Who is it?"

"I didn't ask. Some lady."

Val motions with a tilt of her head toward the back and tells me I can take the call in her office. She takes the paper bag from my hands and barks to the fry cook, "Still waiting on that mushroom-Swiss burger. Let's step it up back there."

I walk to her tiny office at the back of the building. A large window looks out to the fry line, and stained coffee cups line the windowsill like prison guards along a watch tower. I pick the phone receiver up from where it is resting on last year's desk calendar.

"Hello?"

"Debbie? It's me, Dee-Dee."

"Hey, Dee-Dee, it's been a long time. What's up?"

"Mac wanted me to ask if it would be okay to drop off some Christmas gifts for Tara."

"Dee-Dee, he's not allowed to have any contact with me or Tara."

"I know. That's why he wanted me to check and see if it'd be okay for me to bring them to you at work."

I hesitate, unsure of what to do.

"You don't have to tell Tara who they're from, Debbie."

"Alright. You can bring them on my break at 8:00 tonight. But be sure Mac isn't with you because my boyfriend will be here."

"I don't think he would hurt your boyfriend."

"Dee-Dee, my boyfriend is 6'5" and weighs 250 pounds. I'm not worried about Mac hurting him. It's the other way around."

She tries not to laugh but does so anyway and says she'll be there at 8:00 p.m.

SQUIRREL PIE

• • •

At 7:55 p.m. Mac walks into the lobby.

His hair has grown since I last saw him handcuffed in the courtroom. It is now pulled back into a stubby, barely-there ponytail, and the weak chin lies dormant beneath his familiar full beard. The studded belt, chain wallet, and biker boots have all been restored, but Mac looks odd and immature, like a tadpole that just sprouted its back legs.

He strides over to my register with a garbage bag full of stuffed animals in one hand.

"I think I'll just wait here for your Big. Bad. Boyfriend," he snarls in my direction at the register, over-enunciating each word. He tosses the garbage bag full of stuffed animals into a booth near the condiment bar and slides in next to it.

Clearly, Mac does not believe I have a boyfriend. He's in violation of the court order, and I should call the police, but I don't. The law has shown that they don't take a young woman seriously, and I don't feel like being dismissed as the hysterical *little lady* anymore. I feel anxious, but a larger part of me is excited because I'm eager to see Mac's face when Glen walks through those double doors.

I don't have to wait long. Glen is right on time, and I walk him to the back of the dining area. We slide into our regular corner booth, and he makes half a cheeseburger disappear in one bite before pulling me into a hug. He kisses the top of my head, and I steal a glance down the aisleway. Mac is visibly shaken, trying to make himself smaller in the booth.

"He's here, Glen."

"Who's here?"

"Tara's dad, Mac. He's here."

Glen puts down what's left of his burger. He sits up straight and scans the dining room.

"Which one?"

"Glen, I promised Val you wouldn't cause any problems. Please don't start anything."

"I won't start anything, I promise. Now where is he?"

Glen's jaw is clenched so tight I think his teeth might crumble into dust. I hesitate, and Glen repeats his promise not to start trouble.

"The guy with the unibrow, next to the condiment bar."

Glen rises without a word, clutching his plastic food tray. He saunters up the aisle and stops at the condiment bar. Then he slams the tray down onto the counter and Mac jumps in his seat.

Glen stares hard at Mac, who looks at his motorcycle boots on the floor. Without taking his eyes off him, Glen grabs a fist full of condiments and slams them onto the tray. Then another fist full. Then another. Each time he slams the tray, Mac flinches.

Once the tray is piled high with packets of mustard and ketchup, Glen picks it up, takes one step and then drops it on to the Formica table in front of Mac. Condiment packets jump and scatter around the table and into Mac's lap.

"Here you go, pal. Eat up."

Mac does not raise his head or utter a word. Glen bends over and curls the knuckles of both fists onto the table, like a great silverback gorilla.

"If you *ever* come near Debbie again, I will beat you into the dirt—and six feet under it."

I watch from the back of the dining room, recalling the many times Mac loomed over me as I flinched and cowered. He collides with his own karma bus now, and I can't stop the grin creeping across my face. The hammer of retribution is more satisfying than any sword of justice.

Glen returns to our corner booth and pulls me into his chest, kissing the top of my head once more. He took no more than three strides before Mac sprang from his table and vanished out the lobby doors.

"You won't be seeing him around anymore."

I soften into this fortress of a man, hoping he is right.

CHAPTER 44

Last Call

One Styrofoam-stuffed pink bear is salvaged from the trash bag Mac left behind in the Hardee's dining room. The other items are dropped into a Salvation Army donation box. For days I debate whether to give Tara the pink bear. On Christmas Eve, I sit beside her on the bed and present it to her.

"This is from your dad."

"My daddy sent this to me?"

"Yes, he wants you to have a merry Christmas."

"Is he coming over?"

"No, Punkinhead. You might not see your dad for a long time."

"That's okay, Mummy. I don't like sleeping in Daddy's car."

Downstairs the front door opens, and Mark's booming voice rolls down the hallway.

"Ho! Ho! Ho! Anybody home?"

"Uncle Mark is here!"

Tara places the pink bear in the rocking chair and scampers downstairs to be scooped up by her Air Force uncle.

•••

Snow and trepidation blanket our house on Christmas morning. Only Tara seems unaware of the anxiety around her. She sits cross-legged at the Christmas tree with Lucky Bear at her side, mesmerized by its plastic limbs draped in tinsel and more blinking lights than the Vegas strip.

The unnamed pink bear from Mac never stood a chance against the faded green glory of Lucky Bear.

Mark is home on a two-week leave, and Glen shows up early in the morning with a box of gifts. They are additional reinforcements to our domestic infantry unit, and we fan out to double-check locked doors and look for footprints in the snow around the house before joining Tara in the living room.

Dad secures the belt of his full-length robe and sits on the floor. He plays Santa Claus, reading names off tags and handing out gifts. Tara kneels, bouncing up and down with excitement each time a gift is handed to anybody.

When small pyramids of colorfully wrapped boxes sit before everyone, Dad looks around the room, holding a dramatic pause as we wait for him to give the signal. With a half grin, he announces, "Ready… Steady… GO!"

We toss aside bows, tear into the boxes, and display our gifts as we open them, slipping on new flannel pajamas, slippers, and Detroit Red Wings sweatshirts as they're unwrapped. Murmurs of thanks from the adults mingle with giggles of delight from MaryAnne and Tara.

Suddenly, Tara leaps to her feet. "Mummy, I made you something."

She runs up the stairs and returns moments later with a handmade card. It is laminated, with pressed violet flowers on the front. Inside, there is a slanted blue crayon inscription:

*It's Christmas time and
there are presents for you
and presents for me.
But who really cares
when you are right here
with me. I love you.*

Glen reads along over my shoulder, and we are dumbstruck by the simple yet profound words. "Are you sure that kid of yours is only four years old, Deb?" he asks, his voice cracking.

I try to answer, but nothing is getting past the knot in my throat. My hands flutter at my eyes in a useless gesture to quell the tears that have already breached the rims.

It is the best Christmas day I've ever had.

• • •

The warm afterglow of Christmas recedes as the reality of my eighty-hour work week seeps back in. I pick up shifts for the extra ten cents-per-hour holiday bonus. New Year's Eve is the busiest night of the year for the drive-thru, and New Year's Day is the slowest. I work both.

By January third I have worked nine days in a row and am eager to wrap up my shift. I have barely spent any time with Mark, who heads back to Edwards Air Force base in just a few days, but I have tomorrow off and am looking forward to reminiscing with my little brother about our childhood super-hero days as the infamous Avon Street Mustard Men. At 10:00 p.m. Val locks the main lobby doors. It is now drive-thru only until 6:00 a.m., and only three people remain in the building — me, Val, and the fry cook, Phyllis, a middle-aged Polish woman who rarely speaks a word to anybody.

It's a relatively quiet night for a Friday. Val takes over the drive-thru window, sending me off to clean the restrooms. I am pushing the roller bucket of ammonia water into the second stall when Val comes bursting in. Her hands are flailing like a kite trapped in a tree.

"Val, what is it? What's wrong?"

"It's, it's, oh my gosh, Debbie."

"Val, take a breath. You're scaring me."

"Your ex, the guy with the beard, I think he just came through the drive-thru."

I flash back to Phyllis taking trash out to the dumpster about an hour ago.

"Oh my God, Val, the back door!"

Val darts through the dining room and disappears into the back. I check the side doors. They are all locked, and I meet Val near the fry line as she returns from the back of the building.

"Good call, Debbie. The back door was unlocked."

Phyllis watches us with quiet curiosity. Val does her best to reassure her that everything is going to be okay, but it's unnecessary, since Phyllis doesn't appear to be the least bit concerned.

"Is trouble?" she asks Val calmly.

"I'm not sure. Maybe. There was a man in the drive-thru that could be a problem."

"Is no trouble," Phyllis replies.

She turns to pick up the large metal turner used to flip burgers. Phyllis is a stout woman, and her meaty hand swings the turner in a hacking motion, like an axe.

"Is no trouble," she repeats.

Val and I laugh nervously as Phyllis returns to her task of cleaning the large griddle without another word. We inch our way to the front of the building, then over to the dining area, out of ear shot.

"So, I guess Lizzie Borden has been my fry cook for the last three years?" Val quips.

We laugh softly, but I suspect Val is just as comforted to have Phyllis there as I am. We circle the dining room, triple-checking the doors and peering out to the parking lot.

When the drive-thru buzzer squawks, Val insists on taking the order. I return to my abandoned mop and bucket in the restroom. When I have finished cleaning, I return to the register at the drive-thru, ready to take over from Val.

"Why don't you go home early, Debbie?"

"Really?"

"Yeah, go on home and get some rest. I've got this."

I take her up on the offer, eager for the extra hour of sleep. I stuff my brown Hardees hat into my purse and fish out my car keys. Val makes me show them to her before she unlocks the main lobby door and waits until I am in my car, just ten feet away, before locking it again. When I turn on the headlights, she gives a thumbs-up and disappears back into the restaurant.

Interior lights are still on inside the house when I pull up out front. From the front door stoop, I can see and hear Mark laughing inside. He leans against the kitchen sink with a bottle of beer in one hand, talking to somebody out of sight.

When I step through the door, he raises both arms in the air and lumbers down the hallway to wrap me in a bear hug. "Deb! You're home early. Come see who's here."

Mark leaves his arm around my shoulders as he guides me into the kitchen where his former rock band members are scattered around the table. Half empty beer bottles rise in the air to greet me in a welcome home salute.

They tell me to join them, offering cheap beer to lure me in. I decline, saying I am just too tired to stay awake any longer. Halfway up the stairs to bed, I realize that I finally understand the term "bone weary."

The kerosene heater casts an orange glow of tranquility over the attic bedroom. Tara is curled into Lucky Bear, eyes skittering below her lids in a deep REM sleep. My body melts in gratitude when I slip under the covers with her.

Within moments of closing my eyes, the phone begins to ring. It rings only twice before Mark picks it up in the kitchen. My lids lower once again, assuming the call is from another one of Mark's many friends. *They'll be up until daybreak*, I think as I doze off.

A knocking on the bedroom door wakes me. I'm still trying to decide if it is real or imagined when the door creaks open and Mark pokes his head inside.

"Deb? You awake?"

"I am now."

"Sorry, but there's a call for you. Some woman named Dee-Dee with a message about Mac. I told her not to bother you with any bullshit, but she says it's urgent. Do you want to talk to her?"

"Yeah, I'll take it."

I sit up and pull the phone from the nightstand table. Mark retreats to the kitchen and picks up the receiver from where he left it on the table.

SQUIRREL PIE

"Deb, you there?"

"Yeah."

"Okay, I'm hanging up down here. If it's bullshit, Deb, just hang up."

"Thanks, Mark. I got it."

A soft click lets me know he has hung up the kitchen phone.

"Hello, Dee-Dee?"

"Hi, Debbie. Sorry it's so late, but I need to get a phone number for Mac's parents. He's been shot and an ambulance is taking him to the hospital."

"Dee-Dee, is this more mind games from Mac? Did he put you up to this?"

"Debbie, I wouldn't do that. You know me better than that."

"I thought I did until he showed up at Hardees after our last phone call."

"You think I set you up? He used me to find out when your break was, then said he was going himself. I tried to talk him out of it, but you know this man does what he wants."

I sit with her words and turn them over, trying to gauge the sincerity in them.

"Think about it, Debbie. I have five children of my own. I don't have time for games. This is serious."

"Okay, give me a minute."

I throw back the blankets and swing my legs onto the floor. My small address book is in a dresser drawer, and it takes me a few minutes to locate it in the dark.

Dee-Dee writes down the number and thanks me again for taking the call at such a late hour. I tell her that it's okay and I hope it all works out for his parents' sake. I hang up the phone, still not convinced there is an actual emergency but also not concerned enough to keep from falling back asleep.

The gauzy light of pre-dawn is growing under the window curtains when the phone rings again. Mark's friends have left, and the house is quiet. A glance at the alarm clock tells me it is barely after 6:00 am. I pick up when it becomes clear nobody else will.

"Hello?"

"Debbie? Is that you?"

I hear the soft click of somebody picking up on another phone in the house and assume it is Mom.

"Yeah, this is Debbie. Who is this?"

"It's me, Chief. I wanted to let you know that your troubles are over."

"What do you mean?"

"Charles McCall was pronounced dead on arrival from a gunshot wound at Mt. Clemens General Hospital early this morning."

CHAPTER 45

Final Bill

Fifty pounds of anxiety, fear, and stress seem to lift from my shoulders when I hang up the phone. I swing my bedroom door open, and Mom emerges from another door down the hallway. We rush toward each other, hugging and jumping in circles, creating our own one-of-a-kind victory dance.

"I can't believe it, Mom!"

"Thank God! That snake will nae bother us again."

Our hallway reverie halts abruptly a few minutes later when Mom goes still.

"We should'nae be celebrating like this, Deborah. His mother will be mourning right now."

Visions of Mac's mother, Jan, rush into my mind. I imagine his three sisters trying to console her while mourning the loss of their brother at the same time. The reverberance of grief lands closer to home as I think of Ian and Tyan, and then the jolt hits me. *How do I tell Tara?*

Mac's sister, Ruthie, calls the next day with details about his funeral, along with a simple request that Tara be there. The family would really appreciate it, she tells me.

I struggle with the idea for two days. The voice of resentment inside me says I don't owe their family anything. But deep down, my heart knows that Mac's family has always treated me kindly. Well, maybe not James, but the rest of them.

On the morning of the funeral, I make a snap decision to go. Mac was Tara's father, after all, and this is her only chance to say goodbye. I can use the six-hour drive to explain death, funerals, and forever to a four-year-old.

Tara was labeled an old soul at birth by the hospital nurses, and it fits. She seems to ponder the world rather than get caught up in it, and her inquisitive gaze conveys the notion that she figured things out decades ago and is waiting for everyone else to catch up. She casts this gaze at me now from the passenger seat of the beat-up blue Astre.

"Do you know why we are going to Ohio today, Tara?"

"To see my daddy."

"Yes, that's right."

"Will Ian and Tyan be there too?"

"I think so, but I want to talk to you about your daddy right now."

"Okay, Mummy."

"Your daddy is not going to be able to talk to you or play with you. Do you know what it means when somebody dies?"

Tara knits her brows together and fidgets. She takes Lucky Bear from beside her and puts him in her lap, facing her. She kisses his nose and see-saws his arms up and down. It seems she is avoiding my question, but then she sighs and puts Lucky face down across her knees as if he is on a time out.

"Do you mean like Quasimodo?"

Quasimodo was a bubble-eyed goldfish that roamed a one-hundred-gallon aquarium in the living room until a few weeks ago, when he floated, lifeless, back and forth across the water's surface all morning until Mom scooped him out with a net. She held him poised above the toilet bowl, but Tara and MaryAnne discovered her and howled in protest. They placed him in a tissue-lined box and gave him a somber burial in the garden amongst the marigolds.

"Yes, Quasimodo died. People die, too, and that's what happened to your daddy."

Tara turns her head and stares out the passenger side window. She returns Lucky to his position under her arm in a loving choke hold, then turns back to me.

"How did he die?"

I found out only the vaguest details of what happened that night. Mac was living with a friend and his wife. After a night of heavy drinking, Mac let this friend know that he'd been sleeping with his wife for weeks. The man decided to end the affair with a shotgun blast to Mac's neck.

Chief speculates that Mac committed a passive suicide by revealing the affair while knowing a shotgun sat mere feet away. I think back to that night and wonder if it really was Mac that came through the Hardee's drive-thru just hours before being shot. Did he hope to see me one more time? If so, did he have the shotgun or his revolver with him?

I'll never know, because I don't want to know. All I want is to close the whole chapter behind us. I tell Tara I'm not sure how her daddy died and decide that she can learn any details later.

Much later.

• • •

Ian and Tyan run from the doors of the country church when we pull up, mere minutes before the funeral begins. They each clasp one of Tara's hands, and I follow the trio inside.

Ruthie stands just inside the door, greeting people and directing them to take a seat in the chapel area. She is talking to an elderly couple when we enter, and I nod as we pass by. She waves and mouths the words "Thank you," and we head toward the seats that Ian has saved for us.

The simple service wraps up just an hour later, and people funnel out to their cars. A few congregate around Jan, clasping her hands and promising to say prayers on Mac's behalf. She is shattered by the loss, and her eyes look from face to face, as if pleading for somebody to tell her this isn't really happening. Mom was right. This is nothing to celebrate.

Tara and I have a six-hour return trip ahead of us, so we make our rounds with the family to say goodbye. They are all gracious and welcoming, seeming to melt at the sight of Tara holding hands with her siblings.

When I can no longer delay our goodbyes to Mac, I head toward the open casket at the front of the room. Mac's hair is splayed across his collar bone, covering any trace of damage from the shotgun blast. He wears a suit, and it makes me wonder why he never chose to wear one in life because he looks so serene and dignified.

SQUIRREL PIE

I expect to feel some level of grief at the sight of him lifeless in a casket, but I don't. Any trace of intimate feelings I once had were beaten out of me over the last six years, and all I feel now is peace.

I hoist Tara onto my hip and tell her to say goodbye to her daddy. She leans over Mac in the casket and waves her hand. "Bye-bye, Daddy." Then she squirms free and runs off, hand in hand with Ian, to the lawn outside.

• • •

The weeks following Mac's funeral seem like an intermission — as if a curtain has come down and the entire set is being changed out. Judges, courtrooms, and federal agents are replaced with friends, movie nights, and laughter. There is a cosmic push broom sweeping Mac from center stage.

Mr. Burtch meets me at the municipal building one last time to help me get an official death certificate for Mac. We walk out of the county clerk's office with two copies, one of which will accompany the application for Tara's Social Security benefits.

We go to the same restaurant where Mr. Burtch has treated me to lunch several times. It has a catchy name — The Jury Box — and is always full of courthouse clientele. There are paper doilies under the water glasses and linen napkins to lay across your lap. He always picks up the tab, and I always order a side salad, just in case he doesn't.

"Well, Debbie," Mr. Burtch says after the waitress leaves the table. "I can honestly say this was a case unlike any other I've had."

We recount the highlights of the previous ten months with equal parts disbelief, humor, and nostalgia as we clean our plates. The waitress slides the bill discreetly onto the table when we're finished, and Mr. Burtch picks it up immediately.

"I've got this."

"Thank you, Mr. Burtch. Again."

"It's always my pleasure, Debbie. I suppose you won't be needing my services anymore."

FINAL BILL

"I guess not."

"I had my assistant draw up your bill. Pay what you can when you can."

He pulls a white envelope from his breast pocket and slides it across the table to me. My mouth goes dry. I have been dreading this bill for months. During the chaos of the kidnapping, I had asked for a bill from him several times, afraid of being caught off guard by yet another large expense. He always told me I had other things to worry about, and we'd square up at the end.

Now here we are, at the end. I slide the envelope into my purse, too afraid to acknowledge the debt in public. I decide to open it in my car and have my panic attack in private.

We hesitate on the sidewalk in front of the restaurant, both of us awkward with our goodbyes.

"Good luck to you, Debbie. Remember, you won't be in fast food forever."

"I hope you're right, Mr. Burtch."

We head in opposite directions to our parking spots. I sit for a long time in my little blue car, silently adding up my current debts. The private investigator couple sued me for breach of contract after being fired, and I'm now paying monthly installments over the next three years. I also have payments to social services for another ten years, and the increase to my rent has left me with a deficit each payday.

My chest constricts as I begin to calculate the legal bill in my head. At $75 an hour, it is going to be well over $10,000. I picture myself at age fifty still wearing a Hardee's orange plaid uniform. I'll probably replace Phyllis as the fry cook one day.

"Stop torturing yourself, Deb," I say out loud, and rip open the envelope. There is a single sheet of paper with two lines of text:

For legal services rendered: January 1986 to October 1986
Total amount due: $850

There has to be at least one zero missing from that total. His assistant must have made a typo. And then I remember this man who dug through trash bags, drove me up north, and raced around the municipal building like a hummingbird to get critical paperwork filed.

No, I decide, this is not a typo — but it's not charity, either. Mr. Burtch truly believes I can be anything, that I'll shed my polyester uniform and make something of myself.

I've never understood where to find the proverbial bootstraps to pull myself up by, and yet I realize I've just been handed the equivalent of a pair of steel-toed work boots. A seed of endless possibility sprouts within me, and I mentally pull the boots on and prepare for the road ahead.

GALLERY

Steve, MaryAnne, Debbie, and Mark

Carrie and Debbie in the
automotive design shop

Debbie and Glen on
Christmas Day

Carol, Carrie, and Debbie

Tara as a student ambassador in Australia

GALLERY

Tara's graduation

Ian and Tara reunited

Dad and Mom on their 59th wedding anniversary

299

Debbie on the summit of Mt Baker

Debbie with her partner, David, enjoying a night out in Savannah

CHAPTER 46

Homecoming

The morning sun crouches below the horizon, hesitant to rise, as the Boeing 767 rolls to a stop. Outside my passenger window, the pre-dawn landscape of Detroit in January looks hostile. Snow funnels chase each other across the tarmac as I lower the shade in quiet resignation. It has been over twenty-five years since I left Detroit, and I still don't miss the snow.

Slinging my travel backpack over my shoulder, I lumber off the plane in search of the nearest Starbucks. There is still an hour-long drive ahead of me on slick, snow-covered highways. Maybe the caffeine will help keep me focused, or at least awake.

I drain the dredges of my double-shot latte long before the shuttle bus deposits me at the rental car agency. I clutch the empty paper cup to my chest while standing in line and filling out paperwork. Only when I toss my backpack into the passenger seat of the shiny black sedan do I realize I have been caring for this cup like a baby bird. I nest it into the center console before entering my parents' address into the navigation system. Although I can find my way to their home by memory alone, I don't trust my scattered brain today.

Within a few minutes and a few right turns, I am inching my way onto the slushy eastbound entrance ramp of I-94. A smile spreads across my face when I pass the eighty-foot-tall Uniroyal tire, a Detroit icon that feels like an old friend. Decades ago, my brothers and I would plaster our faces against the window of our family station wagon, hoping to spot the beloved landmark. If anyone but Steve saw it first, his rage would explode, with nowhere for us to escape.

The nostalgic behemoth shrinks in my rearview mirror while I search for another childhood memory, one that isn't tarnished with

SQUIRREL PIE

Steve's violence. The car thumps over a crater-like pothole, jolting my consciousness back to the present. When did I merge onto I-75?

Boarded-up windows and crumbling industrial buildings soon give way to modest brick bungalows of the blue-collar suburbs as I drive out of the city. Houses grow larger as the miles pass behind me. Another twenty minutes pass before I spot the slanted red barn surrounded by acres of unkempt farmland and turn left into the development with five-bedroom estates on manicured lawns. My parents bought one of the first homes constructed here over fifteen years ago.

Subzero wind cuts through my flimsy jacket as I dash from the driveway to their front door, and for a moment I'm certain I might freeze to death. The doorknob doesn't budge when I twist it, so I ring the doorbell several times, blowing warm air into my cupped hands and rapping my bare knuckles on the door to emphasize the urgency.

My annoyance melts when I catch sight of Dad through the glass pane that runs alongside the door. Now eighty-three years old, he shuffles towards the door looking comically small.

I stoop to hug his fragile, bony, bent-up body when he opens the door. He struggles to straighten as if there is something heavy on his back, but he quickly wilts back down onto his cane.

The heat of the house is stifling, even after the blood-chilling cold of outside, and I begin shedding my inadequate outerwear. Mom appears in the hallway dressed in navy slacks and a knit sweater, and for a moment I don't recognize her. She has slept more hours of the day than she has been awake over the last twenty years, and it is disorienting to see her without the usual worn flannel nightgown. Mom, too, has shrunk in terms of size, but has not become bent at all, in body or mind.

"Hughie, go put the kettle on."

We settle in at the kitchen table, me with a mug of coffee and my parents with their tea and toast. Deep crevices run along the corners of Mom's mouth, giving her a look of constant disapproval. Dad hunches like a perched sparrow next to her, his bright red suspenders holding up ten-year-old faded blue trousers from thirty pounds ago.

"I wonder how different my life would be if I hadn't married an alcoholic," Mom says, sipping her tea and staring off in the distance.

I look at Dad sitting two feet from her, and he shrugs.

"That's a really mean thing to say, Mom."

"Well, it's the bloody truth! If I had'nae married an alcoholic, then maybe..."

She trails off with a wave of her hand before heaving a sigh of defeat. Her chin quivers almost imperceptibly and she doesn't say any more, but we hear the rest of it anyway: "If I hadn't married an alcoholic, then maybe I wouldn't have a dead son."

Twenty-four hours ago, local sheriffs were summoned to do a wellness check when Steve did not answer his phone all morning. They found him on the bedroom floor of his apartment, where he had died alone during the night.

For decades my brother attempted to quit drinking, but Steve found he was a much kinder person when he drank. His life was a never-ending cycle of uncontrollable rage, quelled only by the soothing effects of alcohol. The anger destroyed his relationships, and the alcohol destroyed his body and took his life.

Dad managed to stop drinking after many years, but not before it took its toll on Mom. She raised four kids almost single handedly — it was her grit and stoic resolve that kept our household running. Although Dad hasn't had a drink in over twenty years, she still has not forgiven him.

Guilt outweighs stone when it's carried for a lifetime, and he accepts each pebble of guilt Mom lays upon his back, unable to forgive himself. Steve's death becomes a boulder hefted upon the pile.

I get up from the table and rinse my mug in the sink. When I turn to face my parents again, they haven't moved an inch. They sit staring off into voids all their own. My intuition tells me this is probably how they pass each day, together but all alone.

"Finish up," I say. "We need to be at the funeral home by noon."

∴

Just past noon, we seat ourselves around a cherry wood table — me, my parents, and Steve's son, Logan. A statuesque bald man with designer glasses joins us, shutting the French doors behind him. He wears the uniform of a funeral director — Italian suit, silk tie, pocket square, an empathetic smile—and utters his condolences before telling us that the death certificate has been issued and Steve is "resting in the cool room."

"Steven is here in this building?" Mom asks.

"Yes, Mrs. Brannigan, Steven is here with us."

"Can I see him?"

Her voice is meek, almost pleading, and this rare display of vulnerability surprises us all. We glance at each other around the table, but nobody reaches out to comfort her.

"We can certainly arrange that. It requires a $300 prep fee and takes twenty-four hours, but Steven will be presentable."

I offer to pay the fee if it gives her some peace, and I also caution Mom that Steve is not going to look like she remembers him. Despite living just thirty miles away, it has been years since she last saw her son, and she has no idea how much he has deteriorated.

Steve died at fifty-six, yet he looked older than our bent-over father. The few teeth left in his mouth had become black with decay, his gray hair was long and stringy, and his skin had become more like parchment paper than flesh.

Mom stares at her hands while she contemplates the idea. She asks if anybody else would like to see him, and we all shake our heads no because, unlike her, we have witnessed his decomposition. Our unison seems to resolve her inner conflict, and her lips return to the formation of an iron rosebud as she tells the funeral director, "No, thank you."

It takes less than thirty minutes to make the final arrangements. We settle on the bare minimum, a basic cremation with no coffin. The funeral director informs us that he needs a payment of $3,200 to get everything ready.

Every head at the table turns to me, and I fish a credit card from my wallet. There is no thank-you or offers to help pay. Later, on the drive home, Mom shouts at me for not financing a more elaborate memorial service. "He's your brother, Deborah!"

It takes all my resolve not to remind her that he is her son.

• • •

Two days later I steer the rental sedan into an industrial park complex. I'm not sure it is the right address until I see Logan waving us to an open parking spot. I ask him to help Dad navigate the icy parking lot, and I do the same for Mom, holding her at the elbow as we skate our way to the sidewalk.

A young woman greets us in the small foyer of the nondescript brown building. There is a logo etched on the reception window that says "Paws and Remember" with a dog and cat silhouette, and I silently pray no one will notice.

She directs us to the viewing area — an eight-foot-square room with floral wallpaper and thinly padded chairs, the kind found in waiting rooms everywhere. We take up positions along the perimeter and attempt small talk while avoiding the large viewing window at one end. Beyond it are girders, cement floors, and an industrial furnace.

The funeral director enters, apologizing for being late although he is exactly on time. He explains the entire cremation procedure to us, ending with: "A fireproof ID tag will be placed with Steven to make sure we always know where he is." He never uses words like "the body" or "the deceased," always referring to Steve as a real person. A deep appreciation wells in my chest for this small dignity.

As if on cue, an unmarked delivery van backs in through the rollup metal door at the rear of the building. Two attendants open the van and lift a long cardboard box onto a short conveyor belt.

This is it. This is how my big brother leaves the world, in a cardboard box at a pet crematorium.

The furnace ignites. I ask Dad if he would like to say a few words, and he shakes his head no, which surprises me because he is a religious man. The funeral director asks if we would like him to recite the Lord's Prayer, and I say yes, surprising myself because I am *not* a religious person.

His beautiful, resonant voice fills the room as the conveyor belt begins to roll. Nobody hugs, holds hands, or cries. Like a row of Easter Island Statues, we stand in silence, looking through the window while Steve rolls into the flames.

A mere thirty minutes after skating our way across the parking lot, we are traversing the same icy terrain in the opposite direction. I hug Logan, promising to be at his dad's apartment to help clear it out after I deposit my parents back home. They sit together in the backseat, wordless, hands in their laps, each staring out opposite windows.

Mom goes directly to her bedroom for a "wee nap." Her slacks and sweater are traded in for the familiar flannel nightgown, and she returns to a dark void of sleep where pain and grief can't reach her.

Dad winces as he eases himself onto the overstuffed living room sofa. The folds pull him in like leather quicksand, making him look even smaller. He rests both hands atop the cane propped between his feet, and it reminds me of an ice axe, ready in case he needs to wrest himself from the Broyhill crevasse.

"Are you going to be okay, Dad?"

"Oh yes, honey, do'nae worry yourself."

"Do you want to talk?"

"About what?"

"About Steve. About how you're feeling. About anything."

"No, no, sweetheart. You've done enough already."

Dad is of a generation that does not talk about feelings, preferring to stuff them down into forgotten spaces until they crop up as tumors or some other physical malady demanding recognition. I have learned his wall is something to be chipped away at, not smashed through with a sledgehammer, so I simply nod and say okay.

A crocheted blanket is piled at his feet, and I gather it up and spread it across his lap. Kissing the top of his head, I promise to bring donuts when I return in the morning. I close the front door behind me and peer back at him through the glass. Dad sits motionless, both hands still resting on the cane, the 70" curved glass of the dark TV screen mirroring his blank expression.

• • •

Logan greets me at the front door of Steve's apartment, and I follow him inside. After just a few feet, I am paralyzed by the scene of garbage, dirty clothes, and mountains of unopened mail scattered everywhere. Steve was always a compulsive neat freak, so none of this makes any sense to me.

Logan asks if I'm okay, like he doesn't see the domestic junkyard in front of us. He takes a step toward me and offers his arm for support. I'm leaning to one side, about to topple over from the immensity of the task in front of me.

"I'm okay, kiddo. Let's get to work."

We wade into the living room and begin clearing through debris like a snowplow. Worn out sweatpants, bloody tissues, fast food wrappers—all of it tumbles into thirty-two-gallon trash bags. Logan heads into the kitchen to tackle the refrigerator, and I move toward the bathroom, pulling from the industrial-sized box of Hefty bags as I go, filling each to the brim before tossing it onto the growing piles around the apartment.

This is too much, Brother, I say under my breath, hoping that Steve is listening somewhere. I want him to know I am angry. I want him to acknowledge the utter chaos he left behind for others to deal with. Twenty years of making good money in the auto industry, and yet his apartment is filled with trash, comic books, and super-hero figurines — not a dime for his family or his own cremation. I want to shake him, tell him to grow up, but it's too late for that.

All my self-righteous anger washes away when I find Steve's false teeth on the bathroom counter. They are garish, made from cheap rubber with bright red gums and oversized incisors. It dawns on me that Steve wore these in public to cover the rotten stumps in his mouth. I can feel his shame and hopelessness, and with tears stinging my eyes, I begin to search for the few fragments of my brother that must still be here, somewhere, amongst this carnage.

I find his art portfolio in the bedroom closet, behind a pile of dirty laundry. Decades-old ink drawings and watercolor images look as if they were just drawn yesterday. I pull out two postcard-sized drawings and remember looking over Steve's shoulder as he drew them. For him, they were practice pieces.

I shake my head at the realization that it has been over forty years since we sat next to each other in Ms. Sorenson's art class. Ms. Sorenson saw these small drawings as fit for the glass display case in our high school hallway, and I decide they should journey home with me tomorrow.

I also select a large eight-paneled storyboard that Steve drew in ink for my sister MaryAnne. They shared a love of graphic novels, and in the morning before I leave, I will ship it to her in Ireland where she has lived for several years. I call Mark while taking a break on Steve's small balcony. He declines my offer to send a memento to him in California.

"He's my brother and I loved him, Deb, but we weren't really close."

Steve regretted how he had bullied Mark while growing up, but he never apologized, and Mark never expected him to. Decades of distance may have created benign resignation between them, but never resentment.

By nightfall, Logan and I have pushed nearly everything from Steve's apartment into the dumpster or a Goodwill donation box. We are bone-weary as we wipe down the bare countertops and floors on our way out. I turn for one last look at the sterile apartment and can't help but think that Steve has just been erased from the canvas of life.

• • •

My carry-on backpack is loaded up long before the sun rises. I am eager to check out of the hotel and catch my flight home. I inch the rental car along a slow line at a Tim Horton's drive-thru to pick up a mixed dozen, and Dad licks his lips like a cartoon character when he sees me walk in the house with the box.

"Bless you, honey," he says, digging a jelly donut from the box.

"Where's Mom?"

"Still in bed."

We both look at the kitchen clock, then back to each other.

"Aye, it's nearly noon. I'll go wake her. Wish me luck."

Dad says this with a wink as he starts a slow tap-shuffle gait with his cane down the hallway to Mom's bedroom door. He knocks lightly but gets no response. He tries again, this time speaking softly through the door.

"Honey? Debbie's here to see you before she heads home."

There is still no response, so he adds, "She's brought a box of fresh donuts."

"Alright, put the kettle on, Hughie."

The kettle has boiled, the tea has steeped, and a brimming Victorian teapot sits on the kitchen table before Mom makes her entrance. The worn flannel night gown swirls around her and obscures her feet. She resembles a Halloween ghost floating across the living room to the kitchen. Dad pours her a cup of tea and opens the box of donuts for her to peruse.

"Hmph. No jellies?"

She plucks a glazed ring from the box, drops it on a small plate, and carries both the plate and cup to her bedroom, leaving us sitting at the kitchen table.

"Is that nae bloody awful?"

"Let it go, Dad."

But it's too late. He hauls himself out of his chair and is shuffling toward the hallway when Mom's bedroom door closes behind her.

"Bridie, your daughter's come here to visit with us."

"She's the one that moved away and left us. Let the poor baby cry her way back to Georgia."

Dad looks apologetically at me, as if he had uttered the words himself. I shake my head and gesture for him to come back to the kitchen table.

I pretend Mom's insults don't bother me anymore, but they do. Steve and MaryAnne cut off all communication with her many years ago, weary of her temper tantrums and bitter words. Mark chose to stay at a distance in California. I have continued to call her every week, but now I contemplate if I should let her go as well. My compassion is buried, and all I can muster right now is resignation.

Maybe tomorrow I can empathize with Mom and try to comprehend her devastation at losing a child.

Maybe tomorrow I can realize that she struggles with processing painful emotions.

Maybe tomorrow I can feel sad about how she cries alone in her bedroom because she doesn't feel safe being vulnerable.

Today, however, I decide to pretend I don't care. Which is exactly what Mom does.

Like most daughters, I have taken on many of my mother's traits, the good with the bad. I walk through life with a sense of adventure and fearlessness — nothing can stand in my way once I have set a course. I inherited this from Mom, and it helped to propel me from fast food to a lucrative career in aerospace design.

I can also unleash stormy rages onto those who don't deserve it and spit words like vinegar from my mouth without considering their consequences. Years after escaping Mac's abuse, my unprocessed trauma continued to fester, oozing out in this unhealthy way. One day I said something hurtful to someone I loved and realized they were not my own words — they were echoes from a long ago past, reverberating from one generation to the next.

Do we unconsciously pass our traumas on to the next generation? To the ones we love most?

I have pulled at this nagging, loose strand in the fabric of my mind for so long that it has unraveled in a heap. It is a daunting task to weave something new from forgiveness, compassion, and vulnerability, especially when it seems I have so few of these raw materials.

Trauma cultivated an entirely different set of resources for me — caution, vigilance, and distrust. There was no room for vulnerability when I was trying to survive, so I forged an emotional suit of armor to protect against it. I continued to don this heavy plating long after my battle ended, convinced it kept me safe.

To shed this protective shell feels threatening, and yet I've learned that life exists beyond the realm of safety. Surviving and living, after all, are not the same thing. Survival requires a fortress or a cave, guarded by constant vigilance. Living requires exposure to the full complexity of life itself, its joys and loves as well as its wounds and pain — and that requires vulnerability.

At an early age Mom learned to push the scared and vulnerable parts of herself into a dark recess of her mind. Decades later, those hidden parts still wait to be told it's safe to come out. On rare occasions they struggle to the surface, through a quivering chin, a faltering of words, or in tears on the brink of release. Always, though, she pushes them back down into the darkness, believing she'll be safe — convinced all of us might be safe — with them hidden and tough-as-nails Bridie on watch.

As always, I wish I could meet Mom there in the dark, to let her know she's not alone.

• • •

"Hey, Dad, let's look through these photos I brought from Steve's apartment."

We sit down again at the kitchen table and rummage through a small collection of photos, each summoning a memory and a story. Dad lifts a photo showing Steve sitting on a velveteen sofa with two-year-old Tara in his lap and laments how quickly time goes by. It is one of the first photos I shot with the new camera Mac gave me for Christmas, and I captured the scene when Steve dropped by for his weekly Tuesday visit.

The only picture I want to keep is this one, and I form the others into a small stack, telling Dad to keep them all. He makes no attempt to argue and thanks me for the walk down memory lane.

His eyelids are drooping, and when he yawns, I gather up my backpack and say I should be getting on the road, although it is still three more hours until my flight. I venture down the hallway to Mom's bedroom door and knock lightly. When there is no response, I knock again.

"Mom, I'm heading out now. I'll call you next week."

On the other side of the door, I hear sheets rustle and her mattress moan.

"Have a safe trip, love."

I know she's not going to come out of the bedroom — that this is all Mom can give right now. I take her offering and tell myself it is enough.

The icy highway and grey skies follow me on the trek to the airport. I long to be back in Savannah, where there is warmth in the air and at home. My partner, David, will have a bouquet of colorful Gerbera daisies on the dining table. He will take my backpack and exchange it for one of his famous Old Fashioned cocktails, and we will sip together on our large, covered porch, waving at neighbors on their way to the dog park.

The departure gate is empty when I arrive two hours early for my flight, so I entertain myself by wandering the strip mall of the concourse, buying souvenir shirts and travel snacks. I pay nearly eight dollars for a Chunky bar and return to the gate, where I remove its shiny silver wrapping. The waxy chocolate is terribly sweet. How did I ever eat these things?

I check my phone, and the red dot for new messages is still there, beside Steve's name. His un-played voicemail is reassuring to me, like he is still here, safe inside my phone. He sits on the velveteen couch, joining me from his 4x6 glossy realm, cradled in my lap.

We sit together in familiar, companionable silence, watching the TV at the gate until it's time to head home.

Epilogue

Air brakes hiss as the bright red rail car comes to a rolling stop. Hydraulic double doors slide apart, framing a perfect, sunlit day in Stuttgart, Germany. I shield my eyes from the October sun and head in the direction of the shopping district. First stop: sunglasses.

The promenade of Königsbau Passagen is more akin to a college campus or sprawling park than a shopping area, with children running across vast green acres of grass as elaborate statues keep watch from posts they took up centuries ago.

Everything in Germany looks tidy, ornate, and ancient to my American eyes. With its Parthenon-like rows of tall colonnades, even the mall is breathtaking. Once the bustling stock exchange building, its austere architecture now houses boutique shops and bistros.

I take the stone stairs two at a time, reaching one of the large glass entrance doors as a set of rubber-coated stroller wheels push against the pane from the inside. A delicate hand reaches out from the stroller but falls short of the door. I pull it open with a sweep of my arm that implies "After you."

Tiny saddle oxford shoes emerge first, followed by bouncing blonde curls framing a little girl's face, then a young mother who looks like she should still be in high school. I stare at the stroller, expecting to see Lucky Bear held tightly in the girl's arms, but he is absent from the scene.

"*Danke*" says the mom without making eye contact. Her blonde ponytail reflects the golden shimmer of the sun, and I watch it sway softly behind her before calling out "*Bitte sehr*" a few beats too late.

"*Danke*" repeats a middle-aged woman brushing past me. It takes me a minute to realize I'm still holding the door open like a hotel doorman for people coming out of the mall.

I release my grip without going inside. Instead, I walk back down the steps to take a seat on a sun-soaked bench. My reality starts to shift and wobble, as it does when you awake from a dream and are unsure which living realm you truly inhabit.

Could it be that my former self has slipped through a galactic black hole? Is she here to pass along some profound message from the universe? Probably not, the cynical engineer inside my head replies. And yet, something's happening…

I travel through a mental wormhole that leads to me as a teenager. Teenage Debbie sobs into her arm, which is draped across the windowsill. Her despair is heavy, as if gravity in the room is twice what it should be. She is ready to sever the thread-like tether of hope, convinced that happiness does not exist.

I wince at the image. It is hard to see my former self, so naïve and lost. She is paralyzed by the world around her, and my first instinct is to close the door and leave her there. But I've done that for far too long now.

You don't need to stay here, I say, mentally placing my hand on her shoulder. *Come with me to Germany and see what's possible.* I clasp her hand and bring her into the present.

Together, we peer at the beautiful, pristine surroundings. I remind her that we were flown first class to Germany by our employer to work with some of the smartest people in engineering, all expenses paid — and that we are worth every penny.

We did it! I say, smiling at her.

I had taken all of this for granted until the moment I held a mall door open for a ponytailed teenage mom and her curly-headed daughter. That small act had catapulted me back in time, to a moment when my younger self was ready to give up.

• • •

When I began writing this book, I found it difficult to write beyond just a few chapters. I kept trying to write what I thought it should be about

— alcoholism, domestic violence, the kidnapping of my daughter. But the book wanted to be something else.

Nobody was more surprised than I was when Mom stepped forward as a prominent figure in my story. Even though I have spent a lot of time in therapy working through the traumatic period at the center of this story, it wasn't until I started writing that some pieces started to fall into place for me.

When I was a teenager, I never understood what Mom meant when she kept telling me to assume responsibility. Now, years later, I believe I have finally done exactly that in my own way. I have examined my past and discovered how the roots of her trauma, especially around the death of her sister, informed and intertwined with my own.

I had a similar realization with Dad, his struggles with self-esteem and shame that colored his entire life and manifested in alcoholism. My parents, and my brother Steve, did the best they could, and yet there was a limit to how much they could give, based on their own wounds and how much they had — or hadn't — healed.

At some point, rather than reap a harvest of their fears, grief, and resentments, I was able to say, "This doesn't work for me" and choose a new way of being, for myself and for my daughter.

I nurture the best characteristics from each parent: Mom's artistic creativity, resilience, and ability to accomplish what others would deem impossible, along with Dad's good humor, warmth, and ability to make friends. I also do my best to mirror Steve's gift of remembering the tiniest details of what matters to someone. The rest has been weeded out to make room for my own creations.

The ability to integrate my past into my present, accepting the good and the bad, has grounded me in a gratitude that emanates from my core, transforming every aspect of my life for the better. And if my story helps others discover their inner resilience and the realization that they can make different choices, then writing this book has been worth it.

SQUIRREL PIE

• • •

So, you may ask, what happened to everybody in the book? Where are they now?

My friend Carrie and I eventually quit our jobs at EWS and went to work at a larger engineering firm for more money. We also became roommates, sharing a great three-bedroom townhome.

Carrie loved Tara like her own niece, and we enjoyed many laughs, parties, and movie nights together. Her friendship gave me a sense of belonging I'd never felt before, and her humor was just the antidote I needed after shedding so many tears.

In 1994, Boeing visited Detroit to recruit automotive engineers. I called for an interview and was hired on the spot. Six weeks later, Tara and I moved to Seattle, Washington. I lived and worked between Portland, Oregon, and Seattle for the next sixteen years. In 2010, I accepted a job in Savannah, Georgia, and immediately fell in love with the sunny weather and my handsome partner, David. I don't plan to live with snow or constant drizzle ever again.

Tara toured Australia and New Zealand as a middle school student ambassador before we relocated to Seattle. She was always an exceptional student and a band geek, graduating with honors in 2000. Almost immediately, she landed a job at Microsoft, kicking off her own twenty-plus-year career in tech and gaming.

Her work has taken her to New Zealand, Germany, and the Netherlands, and she has been a guest speaker at the annual Game Developers Conference (GDC) in San Francisco numerous times. She now resides in Montreal, Quebec, with her adoring partner and two Siberian cats.

Tara and Ian kept in touch for decades, with intermittent meetups whenever possible. In 2008 they were making plans for a road trip to visit Grandma McCall in Ohio when tragedy struck. Ian took his own life just two weeks after his thirty-first birthday, leaving behind a wife and two children.

Tyan struggled to anchor herself in life, falling in and out of communication for years. She died unexpectedly in her sleep in 2020, leaving behind a daughter that was adopted by Darlene.

EPILOGUE

My relationship with Mom continued to be a complex and frustrating one, right up until her death from lung cancer in 2021, just eighteen months after Steve's death. Her diagnosis did little to smooth out the rough edges of her anger; rather, it seemed to intensify it. Barbed words and insults continued to shoot out like porcupine quills to anyone who attempted to get too close.

Mom's hospice nurse told me that emotionally wounded people, especially as they approach death, can often lash out at the ones they know won't abandon them. For better or worse, that person for Mom seemed to be me. It is still an odd comfort to realize, let alone accept, that she considered me her safety net, and that on some unconscious level, she valued me.

Soon after Mom's death, I flew Dad from Michigan to Savannah so he could be closer to me. He arrived at the Savannah airport with a gym bag containing a pair of shorts, a pair of pants, and a few briefs and socks. He never went back for anything else, ready to sell the house and all its contents without hesitation or regret. He soaked up the Georgia sunshine and made dozens of new friends before passing away in the spring of 2023.

Mark left the Air Force after fifteen years and took a management position with the city of Lakeport in northern California. He is married to the love of his life and surrounded by good friends and a loving family, including an eight-year-old granddaughter.

MaryAnne, the only American-born member of our family, got her UK passport and moved to Ireland, where she lives on a picturesque island with stunning sea views.

Glen and I continued to date for another year after Mac's death. We parted ways when I surprised him at the gym on a rare day off from my three jobs and found him kissing a cute young brunette near the squat rack. Val and my coworkers at Hardee's seemed to be more upset than I was, knowing their beloved "Hugo" would no longer be stopping by for dinner breaks.

Graham died in Louisville, Kentucky, in 2017. He had been my shield and ally many times when Mac's temper threatened to spill over onto me and the kids. Decades later, when I obtained copies of the FBI files surrounding the kidnapping, I felt betrayed to learn that Graham aided

Mac in Tara's abduction. It was Graham who drove Tara and Mac out of Michigan in his white van.

As for John Burtch, when we parted from that restaurant in Mt. Clemens, Michigan, I didn't see or talk to him again. I worked three jobs for two years following Mac's death, and before I knew it, decades had passed.

In 2019, I set an intention to say thank you to the people who had helped me along my life's mile markers. John Burtch was one of those people. I had never thanked him for his generosity or told him how he had positively affected the direction of my life with his encouragement about making conscious choices.

I tracked down two addresses and sent a letter to both. Within a week, Mr. Burtch called me and we reconnected. He had never forgotten my case and told me I should really write a book. I toyed with the idea for over a year but never composed anything. Steve's death in 2020 reminded me that time is short, so I got serious about it. This book was born from my year of gratitude, and once again, I owe my thanks to John Burtch.

I have been unable to locate Mary McCarty, so instead I send a silent thank you out to her each year on Mother's Day. Without her selfless cooperation with the FBI, I don't know how my saga would have ended.

It has been over thirty years since Mac's death, and I still cannot put a phone to my ear without my heart racing, palms sweating, and anxiety blinding me. Years of therapy have helped me to better navigate the CPTSD obstacle course within my mind, and yet my body has its own memory, one that doesn't easily forget.

I was too young at sixteen to grasp how the acceptance of physical violence and lack of emotional connection within my family had extended to an acceptance of Mac's abuse. I developed the faulty belief that somehow my abusive situation was typical.

For years I felt unloved, unseen, unappreciated, unwanted, not good enough, not smart enough, not powerful or attractive enough. Eventually, I just stopped feeling.

These false narratives ran on a continuous loop in my head, until they crowded out all potential for joy, love, and ease in my life. I became a thin-penciled outline of a person, lacking any dimension or color, and I longed for a jumbo Crayola box of crayons to fill myself in.

I hoped to find that dimension and color by working hard and playing even harder. I worked fifty-five hours a week, joined a mountaineering team to summit mountains on weekends, and dated…a lot!

But the harder I tried, the wider and darker my interior void grew and the angrier I became. My pencil outline had started to resemble my parents, and I realized my problems weren't "out there." I was the common denominator. That's when I found a therapist and slowly began laying down the burdens I carried — especially the one that implied I was undeserving of love because I hadn't done enough to earn it.

My road to recovery is a lifetime journey, but it is one that I can now walk consciously, step by step. Love and happiness are an inside job, and you don't have to earn either of them. You simply choose them — every single day — and it starts with the person staring back at you in the mirror.

All the people in this book, myself included, had choices to make. I believe we each did the best we could at the time, given our own unique burdens. Had we made different choices, maybe things would have turned out differently, but we didn't, and there's no point regretting any of it. All we can do is learn from our mistakes and keep moving forward.

After all, at the end of our time here on earth, our lives will have been lived only by us. We determine how much power to give the past, and how much it will define the future. My decision has been to strive for compassion and understanding, and to keep my thoughts anchored in the present moment.

I am no longer ashamed of my sixteen-year-old self. I once saw her as helpless, needy, and pathetic. Now I see how strong, resilient, and smart she was — I mean, when life gave this girl dead squirrels, she made pies!

If I could go back and give her some advice, I would tell her to stop trying to hold the entire universe together. Instead, I would encourage her to find her allies and ask for help because, when she finally started to ask, her world began to change for the better. All the things she wanted most — that joy, love, and ease — were waiting for her all along.

The End

Resources

If you or someone you love is caught up in a cycle of violence and abuse, please encourage them to ask for help. Reaching out is a powerful first step, and here are some organizations that would love to be your ally:

National Domestic Violence Hotline
Call 1-800-799-SAFE (7233)
Text "START" to 88788
Or live chat at www.thehotline.org

CPTSD Foundation
www.cptsdfoundation.org

Books That Helped Me:
Breaking the Habit of Being Yourself, Dr. Joe Dispenza
Codependent No More, Melody Beattie
Adult Children of Emotionally Immature Parents: How to Heal from Distant, Rejecting, or Self-Involved Parents, Lindsay C. Gibson, PsyD
What My Bones Know: A Memoir of Healing from Complex Trauma, Stephanie Foo
The Body Keeps the Score, Bessel A. Van der Kolk
The Power of Now, Eckhart Tolle
No Visible Bruises: What We Don't Know About Domestic Violence Can Kill Us, Rachel Louise Snyder

Acknowledgements

You may assume, as I did, that writing a memoir is a long and lonely journey. While *Squirrel Pie* did take five long years to complete, it was not a solitary trek.

I could not have completed this daunting task without the patience and guidance of Joanna Bender. Her soothing voice and calm demeanor were always there, talking me out of a doom spiral or vicious attack of imposter syndrome. She taught me how to structure a story, ground myself in feelings and become a better writer.

This project required a safe space to explore unpleasant memories and uncomfortable feelings. My partner of thirteen years, David Murphy, provided me with just such a space. The words *thank you* seem trivial to express my gratitude for the countless hours we spent drinking coffee and talking through the tough emotions that surfaced in this book. Ten thousand thank-you's will never be enough, but I will start with this one: *Thank You.*

To my sister, MaryAnne, I thank you for always being my biggest cheerleader. Your love, time and thoughtfulness are always given freely, and you are still the bravest person I know. I love you to the moon and back!

Lastly, I owe a debt of gratitude to my early readers, the friends that kept me motivated and moving forward on the worst of days: Aileen Gabbey, the Brill sisters, Lenora Edwards, Patty Ruiz, and Shannon Sansoterra. You are daily reminders of the magnificent life I now live.

Thank you all.

About the Author

Debbie Brannigan immigrated to the United States from Glasgow, Scotland as a toddler. While her love for writing was evident during her childhood in Detroit, a tumultuous life demanded that Brannigan focus her energies elsewhere. She quit high school at 16 and began an unusual and circuitous route to a highly successful career as a design engineer in the automotive and aerospace industries.

Brannigan produced a successful film competition that spotlighted small businesses making a difference in the community, earning a regional Emmy award in the process. An avid mountaineer and traveler, she has also summited numerous northwest peaks, lived and worked across North America and in Germany, and traveled in Central and South America, New Zealand, and throughout Europe.

Book Club Questions

- Which characters were impacted by domestic violence in this book, and how were they affected by it?

- Was this issue of domestic violence connected to other social problems faced by the characters (e.g., child abuse, racism, alcoholism)? If so, how?

- In what ways did other characters in the book help Debbie stay safe? If they didn't reach out to help her, why didn't they and how could they have?

- Often, women involved in domestic violence situations can be reluctant to ask for help, even if they have opportunities to do so. What might prevent them from doing this?

- How did this book make you feel? Did it remind you of a situation you have experienced yourself? If so, how has that experience affected you?

- What scenes from the book have stuck with you the most? Did you reread any passages? If so, which ones?

- Discuss the book's structure and the author's use of language and writing style. How does the author draw the reader in and keep them engaged? Does the author convey her story with comedy, self-pity, something else?

- What do you think the author's most admirable quality is? Is this someone you would want to know or have known?

- Are there lingering questions from the book you're still thinking about? If you could ask the author anything, what would it be?

- Compare this book to other memoirs your group has read. Is it similar to any of them? Did you like it more or less than the other books you've read? How did the book impact you and what do you think will be your lasting impression of the book?

- Would you recommend this book to a friend? Do you want to read more works by this author?

Made in the USA
Columbia, SC
23 July 2025

fddce0f6-c163-4e40-9223-3df0ba58f9f7R01